# FINANCIAL INTELLIGENCE

## FOR HR PROFESSIONALS

# FINANCIAL INTELLIGENCE

## FOR HR PROFESSIONALS

### What You Really Need to Know
### About the Numbers

**KAREN BERMAN**

**JOE KNIGHT**

with John Case

HARVARD BUSINESS PRESS
BOSTON, MASSACHUSETTS

Copyright 2008 Business Literacy Institute, Inc.
All rights reserved
Printed in the United States of America
12  11  10  09  08     5  4  3  2  1

Library of Congress Cataloging-in-Publication Data
Berman, Karen, 1962–
    Financial intelligence for HR professionals : what you really need to know about the numbers / Karen Berman, Joe Knight with John Case.
      p.   cm.
    Includes bibliographical references and index.
    ISBN-13: 978-1-4221-1913-6
    1. Personnel management  2. Finance.  I. Knight, Joe, 1963–  II. Case, John, 1944–
III. Title.
HF5549.B4484   2008
658.15088'6583—dc22

                                                      2007051756

*Karen dedicates this book to*
*her husband Young Riddle*
*and to their daughter Marie.*

*Joe dedicates this book to his wife,*
*Donielle, and to the seven Js—*
*Jacob, Jordan, Jewel, Jessica, James, Jonah,*
*and Joseph Christian (JC).*

# CONTENTS

# THE BALANCE SHEET REVEALS THE MOST

# CASH IS KING

## PART EIGHT
## CREATING A FINANCIALLY INTELLIGENT HR DEPARTMENT (AND ORGANIZATION)

## WHAT IS FINANCIAL INTELLIGENCE?

We have worked with thousands of employees, managers, and leaders in American companies, teaching them about the financial side of business. Our philosophy is that everyone in a company does better when they understand how financial success is measured and how they have an impact on the company's performance. Our term for that understanding is *financial intelligence*. Greater financial intelligence, we've learned, helps people feel more involved and committed. They understand better what they are a part of, what the organization is trying to achieve, and how they affect results. Trust increases, turnover decreases, and financial results improve.

When we say "everyone," we mean everyone: the original edition of this book was written for nonfinancial managers of every stripe, engineers and marketers and operations people alike. This edition has been developed specifically for human resource professionals. It is for the senior HR executive who has not yet picked up the financial skills he or she needs to become an effective advocate, leader, and business partner. It is also for junior and midlevel people on their way to positions of greater responsibility—the HR leaders of the future.

Given that focus, we should begin with an observation that we think many—perhaps not all—of our readers will agree with. HR people are ambivalent about finance. On the one hand, it is often they who call us, asking us to develop and deliver training courses for other managers or leaders in their organization. They seem to understand the importance of nonfinancial people learning the financial side of the business—the statements, the measures, the tools. On the other hand, some HR folks aren't sure about applying the lesson to themselves. HR in the past concerned itself only with the people side of the business and with a few specific financial metrics, such as the cost of turnover. Some HR professionals still don't think or talk much about the broader financial side of their organization.

We know that human resources as a discipline has been chipping away at this limitation for many years now. Journals, conferences, and books have all made the point that HR people need to speak the language of business if they want a seat at the strategic table. Most senior HR leaders have gotten the message and are urging others in the field to learn more about business. Larry Godfrey, the assistant dean of the College of Human Resources and Labor Relations at General Motors, puts it this way: "We need to be businesspeople who do HR, as opposed to HR people who support the business. I think there is a pretty significant difference in the phrasing of that." We agree.

But perceptions are hard to change, so people in your organization— even those in your department—may still see HR as focused only on the "soft" side of business. Boosting your financial intelligence can help change that perception. If you can speak the language, ask questions, and use the information, you will be a part of the wave of change in HR, and you will help give your department a stronger voice in business decisions.

We came to our philosophy about financial intelligence by different routes. Karen took the academic path. Her PhD dissertation focused on the question of whether information sharing and financial understanding on the part of employees and managers positively affects a company's financial performance. (It does.) Karen went on to become a financial trainer and started an organization, the Business Literacy Institute, devoted to helping others learn about finance. Joe earned an MBA in finance, but most of his experience with financial training in organizations has been on the practical side. After stints at Ford Motor Company and several small companies, he joined a start-up business, Setpoint, which manufactures roller coasters and factory-automation equipment. As chief financial officer (CFO) of Setpoint, he learned firsthand the importance of training engineers and other employees in how the business worked. In 2003 Joe joined Karen as co-owner of the Business Literacy Institute and since then has worked with dozens of companies as a financial trainer.

What do we mean by financial intelligence? It isn't some innate ability that you either have or don't have. Granted, some people are better at numbers than others, and a few legendary folks seem to have an intuitive grasp of finance that eludes the rest of us. But that's not what we're talking about here. For most businesspeople—HR included—financial intelligence is no more than a set of skills that must be, and can be, learned. People who work in finance learn these skills early on, and for the rest of their careers they are able to talk with one another in a specialized language that can sound like Greek to the uninitiated. Most senior executives either come out of finance or pick up the skills during their rise to the top, just because it's tough to run a business unless you know what the financial folks are saying. Managers who don't work in finance, however, too often are out of luck. They never picked up the skills, so in some ways they've been relegated to the sidelines.

Fundamentally, financial intelligence boils down to four distinct skill sets, and when you finish the book, you should be competent in all of them. They are:

- *Understanding the foundation.* HR managers who are financially intelligent understand the basics of financial measurement. They can read an income statement, a balance sheet, and a cash flow statement. They know the difference between profit and cash. They understand why the balance sheet balances. The numbers neither scare nor mystify them.

- *Understanding the art.* Finance and accounting are an art as well as a science. The two disciplines must try to quantify what can't always be quantified, and so they must rely on rules, estimates, and assumptions. Financially intelligent HR managers can identify where the artful aspects of finance have been applied to the numbers, and they know how applying the numbers differently might lead to different conclusions. They thus are prepared, when appropriate, to question and challenge the numbers.

- *Understanding analysis.* Once you have the foundation and an appreciation of the art of finance, you can use the information to analyze the numbers in greater depth. Financially intelligent HR managers don't shrink from ratios, return on investment (ROI) analysis, and the like. They use these analyses to inform their decisions and thus make better decisions.

- *Understanding the big picture.* Finally, although we teach finance, and although we think that everyone should understand the numbers side of business, we are equally firm in our belief that numbers can't and don't tell the whole story. A business's financial results must always be understood in context—that is, within the framework of the big picture. Factors such as the economy, the competitive environment, regulations, changing customer needs and expectations, and new technologies all affect how numbers are interpreted and what decisions should be made.

Financial intelligence begins but doesn't end with book learning. Like most disciplines and skill sets, it must not only be learned; it must also be practiced and applied. On the practical side, we hope and expect this book will prepare you to take actions such as the following:

- *Speak the language.* Finance is the language of business. Whether it is comfortable for you or not, the one thing every organization has in common is numbers and how those numbers are tabulated, analyzed, and reported. In HR you need to *use* the language to be taken seriously and to communicate effectively. As with any new language, you can't speak fluently at first. Never mind—jump in and try something. You'll gain confidence as you go.

- *Ask questions.* We want you to look at financial reports and analysis with a questioning eye. It's not that we think anything is necessarily wrong with the numbers you will see. We merely believe it is tremendously important to understand the what, why, and how of the numbers you are using to make decisions. Since every company is different, sometimes the only way to figure out all those parameters is to ask questions.

• *Use the information.* After reading this book, you should know a lot.
So use it! Use it to help the business unit you support improve cash
flow. Use it to analyze an outsourcing decision. Use it to assess your
company's results. Your job will be more fun, and your impact on the
company's performance will be greater. From our vantage point, we
love to see everyone in HR connect the dots between financial results
and their jobs.

So this book, we hope, will support the development of your financial
intelligence. We hope it will enable you to achieve greater success, both
personally and professionally. We hope it helps your company be more
successful as well. But most of all, we think, after reading this book, you'll
be just a bit more motivated, a bit more interested, and a bit more excited
to understand a whole new aspect of business.

# The Art of Finance
# (and Why It Matters to HR)

# You Can't Always Trust the Numbers

If you read the papers regularly, you have learned a good deal in recent years about all the wonderful ways people cook their companies' books. They record phantom sales. They hide expenses. Some of the techniques are pleasantly simple, like the software company a few years back that boosted revenues by shipping its customers empty cartons just before the end of a quarter. (The customers sent the cartons back, of course—but not until the following quarter.) Other techniques are complex to the point of near incomprehensibility. (It took years for accountants and prosecutors to sort out all of Enron's spurious transactions.) As long as there are liars and thieves on this earth, some of them will no doubt find ways to commit fraud and embezzlement.

But maybe you have also noticed something else about the arcane world of finance, namely that many companies find perfectly legal ways to make their books look better than they otherwise would. Granted, these legitimate tools aren't quite as powerful as outright fraud: they can't make a bankrupt company look like a profitable one—at least, not for long. But it's amazing what they can do. For example, a little technique called a *one-time charge* allows a company to take a whole bunch of bad news and cram it into one quarter's financial results so that future quarters will look better. Alternatively, some shuffling of expenses from one category into another can pretty up a company's quarterly earnings picture and boost its stock price. While we were writing this book, the *Wall Street Journal* ran a front-page story on how companies fatten their bottom lines by reducing retirees' benefit accruals—even though they may not spend a nickel less on those benefits.

Everybody who isn't a financial professional is likely to greet such maneuvers with a certain amount of mystification. Human resources—like most other aspects of business, including marketing, research and development, and strategy formulation—is at least partly subjective, a matter dependent on experience and judgment as well as data. But finance? Accounting? Surely, the numbers produced by these departments are objective, black and white, indisputable. Surely, a company sold what it sold, spent what it spent, earned what it earned. Even where fraud is concerned, unless a company really does ship empty boxes, how can its executives so easily make things look so different than they really are? And short of fraud, how can executives so easily manipulate the business's bottom line?

## THE ART OF FINANCE

The fact is, accounting and finance, like all those other business disciplines, really are as much art as they are science. You might call this the CFO's or the controller's hidden secret—except that it isn't really a secret; it's a widely acknowledged truth that everyone in finance knows. Trouble is, the rest of us tend to forget it. Or maybe we suspected it based on the interactions we've had with the finance department, but we never felt confident enough to pursue the matter. It seems like if a number shows up on the financial statements or on the finance department's reports to management, it must accurately represent reality.

In fact, of course, that can't always be true, if only because even the number jockeys can't know everything. They can't know exactly what people in human resources (and in all the other departments) do every day, so they don't know exactly how to allocate costs. They can't know exactly how long a piece of equipment will last, so they don't know how much of its original cost to record in any given year. They can't predict exact payouts for incentive plans, so they don't know exactly how much to budget. *The art of accounting and finance is the art of using limited data to come as close as possible to an accurate description of how well a company is performing.*

Accounting and finance are not reality; they are a reflection of reality. The accuracy of that reflection depends on the ability of accountants and finance professionals to make reasonable assumptions and to calculate reasonable estimates.

It's a tough job. Sometimes they have to quantify what can't easily be quantified. Sometimes they have to make difficult judgments about how to categorize a given item. None of these complications necessarily arises because they are trying to cook the books or because they are incompetent. The complications arise because accountants and financial folks must make educated guesses related to the numbers side of the business all day long.

The result of these assumptions and estimates is, typically, a bias in the numbers. Please don't get the idea that by using the word *bias* we are impugning anybody's integrity. (Some of our best friends are accountants—no, really—and one of us, Joe, actually carries the title *CFO* on his business card.) Where financial results are concerned, bias means only that the numbers might be skewed in one direction or another. It means only that accountants and finance professionals have used certain assumptions and estimates rather than others when they put their reports together. Enabling you to understand this bias, to correct for it where necessary, and even to use it to your own (and your company's) advantage is one objective of this book. To understand it, you must know what questions to ask about these assumptions and estimates. Armed with that information, you can make well-considered, appropriate decisions.

In issues related to human resources, you have to make judgment calls every day. Understanding the thought process behind those decisions helps you and others see the reasoning behind your conclusions. It's the same in

## Box Definitions

We want to make finance as easy as possible. Most finance books make us flip back and forth between the page we're on and the glossary to learn the definition of a word we don't know. By the time we find it and get back to our page, we've lost our train of thought. So here we are going to give you the definitions right where you need them, near the first time we use the word.

finance. As an HR manager, you should strive to understand the assumptions behind the numbers that the accounting department presents.

## JUDGMENT CALLS

For example, let's look at one of the variables that is frequently estimated—one that you wouldn't think needed to be estimated at all. *Revenue* or *sales* refers to the value of what a company sold to its customers during a given period. You'd think that would be an easy matter to determine. But the question is when revenue should be recorded (or "recognized," as accountants like to say). Here are some possibilities:

- When a contract is signed

- When the product or service is delivered

- When the invoice is sent out

- When the bill is paid

If you said, "When the product or service is delivered," you're correct; as we'll see in chapter 6, that's the fundamental rule that determines when a sale should show up on the income statement. Still, the rule isn't simple. Implementing it requires making a number of assumptions, and in fact the whole question of "when is a sale a sale?" was a hot topic in many of the fraud cases dating from the late 1990s.

Imagine, for instance, that a company sells a customer a copier, complete with a maintenance contract, all wrapped up in one financial pack-

### Income Statement

The income statement shows revenues, expenses, and profit for a period of time, such as a month, quarter, or year. It's also called a profit and loss statement, P&L, statement of earnings, or statement of operations. Sometimes the word *consolidated* is thrown in front of those phrases, but it's still just an income statement. The bottom line of the income statement is net profit, also known as net income or net earnings.

age. Suppose the machine is delivered in October, but the maintenance contract is good for the following twelve months. Now, how much of the initial purchase price should be recorded on the books for October? After all, the company hasn't yet delivered all the services that it is responsible for during the year. Accountants can make estimates of the value of those services, of course, and adjust the revenue accordingly. But that requires a big judgment call.

Nor is this example merely hypothetical. Witness Xerox, which played the revenue recognition game on such a massive scale that it was later found to have improperly recognized a whopping $6 billion of sales. The issue? Xerox was selling equipment on four-year leases, including service and maintenance. So how much of the price covered the cost of the equipment, and how much was for the subsequent services? Fearful that the company's sagging profits would cause its stock price to plummet, Xerox's executives decided to book ever-increasing percentages of the anticipated revenues—along with the associated profits—up front. Before long, nearly all the revenue on these contracts was being recognized at the time of the sale. Suppose you worked in HR for Xerox. You probably wouldn't have known that the revenue number wasn't matched appropriately to actual sales. Yet that number might have been used for incentive-plan compensation and for commission checks. It might have been used to determine which salespeople needed extra training and which didn't. And those decisions that you would have made would have been dramatically affected by the decision to change how revenue was being recognized.

Xerox had clearly lost its way and was trying to use accounting to cover up its business failings. But you can see the point here: there's plenty of room, short of outright book-cooking, to make the numbers look one way or another. And the implications for managers who can't ask the right questions are huge.

A second example of the artful work of finance—and another one that played a huge role in recent financial scandals—is determining whether a given cost is a capital expenditure or an operating expense. We'll get to all the details later; for the moment, all you need to know is that an operating expense reduces the bottom line immediately, and a capital expenditure spreads the hit out over several accounting periods. You can see the temptation here. *Wait. You mean if we take all those office supply purchases and*

## Operating Expenses

Operating expenses are the costs that are required to keep the business going day to day. They include salaries, benefits, and insurance costs, among a host of other items. Many companies' largest operating expense is labor costs. Understanding the components of labor costs and what drives them is a key part of finance as it relates to HR. Operating expenses are listed on the income statement and are subtracted from revenue to determine profit.

call them capital expenditures, we can increase our profit accordingly? HR isn't immune to this kind of thinking. The department is usually seen as a cost center, so anything you can do to reduce expenses might seem like a good thing. But it's the sort of thinking that can get you into trouble. To prevent such temptation, both the accounting profession and individual companies have rules about what must be classified where. But the rules leave a good deal up to individual judgment and discretion. Again, those judgments can affect a company's profit, and hence its stock price, dramatically.

Now, we are writing this book primarily for HR leaders in companies, not for investors. So why should HR people worry about any of this? The reason, of course, is that they use numbers to make decisions. You yourself make judgments about budgets, capital expenditures, staffing, and a dozen other matters—or your boss does—based on an assessment of the company's or your business unit's financial situation. You are supporting parts of the organization that deal with the numbers every day—and you provide advice and information based in part on how they are doing financially. Moreover, what you do affects the financials of those departments and units. If you aren't aware of the assumptions and estimates that underlie the numbers and how those assumptions and estimates affect the numbers in one direction or another, your decisions, advice, support, and information may all be faulty.

Financial intelligence means understanding where the numbers are "hard" (that is, well supported and relatively uncontroversial) and where they

## Capital Expenditures

A capital expenditure is the purchase of an item that's considered a long-term investment, such as computer systems and equipment. Most companies follow the rule that any purchase over a certain dollar amount counts as a capital expenditure; anything less is an operating expense. Operating expenses show up on the income statement and thus reduce profit. Capital expenditures show up on the balance sheet; only the *depreciation* of a piece of capital equipment appears on the income statement. More on this in chapters 4 and 10.

are "soft" (that is, highly dependent on judgment calls). What's more, outside investors, bankers, vendors, customers, and others will be using your company's numbers as a basis for their own decisions. If you don't have a good working understanding of the financial statements and don't know what those folks are looking at or why, you are at their mercy.

# Spotting Assumptions, Estimates, and Biases

So let's plunge a little deeper into the "artistic" aspects of finance. We'll look at three examples and ask some simple but critical questions:

- What were the assumptions in this number?

- Are there any estimates in the numbers?

- What is the bias those assumptions and estimates lead to?

- What are the implications?

The examples we'll look at are accruals and allocations, depreciation, and valuation. If these words sound like part of that strange language the financial folks speak, don't worry. You'll be surprised how quickly you can pick up enough to get around.

## ACCRUALS AND ALLOCATIONS: LOTS OF ASSUMPTIONS AND ESTIMATES

At a certain time every month, you know that your company's controller is busy "closing the books." The controller asks you for additional information, maybe information that seems too detailed to matter, and he or she needs it right away. Here, too, is a financial puzzle: why on earth does it take as long as it does? And why does the accounting department need all that information? If you haven't worked in accounting, you might think it could take a day to add up all the end-of-the-month figures. But two or three *weeks*?

Well, one step that takes a lot of time is figuring out all the accruals and allocations. There's no need to understand the details now—we'll get to that in chapters 10 and 11. For the moment, read the definitions in the boxes, and focus on the fact that the accountants use accruals and allocations to try to create an accurate picture of the business for the month. After all, it doesn't help anybody if the financial reports don't tell us how much it cost us to produce the products and services we sold last month. That is what the controller's staff is trying so hard to do, and that is one reason why it takes as long as it does. And even though HR people aren't usually directly involved in the development or delivery of products or services, the accountants must still figure out where to put HR expenses to create that accurate picture of reality. Many of these expenses require accruals. How the accruals are handled can affect the bottom line on the income statement.

Determining accruals and allocations nearly always entails making assumptions and estimates. For example, say that you are an organizational development specialist in HR. In June you supported a team that was developing a new product line. Team members needed your expertise to help them through the difficulties of developing the new product. The company launched the new product in July, and you kept on working with the

## Accruals

An accrual is the portion of a given revenue or expense item that is recorded for a particular time span. Product development costs, for instance, are likely to be spread out over several accounting periods, and so a portion of the total cost will be accrued each month. The purpose of accruals is to match revenues to costs in a given time period as accurately as possible.

## Allocations

Allocations are apportionments of costs to different departments or activities within a company. For instance, overhead costs, such as some HR salaries, are often allocated to the company's operating units. Many HR professionals know firsthand about allocations, partly because they hear the complaints from operating managers about being "charged" for HR.

team through the product's initial market test. Now the accountant determining the allocations has to estimate how much of your salary should be considered development costs (because you worked with the team on the initial development of the product) and how much should be charged to product costs (because you continued to work with the team after the product was generating revenue). She must also decide how to accrue for June versus July. Her decisions affect the income statement. Product costs go into cost of goods sold. If product costs go up, gross profit goes down—and gross profit is a key measure for assessing product profitability. Development costs, however, go into research and development, which are included in the operating-expense section of the income statement and don't affect gross profit at all.

So let's say the accountant determined that all your salary should go into the development cost in June, rather than the product cost in July. Her assumption is that your work wasn't directly related to the manufacturing of the product and therefore shouldn't be categorized as product cost. But a twofold bias results:

- First, development costs are larger than they otherwise would be. An executive who analyzes those costs later on may decide that product development is too expensive and that the company shouldn't take that risk again. If that's what happens, the company might do less product development, thereby jeopardizing its future.

- Second, the product cost is smaller than it otherwise would be. That, in turn, will affect key decisions, such as pricing and hiring. Maybe the product will be priced too low. Maybe more people will be hired to put out what looks like a profitable product—even though the profit reflects some dubious assumptions.

Of course, any individual's salary won't make much of a difference in most companies. But the assumptions that govern one person are likely to be applied across the board. To paraphrase a familiar saying in Washington, D.C., a salary here and a salary there and pretty soon you're talking real money. At any rate, this case is simple enough that you can easily see the answers to the questions we posed earlier. *The assumptions in the numbers?* Your time spent supporting the development team didn't really have much to do with the production of the product that was sold in July. *The estimates?* How your salary should be split, if at all, between development and product cost. *The bias?* Higher development costs and lower product costs. *And the implications?* Concern about the high cost of development; product pricing that may be too low. The way these issues are handled could directly impact the staffing decisions in the relevant departments. Some of the most expensive mistakes people make in business are related to the hiring or firing of personnel. You would want to understand how these costs are allocated before making critical staffing decisions.

Who said there is no poignancy or subtlety in finance? Accounting and finance professionals labor to give the most accurate picture possible of the company's performance. That is why they ask all those questions of you. But all the while they know that they will never, ever capture the exact numbers.

## DISCRETION ABOUT DEPRECIATION

A second example is the use of depreciation. The notion of depreciation isn't complicated. Say a company buys some expensive machinery or vehicles that it expects to use for several years. Accountants think about such an event like this: rather than subtracting the entire cost from one month's revenues—perhaps plunging the company or business unit into the red for that month—we should spread the cost out over the equipment's useful life. If we think a machine will last three years, for instance, we can record ("depreciate") one-third of the cost per year, or one-thirty-sixth per month, using a simple method of depreciation. That's a better way of estimating

> ## Depreciation
>
> Depreciation is the method accountants use to allocate the cost of equipment and other assets to the total cost of products and services as shown on the income statement. It is based on the same idea as accruals: we want to match as closely as possible the costs of our products and services with what was sold. Most capital expenditures are depreciated. (Land is an example of one that isn't.) Accountants attempt to spread the cost of the expenditure over the useful life of the item. More about depreciation in parts 2 and 3.

the company's true costs in any given month or year than if we recorded it all at once. Furthermore, it better matches the equipment's cost to the revenue that it helps generate—an important idea that we will explore at length in chapter 4.

The theory makes perfect sense. In practice, however, accountants have a good deal of discretion about exactly how a piece of equipment should be depreciated. And that discretion can have a considerable impact. Take the airline industry. Some years back, airlines realized that their planes were lasting longer than anticipated. So the industry's accountants changed their depreciation schedules to reflect that longer life. As a result, they subtracted less depreciation from revenue each month. And guess what? The industry's profits rose significantly, reflecting the fact that the airlines wouldn't have to be buying planes as soon as they had thought. But note that the accountants had to assume that they could predict how long a plane would be useful. On that judgment—and it is a judgment—hung the resulting upward bias in the profit numbers. On that judgment, too, hung all the implications: investors deciding to buy more stock, airline executives figuring they could afford to give out better raises, and so on.

## THE MANY METHODS OF VALUATION

A final example of the art of finance has to do with the valuation of a company—that is, figuring out how much a company is worth. Publicly traded companies, of course, are valued every day by the stock market. They are worth whatever their stock price is multiplied by the number of shares outstanding, a figure known as their *market capitalization* or just market cap. But even that doesn't necessarily capture their value in certain circumstances. A competitor bent on takeover, for instance, might decide to offer a premium for the company's shares because the target company is worth more to that competitor than it is on the open market. Of course, the millions of companies that are privately held aren't valued at all on the market. When they are bought or sold, the buyers and sellers must rely on other methods of valuation.

Talk about the art of finance: much of the art here lies in choosing the valuation method. Different methods produce different results—which, of course, injects a bias into the numbers.

Suppose, for example, your company proposes to acquire a closely held manufacturer of industrial valves. It's a good fit with your business—it's a "strategic" acquisition—but how much should you pay? Well, you could look at the valve company's earnings (another word for profits) and then go to the public markets to see how the market values similar companies in relation to their earnings. (This is known as the *price-to-earnings ratio method.*) Or you could look at how much cash the valve company generates each year and figure that you are, in effect, buying that stream of cash. Then you would use some interest rate to determine what that stream of future cash is worth today. (This is the *discounted cash flow method.*) Alternatively, you could simply look at the company's assets—its plant, equipment, inventory, and so on, along with intangibles such as its reputation and customer list—and make estimates about what those assets are worth (the *asset valuation method*).

Needless to say, each method entails a whole passel of assumptions and estimates. The price-to-earnings method, for example, assumes that the stock market is somehow rational and that the prices it sets are therefore accurate. But of course, the market isn't wholly rational; if the market is high, the value of your target company will be higher than it is when the market is low. And besides, that earnings number, as we'll see in part 2, is *itself* an estimate. And you thought HR was subjective! We think there is nearly as much subjectivity in accounting and finance.

So maybe, you might think, we should use a more objective tool, such as the discounted cash flow method. The question with this method is,

What is the right interest or discount rate to use when we're calculating the value of that stream of cash? Depending on how we set it, the price could vary enormously. And of course, the asset valuation method itself is merely a collection of guesses about what each asset might be worth.

As if these uncertainties weren't enough, think back to that delightful, outrageous, nerve-racking period known as the dot-com boom. Ambitious young Internet companies were springing up all over, fed and watered by a torrent of enthusiastic venture capital. But when investors such as venture capitalists (VCs) put their money into something, they like to know what their investment—and hence what the company—is worth. When a company is just starting up, that's tough to know. Earnings? Zero. Operating cash flow? Also zero. Assets? Negligible. In ordinary times, that's one reason VCs shy away from early-stage investments. But in the dot-com era, they were throwing caution to the wind, relying on what we can only call unusual methods of valuation. They looked at the number of engineers on a company's payroll. They counted the number of hits ("eyeballs") a company got every month on its Web site. One energetic young CEO of our acquaintance raised millions of dollars based almost entirely on the fact that he had hired a large staff of software engineers. Unfortunately, we observed a "For Lease" sign in front of this company's office less than a year later.

The dot-com methods of valuation look foolish now, even though they didn't seem so bad back then, given how little we knew about what the future held. But the other methods described earlier are all reasonable. Trouble is, each has a bias that leads to different results. And the implications are far reaching. Companies are bought and sold based on these valuations. They get loans based on them. If you hold stock in a privately held company, the value of that stock is dependent on an appropriate valuation. It seems reasonable to us that your financial intelligence should include an understanding of how those numbers are calculated.

# Why Increase Your Financial Intelligence?

**S**o far our discussion has been pretty abstract. We have been introducing you to the art of finance and explaining why understanding it is an essential ingredient of financial intelligence. But who needs financial intelligence, anyway? To put it bluntly, why is this book worth reading?

For starters, we want to emphasize that this book is different from other finance books. It doesn't presuppose any financial knowledge. But neither is it another version of *Accounting for Dummies*. We will never mention debits and credits. We won't ever refer to the general ledger or trial balances. This book is about financial intelligence, or, as the subtitle says, *what you really need to know about the numbers*. It's written not for would-be accountants but for everyone in human resources.

This book is also different from other numbers-oriented books aimed at HR. Those books typically focus on metrics that are specific to human resources, including those related to hiring, staffing, compensation, retention programs, training, and the like. This book, by contrast, is about general financial metrics. These are the numbers that senior managers use to gauge a business's performance. They are the basis for many of the fundamental decisions a company's leaders must make day in and day out.

HR professionals sometimes—maybe even many times—get a bum rap. They focus on the "soft" side of business, so it is said, rather than on the "hard" numbers side. It's a bum rap because the numbers ultimately depend on people, and HR is the department that is most responsible for the people in a company. Still, it may be true that HR folks tend to shy away from discussions and decisions that involve finance. That hurts the company because senior management may miss out on the HR perspective. But it also hurts HR people themselves. Why? The fact is, business will always be a game of numbers, and the real players are the people who understand what the numbers mean. If you want to be seen as an integral part of the success of your company, if you want your department to be seated at the strategic table, if you want to be a true business partner to the operational unit you are supporting, then you need to be financially intelligent. "If you're going to be in business and you're going to work in HR, then you better understand finance," says John Hofmeister, president of Shell Oil Company, which is Royal Dutch Shell's U.S. division. Asked exactly what an HR professional should understand about finance, he replied, "To be blunt, everything that a business line manager should understand."

Hofmeister believes that HR people should be able to read and understand their company's income statement, balance sheet, and cash flow statement and that they should be able to "deal with the whole budgeting process, capital investments, depreciation, and so on." That's precisely what we propose to teach you in this book. You'll learn how to read the financial statements and how to use the information they contain to do your job better. You'll learn how to calculate ratios. You'll learn about return on investment (ROI) and working capital management, two concepts that you can use to improve your decision-making skills and boost your impact on the organization. You'll see pretty quickly that it isn't hard—the concepts are straightforward, the calculations simple.

A few years ago, the directors in a sample of *Fortune* 500 companies took a simple financial-literacy test—and got an average of 32 percent of the questions right.[1] If you read this book, you should get 100 percent.

## THE BENEFITS OF FINANCIAL LITERACY

But it isn't just a matter of scoring well on a test; financial literacy brings with it a host of practical benefits. Here's a short list of the advantages you'll gain.

## The Ability to Move HR from a Tactical to a Strategic Organization

Historically, the human resource department was tactical in nature. Its job was to ensure that hiring and firing were done properly, that labor laws were followed, that employee benefits were properly managed, and so on. Over the past decade, however, HR has begun to transform itself. HR professionals have deepened their expertise in key fields such as organizational development and talent development. Leading-edge departments have also begun expecting HR people to understand the business and to take part in business-related discussions and decisions. General Motors, for example, has identified four critical capability arenas for HR professionals. One is pure functional expertise—all the traditional stuff that HR does, which any professional must master. Right behind it, however, is business acumen. (Change management is the third on GM's list, and relationships and partnerships is the fourth.) HR departments that follow these priorities are on their way to becoming a strategic part of their company. If you want to be a part of that transformation—and if you want to help your department make the shift—you need to be financially intelligent.

## The Ability to Evaluate Your Company Critically

Maybe you've had nightmares in which you worked at Enron, Global Crossing, or Sunbeam. Many of the people at these troubled companies—including the HR people who continued to supervise hiring—had no inkling of their precarious situation.

Suppose, for instance, you worked at the big telecommunications company WorldCom (later known as MCI) during the late 1990s. WorldCom's strategy was to grow through acquisition. Trouble was, the company wasn't generating enough cash for the acquisitions it wanted to make. So it used stock as currency and paid for the companies it acquired partly with World-Com shares. That meant it had to keep its share price high; otherwise, the acquisitions would be too expensive. It also meant keeping profits high so that Wall Street would give it a high valuation. WorldCom paid for the acquisitions through borrowing. A company doing a lot of borrowing has to keep its profits up, or the banks will stop lending it money. So on two fronts WorldCom was under severe pressure to report high profits.

That, of course, was the source of the fraud that was ultimately uncovered. The company artificially boosted profits "with a variety of accounting tricks, including understating expenses and treating operating costs as capital expenditures," as *BusinessWeek* summarized the Justice Department's indictment.[2] When we all learned that WorldCom was not as profitable as it had claimed, the house of cards came tumbling down. Many of the employees that HR had helped hire suddenly had to be laid off. But even if there hadn't been fraud, WorldCom's ability to generate cash was out of step with its growth-by-acquisitions strategy. It could live on borrowing and stock for a while, but not forever.

Or look at Tyco International. For all the news stories about Dennis Kozlowski's elaborate birthday party and zillion-dollar umbrella stand, there is another story that wasn't widely reported. During the 1990s, Tyco also was a big acquirer of companies. In fact, it bought some six hundred companies in just two years, or more than one every working day. With all those acquisitions, the goodwill number on Tyco's balance sheet grew to the point where bankers began to get nervous. Bankers and investors don't like to see too much goodwill on a balance sheet; they prefer assets that you can touch (and in a pinch, sell off). So when word spread that there might be some accounting irregularities at Tyco, the capital markets effectively shut Tyco off from further acquisitions. Today Tyco is focusing on organic growth and operational excellence rather than on acquisitions; its financial

## Goodwill

Goodwill comes into play when one company acquires another company. It is the difference between the net assets acquired (that is, the fair market value of the assets less the assumed liabilities) and the amount of money the acquiring company pays for them. For example, if a company's net assets are valued at $1 million and the acquirer pays $3 million, then goodwill of $2 million goes onto the acquirer's balance sheet. That $2 million reflects all the value that is not reflected in the acquiree's tangible assets—for example, its name, its reputation, its customer lists, the talent that it has developed, and so on.

picture matches its strategy. A strategy of organic growth and operational excellence can mean a high level of strategic involvement by HR. Companies such as today's Tyco may present great opportunities for financially intelligent HR professionals.

Now, we're not arguing that every financially intelligent HR manager would have been able to spot WorldCom's or Tyco's precarious situation. Plenty of seemingly savvy Wall Street types were fooled by the two companies. Still, a little more knowledge will give you the tools to watch trends at your company and understand more of the stories behind the numbers. While you might not have all the answers, you should know what questions to ask when you don't. It's always worth your while to assess your company's performance and prospects. You'll learn to gauge how it's doing and to figure out how you can best support those goals and be successful yourself.

## The Ability to Understand the Business

Hofmeister, of Shell Oil, says that anyone working in a business is a businessperson—so HR people, for example, are businesspeople with a specialty in human resources. And what do businesspeople know? They understand how their company makes money. They know how its business model works. They can talk about how its accounting procedures affect its results. If you don't understand all that, adds Hofmeister, you're not a businessperson, and you can't be an effective HR professional.

Tough stuff, but true. Think about it. You are working in a business. How can you be effective if you don't know how the company makes

## Balance Sheet

The balance sheet reflects the assets, liabilities, and owners' equity at a point in time. In other words, it shows, on a specific day, what the company owned, what it owed, and how much it was worth. The balance sheet is called such because it balances—assets always must equal liabilities plus owners' equity. A financially savvy manager knows that all the financial statements ultimately flow to the balance sheet. We'll explain all these notions in part 3.

money? Or what the numbers mean? Or how the company decides what to invest in? Imagine if you started your own business. How long would it be successful if you yourself didn't work toward ensuring that it was successful? If your current employer is to succeed, it will need your help.

### The Ability to Understand the Bias in the Numbers

We've already discussed the bias that is built into many numbers. But so what? What will understanding the bias do for you? One very big thing: it will give you the knowledge and the confidence—the financial intelligence—to challenge the data provided by your finance and accounting department. You will be able to identify the hard data, the assumptions, and the estimates. These projections and estimates often affect critical staffing decisions. In a tight labor market, for instance, layoffs can have hidden costs. HR professionals should know what assumptions and estimates underlie a decision to reduce headcount so that they can play an effective role in the conversation. You will know—and others will, too—when your decisions and actions are on solid ground.

And it isn't just staffing decisions that are at stake. Let's say you are proposing to expand your existing human resource information system (HRIS) with additional kiosks so that employees in the field can have direct access to their information. Your boss says he'll listen, but he wants you to justify the purchase. That means digging up data from finance, including cash flow analysis for the kiosks, working capital requirements, and depreciation schedules. All these numbers—surprise!—are based on assumptions and estimates. If you know what they are, you can examine them to see whether they make sense. If they don't, you can change the assumptions, modify the estimates, and put together an analysis that is realistic and that (hopefully) supports your proposal. Joe, for example, likes to tell audiences that he's a veteran finance professional and could easily come up with an analysis to show why his company should buy him a $5,000 computer. He would assume that he could save an hour a day because of the new computer's features and processing speed; he would calculate the value of an hour per day of his time over a year; and presto, he would show that buying the computer is a no-brainer. A financially intelligent boss, however, would take a look at those assumptions and posit some alternatives, such as that

Joe might actually lose an hour a day of work because it is now so easy for him to surf the Web and download music.

It's amazing, in fact, how easily a financially knowledgeable manager can change the terms of discussion so that better decisions get made. When he worked for Ford Motor Company, Joe had an experience that underlined just that lesson. He and several other finance folks were presenting financial results to a senior marketing director. After they sat down, the director looked straight at them and said, "Before I open these finance reports, I need to know . . . for how long and at what temperature?" Joe and the others had no idea what he was talking about. Then the light went on and Joe replied, "Yes, sir, they were in for two hours at 350°." The director said, "OK, now that I know how long you cooked 'em, let's begin." He was telling the finance people that he knew there were assumptions and estimates in the numbers and that he was going to ask questions. When he asked in the meeting how solid a given number was, the financial people were comfortable explaining where the number came from and the assumptions, if any, they had made. The director could then take the numbers and use them to make decisions he was comfortable with.

Absent such knowledge, what happens? It's simple: the people from accounting and finance control the decisions. We use the word *control* because when decisions are made based on numbers, and when the numbers are based on accountants' assumptions and estimates, then the accountants and finance folks have effective control (even if they aren't trying to control anything). That's why you need to know what questions to ask.

## The Ability to Form Relationships with Finance

From a purely functional perspective, there might never be a reason for HR and finance to form close relationships. Their functions are so different. But that is exactly the point. Imagine what might be different if finance and HR worked together during the budgeting process, instead of at cross-purposes. Imagine how layoffs might be handled if finance and HR collaborated, rather than finance letting HR know at the last minute what had been decided. To develop those relationships, says Connie Haney, vice president of compensation and benefits at Mentor Graphics Corporation, "you have to be able to talk the talk of the business." Haney is in human resources, but she has hired people with a finance or economics background because everyone in compensation must speak the language of finance.

### The Ability to Use Numbers and Financial Tools to Make and Analyze Decisions

What is the ROI of that project? Why can't we spend money when our company is profitable? Why do I have to (and how can I) focus on accounts receivable when I am in HR, not the accounting department? You ask yourself these and other questions every day (or someone else asks them—and assumes you know the answers!). You are expected to use financial knowledge to make decisions, to direct your subordinates, and to plan the future of your department. We will show you how to do that, give you examples, and discuss what to do with the results. In the process, we'll try to use as little financial jargon as possible.

For example, let's look at why the finance department might tell you not to spend any money, even though the company is profitable.

We'll start with the basic fact that cash and profit are different. In chapter 15 we'll explain why, but right now let's just focus on the basics. Profit is based on revenue. Revenue, remember, is recognized when a product or service is delivered, not when the bill is paid. So the top line of the income statement, the line from which we subtract expenses to determine profit, is often no more than a promise. Customers have not paid yet, so the revenue number does not reflect real money and neither does the profit line at the bottom. If everything goes well, the company will eventually collect its receivables and have cash corresponding to that profit. In the meantime, it doesn't.

Now suppose you're working for a fast-growing business-services company. The company is selling a lot of services at a good price, so its revenues and profits are high. HR is busy helping the company hire people as fast as possible, and of course, those people have to be paid as soon as they come on board. But all the profit that these people are earning won't turn into cash until thirty days or maybe sixty days after it is billed out. That's one reason why even the CFO of a highly profitable company may sometimes ask you not to spend any money right now because cash is tight.

Although this book focuses on increasing your financial intelligence in business, you can also apply what you learn in your personal life. Consider your decisions to purchase a house, a car, or a boat. The knowledge you'll

## Cash

Cash as presented on the balance sheet means the money a company has in the bank, plus anything else (like stocks and bonds) that can readily be turned into cash. Really, it is that simple. Later we will discuss measures of cash flow. For now, just know that when companies talk about cash, it really is the cold, hard stuff.

gain can apply to those decisions as well. Or consider how you plan for the future and decide how to invest. This book is not about investing, but it is about understanding company financials, which will help you analyze possible investment opportunities.

## HOW IT BENEFITS A COMPANY

We are the owners of an organization called the Business Literacy Institute. Our job is to teach financial literacy, thereby (we hope) increasing the financial intelligence of the leaders, managers, and employees who are our students. So naturally, we think it's an important subject for our students to learn. But what we have also seen in our work is how much financial litereracy benefits companies. Again, here is a short list of advantages.

### Strength and Balance Throughout the Organization

Do the finance folks dominate decisions? They shouldn't. The strength of their department should be balanced by the strength of human resources, of operations, of marketing, of customer service, of information technology, and so on. If the managers of HR and those other departments are not financially savvy, if they don't understand how financial results are measured and how to use those results to critically evaluate the company, then accounting and finance have the upper hand. The bias they inject into the numbers affects and can even determine decision making.

### Better Decisions

Managers routinely incorporate what they know about the marketplace, the competition, the customers, and so on into their decisions. When they also incorporate financial analysis, their decisions are better. Yes, HR is in a support position—but it can help the department or unit it is supporting make better decisions. When you are participating in meetings, discussing plans, or working through issues with the manager you support, your ideas and advice are going to be better if you understand the financials of that unit or department. We are not big believers in making decisions based solely on the numbers. But we do think that ignoring what the numbers tell you is pretty silly. Good financial analysis gives managers a window into the future and helps them make smarter, more informed choices.

### Greater Alignment

Imagine the power in your organization if everyone understood the financial side of the business. Everyone might actually work in alignment with the strategy and goals. Everyone might work as a team to achieve healthy profitability and cash flow. Everyone might communicate in the language of business instead of jockeying for position through office politics. Wow. HR could have two roles to play here. One is to encourage its own staff to understand finance so that they, too, are aligned. The other is to help create such an alignment for everybody else through training, organizational development, and the other tools of the field. What an opportunity for HR to support the strategy of the company!

## ROADBLOCKS TO FINANCIAL SAVVY

We have worked with enough people and companies to know that while the results everyone wants might be great, they aren't so easy to attain. In fact, we run into several predictable obstacles, both personal and organizational.

One obstacle might be that you hate math, fear math, and don't want to do math. Well, join the club. It might surprise you to know that, for the most part, finance involves addition and subtraction. When finance people get really fancy, they multiply and divide. So have no fear: the math is easy. (And calculators are cheap.) You don't need to be a rocket scientist to be financially intelligent.

A second possible obstacle: the accounting and finance departments hold on tightly to all the information. Are your finance folks stuck in the old approach to their field—keepers and controllers of the numbers, reluctant participants in the communication process? Are they focused on control and compliance? If so, that means you may have a difficult time getting access to data. HR and finance have traditionally not had close relationships, except perhaps in matters of compensation—and even there, the relationship was probably not one of open communication and sharing. But you can still use what you learn to talk about the numbers at your management meetings. You can use the tools to help you make a decision or to ask questions about the assumptions and estimates behind the numbers. In fact, you'll probably surprise and maybe delight your accountants and finance people. And who knows? Those relationships might start to develop. We would love to see it happen (please let us know).

A third possibility is that your boss doesn't want you to question the numbers. If that's the case, he himself may not be comfortable with financials. He probably doesn't know about the assumptions, estimates, and resulting bias. Your boss is a victim of the numbers! Our advice is to keep going; eventually, bosses usually see the benefit to themselves, their departments, and their companies. You can help them along. The more people who do so, the more financially intelligent the entire organization will be. You can also begin to take some risks. Your financial knowledge will give you newfound power, and you can ask some probing questions. Asking questions, as PBS Kids tells our children, is a good way to find things out.

A fourth possibility: you don't have time. Just give us enough time to read this book. If you fly for business, take it with you on a trip or two. In just a few hours, you will become a lot more knowledgeable about finance. Alternatively, keep it somewhere handy. The chapters are deliberately short, and you can read one whenever you have a few spare moments. Incidentally, we've included some stories about the fancy financial shenanigans pulled by some of the corporate villains in the late 1990s, just to make it a little more entertaining—and to show you how slippery some of these slopes can be. We don't mean to imply that every company is like them; on the contrary, most are doing their best to present a fair and honest picture of their performance. But it's always fun to read about the bad guys.

If you can overcome these obstacles, you will have a healthy appreciation of the art of finance, and you will increase your financial intelligence. You won't magically acquire an MBA in finance, but you will become more of a businessperson, more an appreciative consumer of the numbers, someone who's capable of understanding and assessing what the financial folks are showing you and asking them appropriate questions. The numbers will no longer scare you.

It won't take long, it's relatively painless, and it will mean a lot to your career. Let's begin.

# Part One
# TOOLBOX

## GETTING WHAT YOU WANT

Imagine the shock on your boss's face if you made a case for a raise—and part of your case included a detailed analysis of the company's financial picture, showing exactly how human resources has contributed.

Far-fetched? Not really. Once you read this book, you'll know how to gather and interpret data such as the following:

- *The company's revenue growth, profit growth, and margin improvements over the past year.* If the business is doing well, members of senior management may be thinking about new plans and opportunities. They'll need experienced people—like those you are about to recruit into the business.

- *The company's remaining financial challenges.* Could inventory turns be improved? What about gross margin or receivable days? If you can suggest specific ways to better the business's financial performance— and show how human resources can support that improvement— both you and your boss will look smart.

- *The company's cash flow position.* Maybe you'll be able to show that your company has lots of free cash flow for raises for its hard-working employees.

The same goes for when you apply for that next job. The experts always tell job seekers to ask questions of the interviewer—and if you ask financial questions, you'll show that you understand the financial side of the business. Try questions like these:

- Is the company profitable?

- Does it have positive equity?

- Does it have a current ratio that can support payroll?

- Are revenues growing or declining?

  If you don't know how to assess all these, read on—you'll learn.

## THE PLAYERS AND WHAT THEY DO

Who's really in charge of finance and accounting? Titles and responsibilities differ from one company to another, but here's an overview of who usually does what in the upper echelons of these departments:

- *Chief financial officer (CFO).* The CFO is involved in the management and strategy of the organization from a financial perspective. He or she oversees all financial functions; the company controller and treasurer report to the CFO. The CFO is usually part of the executive committee and often sits on the board of directors. For financial matters, the buck stops here. Sometimes human resources reports to the CFO, which, on the face of it, doesn't quite fit. But from our perspective it is perfect, so long as the CFO has a strong understanding of the role human resources should play in the organization. When HR reports to the CFO, it forces everyone in that department to speak the language of business.

- *Treasurer.* The treasurer focuses outside the company as well as inside. He or she is responsible for building and maintaining banking relationships, managing cash flow, forecasting, and making equity and capital-structure decisions. The treasurer is also responsible for investor relations and stock-based equity decisions. Some would say that the ideal treasurer is a finance professional with a personality.

- *Controller.* The focus of the controller—sometimes spelled *comptroller*—is purely internal. His or her job is providing reliable and accurate financial reports. The controller is responsible for general accounting, financial reporting, business analysis, financial planning, asset management, and internal controls. He or she ensures that day-to-day transactions are recorded accurately and correctly. Without good, consistent data from the controller, the CFO and the treasurer can't do their jobs.

## DUE DILIGENCE: NOT JUST FOR FINANCE ANYMORE

When two companies consider a merger or an acquisition, a lot goes on in the finance department. (By the way, there is never really a merger, no matter what the press release says. One company is always acquiring another.) All that activity is called due diligence, which really means that the company's managers are doing their homework. They make sure what the seller told them is true. They check out what they are buying, and they determine how best to structure the financial deal. Due diligence of this sort is critically important—when deals involve millions or even billions of dollars, a buyer better be sure it is doing the right thing.

But finance shouldn't be—and more and more isn't—the only department doing the due diligence. More often than not, a failed acquisition is a result of cultural issues. So HR needs to be involved up front in the process, working hand in hand with finance. This "human due diligence," as *Harvard Business Review* authors David Harding and Ted Rouse have termed it, can often make the difference between success and failure in mergers and acquisitions.[1]

# The (Many) Peculiarities of the Income Statement

# Profit Is an Estimate

In a familiar phrase generally attributed to Peter Drucker, profit is the sovereign criterion of the enterprise. The use of the word *sovereign* is right on the money. A profitable company charts its own course. Its managers can run it the way they wish to. When a company stops being profitable, other people begin to poke their noses into the business. Although you may not see a link right away, profitability is also how you as an HR professional are likely to be judged, just as all managers are ultimately judged. Are you contributing to the company's profitability or detracting from it? Are you figuring out ways to increase profitability every day, or are you just doing your job and hoping everything will work out? Most HR departments are cost centers. But what about the part of the organization you are supporting? Are the initiatives you are involved in targeted to improve profitability, either in the short term or in the long term? Does what you do in supporting others help them improve profitability?

Another familiar saying, this one attributed to Laurence J. Peter of *The Peter Principle*, tells us that if we don't know where we're going, we'll probably end up somewhere else. If people in the human resource function don't know how to contribute to profitability, they are unlikely to do so effectively.

In fact, too many people in business don't understand what profit really is, let alone how it is calculated. Nor do they understand that a company's profit in any given period reflects a whole host of estimates and assumptions. The art of finance might just as easily be termed the art of making a profit—or, in some cases, the art of making profits look better than they really are.

We'll see in this part of the book how companies can do this, both legally and illegally. Our experience is that most companies play it pretty straight, though there are always a few that end up pushing the limits. We'll focus on the basics of understanding an income statement because "profit" is no more and no less than what shows up there. Learn to decipher this document, and you will be able to understand and evaluate your company's overall profitability and the profitability of the organizations you support. Learn to manage the lines on the income statement that you can affect, and you will know how to contribute to that profitability. Learn how the department or unit that you support affects overall profit, and you'll be able to contribute to its financial success. Learn the art involved in determining profit, and you will definitely increase your financial intelligence. You might even get where you are going.

## A (VERY) LITTLE ACCOUNTING

We told you early on that we wouldn't teach you accounting, and so we won't. There is one accounting idea, however, that we will explain to you in this chapter, because once you understand it, you will grasp exactly what the income statement is and what it is trying to tell you. First, though, we want to back up one step and make sure there isn't a major misconception lurking in your mind.

You know that the income statement is supposed to show a company's profit for a given period—usually a month, a quarter, or a year. It's only a short leap of imagination to conclude that the income statement shows how much cash the company took in during that period, how much it spent, and how much was left over. That leftover amount would then be the company's profit, right?

Alas, no. Except for some very small businesses that do their accounting this way—it's called cash-based accounting—that notion of an income statement and profit is based on a fundamental misconception. In fact, an income statement measures something quite different from cash in the door, cash out the door, and cash left over. It measures *sales* or *revenues*, *costs* or *expenses*, and *profit* or *income*.

Any income statement begins with sales. When a business delivers a product or a service to a customer, accountants say it has made a sale. Never mind if the customer hasn't paid for the product or service yet—the business may count the amount of the sale on the top line of its income statement for the period in question. No money at all may have changed hands. Of course, for cash-based businesses such as retailers and restaurants, sales and cash coming in are pretty much the same. But most businesses have to wait thirty days or more to collect on their sales, and manufacturers of big products, such as airplanes, may have to wait many months. (You can see that managing a company like Boeing would entail having a lot of cash on hand to cover payroll and operating costs until the company is paid for its work. We'll get to a concept known as working capital, which helps you assess such matters, later in the book.)

And the "cost" lines of the income statement? Well, the costs and expenses a company reports are not necessarily the ones it wrote checks for during that period. The costs and expenses on the income statement are those it *incurred* in generating the sales recorded during that time period. Accountants call this the *matching principle*—that appropriate costs should be *matched* to all the sales for the period represented in the income statement—and it's the key to understanding how profit is determined. Just as HR tries to match people to the right job, accounting tries to match the appropriate costs to revenue. So really good HR and really good accounting are closely related. (OK, maybe this is a slight stretch.)

## The Matching Principle

The matching principle is a fundamental accounting rule for preparing an income statement. It simply states, "Match the sale with its associated costs to determine profits in a given period of time—usually a month, quarter, or year." In other words, one of the accountants' primary jobs is to figure out and properly record all the costs incurred in generating sales.

The matching principle is the little bit of accounting you need to learn. For example:

- If an ink-and-toner company buys a truckload of cartridges in June to resell to customers over the next several months, it does *not* record the cost of all those cartridges in June. Rather, it records the cost of each cartridge when the cartridge is sold. The reason is the matching principle.

- And if a delivery company buys a truck in January that it plans to use over the next three years, the cost of the truck doesn't show up on the income statement for January. Rather, the truck is depreciated over the whole three years, with one-thirty-sixth of the truck's cost appearing as an expense on the income statement each month (assuming a simple straight-line method of depreciation). Why? The matching principle. The truck is one of the many costs associated with that month's work—the work that shows up in January's sales.

- In human resources, the matching principle applies to any big purchases designed to be used over several accounting periods. These are called capital expenditures, and we'll discuss them in detail in part 6. It also applies to vacation and other benefits. In Joe's small company, Setpoint, productivity typically declines every October because many of the employees take their vacation to go deer hunting. To offset this lower productivity in October, vacation is accrued as a charge in other months, when everyone is working and earning time off. In October, the company doesn't have to charge so much vacation and thus better matches cost with revenue.

- The matching principle even extends to items like taxes. A company may pay its tax bill once a quarter—but every month the accountants will tuck into the income statement a figure reflecting the taxes owed on that month's profits.

- The matching principle applies to service companies as well as product companies. A consulting firm, for example, sells billable hours, which refers to the time each consultant spends working with a client.

Accountants still need to match all the expenses associated with the time—marketing costs, materials costs, research costs, and so on—to the associated revenue.

You can see how far we are from cash in and cash out. Tracking the flow of cash in and out the door is the job of another financial document, namely the cash flow statement (part 4). You can also see how far we are from simple objective reality. Accountants can't just tote up the flow of dollars; they have to *decide* which costs are associated with the sales. They have to make assumptions and come up with estimates. In the process, they may introduce bias into the numbers.

## THE PURPOSE OF THE INCOME STATEMENT

In principle, the income statement tries to measure whether the products or services that a company provides are profitable when everything is added up. It's the accountants' best effort to show the sales the company generated during a given time period, the costs incurred in making those sales, and the profit, if any, that is left over. The costs incurred are all the costs of operating the business for that span of time—which, of course, includes human resource costs (like salaries, training, supplies, consultants, incentive compensation, and recruiting). Possible bias aside, this is a critically important endeavor for nearly every manager in a business to understand. A human resource manager should know the profitability of his company's products or services so that he knows where the company's strategic priorities are likely to lie when he is recruiting new people. He should also know the changes in profitability of various parts of the business so that he can be prepared for operational changes that may need to occur, such as adding specific types of talent, retraining, relocating, and the like. Similarly, a sales manager needs to know what kind of profits she and her team are generating so that she can make decisions about discounts, terms, which customers to pursue, and so on. A marketing manager needs to know which products are most profitable so that those can be emphasized in marketing campaigns.

Over time, the income statement and the cash flow statement in a well-run company will track one another. *Profit* will be turned into *cash*. As we saw in chapter 3, however, just because a company is making a profit in any given time period doesn't mean it will have the cash to pay its bills. Profit is always an estimate—and you can't spend estimates.

With that lesson under our belts, let's turn to the business of decoding the income statement.

# Cracking the Code of the Income Statement

**N**ote the word we used in the title to this chapter: *code*. Unfortunately, an income statement can often seem like a code that needs to be deciphered.

Here's the reason. In books like this one—and even later in this book—you will often find cute little sample income statements. They look something like this:

| | |
|---|---|
| Revenue | $100 |
| Cost of goods sold | 50 |
| Gross profit | 50 |
| Expenses | 30 |
| Taxes | 5 |
| Net profit | $ 15 |

A bright fourth grader wouldn't need much help figuring out that one, once she had a little help with definitions. She could even do the math without a calculator. But now check out a real-world income statement—your own company's or one that you find in some other company's annual report. If it's a detailed statement, it may go on for pages—line after line after line of numbers, usually in print so small you can barely read it. Even if it's a "consolidated" statement like those you find in annual reports, it's likely to contain a whole bunch of lines with arcane labels like "enterprise investments/other" (that's from IBM) or "consolidated, liquidating securitization entities" (that's from General Electric). It's enough to make anybody but a financial professional throw up his hands in dismay.

So bear with us while we run through some simple procedures for curling up with an income statement. Boosting your financial intelligence shouldn't involve an attack of heartburn, and learning these steps may save you from just that.

## READING AN INCOME STATEMENT

Before you even start contemplating the numbers, you need some context for understanding the document.

### The Label

Does the document say "income statement" at the top? It may not. It may instead say "profit and loss statement" or "P&L statement," "operating statement" or "statement of operations," "statement of earnings" or "earnings statement." Often the word *consolidated* is in front of these phrases. We work with a client that calls the income statement in its annual report the statement of earnings. Meanwhile, one of the company's major divisions calls its income statement an income statement—and another major division calls it the profit and loss statement! With all these terms for the same thing, one might get the idea that our friends in finance and accounting don't want us to know what is going on. Or maybe they just take it for granted that everybody knows that all these different terms mean the same thing. However that may be, in this book we will always use the term *income statement*.

Incidentally, if you see "balance sheet" or "statement of cash flows" at the top, you have the wrong document. The label pretty much has to include one of those phrases we just mentioned.

### What It's Measuring

Is this income statement for an entire company? Is it for a division or business unit? Is it for a region? Larger companies typically produce income statements for various parts of the business as well as for the whole organization. H. Thomas Johnson and Robert S. Kaplan, in their classic book

*Relevance Lost*, tell how General Motors developed the divisional system—with income statements for each division—in the first half of the twentieth century.[1] We can be glad it did. Creating income statements for smaller business units has provided managers in large corporations with enormous insights into their financial performance. As an HR manager, you'll probably want to study at least two and probably three income statements: the income statement or cost center report for human resources, the income statement for the unit that you are supporting, and the income statement for the entire company. We believe that you should understand the big-picture context of the company and then understand how your income statement or cost center results fit into that. Incidentally, if all you see in HR is a cost center report or budget results, don't let that stop you. These documents typically include line items similar to the expenses listed in an income statement, so you can use them in the same way to understand your function's goals and results.

Once you have identified the relevant entity, you need to check the time period. An income statement, like a report card in school, is always for a span of time: a month, quarter, year, or maybe year-to-date. Some companies produce income statements for a time span as short as a week. Incidentally, the figures on large companies' income statements are usually rounded off, and the last zeros are omitted. So look for a little note at the top: "in millions" (add six zeros to the numbers) or "in thousands" (add three zeros). This may sound like common sense, but we have found that seemingly trivial details such as this one are often overlooked by financial newcomers.

## "Actual" Versus "Pro Forma"

Most income statements are "actual," and if there's no other label, you can assume that is what you're looking at. They show what "actually" happened to revenues, costs, and profits during that time period according to the rules of accounting. (We put "actually" in quotes to remind you that *any* income statement has those built-in estimates, assumptions, and biases, which we will discuss in more detail later in this part of the book.)

Then there are what's known as *pro forma* income statements. Sometimes pro forma means that the income statement is a projection. You might be asked, for example, to participate in drawing up a plan for a new business. Your role might be to help project salary and benefit expenses for the first year or two—in other words, what you hope and expect will happen in terms of personnel expenses. That projection is called a pro forma. But pro forma can also mean an income statement that excludes any unusual or one-time charges. Say a company has to take a big write-off in a particular year, resulting in a loss on the bottom line. (More on write-offs later in this part.) Along with its actual income statement, it might prepare one that shows what would have happened without the write-off.

Be careful of this kind of pro forma! Its ostensible purpose is to let you compare last year (when there was no write-off) with this year (if there hadn't been that ugly write-off). But there is often a subliminal message, something along the lines of, "Hey, things aren't really as bad as they look—we just lost money because of that write-off." Of course, the write-off really did happen, and the company really did lose money. Most of the time, you want to look at the actuals as well as the pro formas, and if you have to choose just one, the actuals are probably the better bet. Cynics sometimes describe pro formas as income statements with all the bad stuff taken out, which is how it sometimes appears.

## The Big Numbers

No matter whose income statement you're looking at, there will be three main categories. One is sales, which may be called revenue (it's the same thing). Sales or revenue is always at the top. When people refer to "top-line growth," that's what they mean: sales growth. Costs and expenses are in the middle, and profit is at the bottom. (If the income statement you're looking at is for a nonprofit, "profit" may be called "surplus/deficit" or "net revenue.") There are subsets of profit that may be listed as you go along, too—gross profit, for example. We'll explain the different forms of profit in chapter 8.

You can usually tell what's important to a company by looking at the biggest numbers relative to sales. For example, the "sales" line is usually followed by "cost of goods sold," or COGS. In a service business, the line is often "cost of services," or COS. If that line is a large fraction of sales, you can bet that management in that company watches COGS or COS very closely. In your own company, you will want to know exactly what is included in line items that are relevant to your job.

If you are looking at the income statement found in your company's annual report, HR expenses will most likely be found in the "sales, general, and administrative" or SG&A category (more on that in chapter 7). If you are looking at your own department's income statement or budget, you'll need to focus on the specifics of your job and the jobs of those who report to you.

As for the income statement for the unit that you support, you'll probably want to take a look at the big picture—how the unit is doing overall—and then study specific line items relevant to the activities you're engaged in. If you are supporting the marketing department, for instance, part of your role may be to ensure that the department is properly staffed. You will want to identify where the payroll expenses for the marketing department show up on the report. If you are focused on benefits, you should know where benefits show up and what percentage of overall payroll expenses they account for. This information should be split out on a detailed income statement for your unit.

By the way, unless you're a financial professional, you can usually ignore items like "consolidated, liquidating securitization entities." Most lines with labels like that aren't material to the bottom line anyway. And if they are, they ought to be explained in the footnotes.

## Comparative Data

The consolidated income statements presented in annual reports typically have three columns of figures, reflecting what happened during the past three years. Internal income statements may have many more columns. You may see something like this, for example:

| Actual % of sales | Budget % of sales | Variance % |
|---|---|---|

Or like this:

| Actual previous period | $ Change (+/−) | % Change |
|---|---|---|

Tables of numbers like these can be intimidating. But they don't need to be.

In the first case, "% of sales" is simply a way of showing the magnitude of an expense number relative to revenue. The revenue line is taken as a given—a fixed point—and everything else is compared with it. Many companies set percent-of-sales targets for given line items and then take action if they miss the target by a significant amount. For instance, maybe senior executives have decided that selling expenses shouldn't be more than 12 percent of sales. If the number creeps up much above 12 percent, the sales organization had better watch out. And many companies have targets for personnel costs. For example, management might set a target that overall personnel expenses should never exceed 70 percent of total expenses and that benefits should never exceed a certain percentage of personnel costs. If these targets are broken, you can be sure someone in management will want to know why. It's the same with the budget and variance numbers. ("Variance" just means difference.) If the actual number is way off budget—that is, if the variance is high—that, too, will draw attention. Financially savvy managers always identify significant variances to budget and find out why they occurred.

In the second case, the statement simply shows how the company is doing compared with last quarter or last year. Sometimes the point of comparison will be "same quarter last year." Again, if a number has moved in the wrong direction by a sizable amount, someone will want to know why.

In short, the point of these comparative income statements is to highlight what is changing, which numbers are where they are supposed to be, and which ones are not.

## Footnotes

An internal income statement may or may not include footnotes. If it does, we recommend reading them very carefully. They are probably going to tell you something that the accountants think everybody should be aware of. External income statements, like those found in annual reports, are a little different. They usually include many, many footnotes. You may want to scan them: some may be interesting; others not so much.

Why all the footnotes? In cases where there is any question, the rules of accounting require the financial folks to explain how they arrived at their totals. So most of the notes are like windows into how the numbers were determined. Some are simple and straightforward, such as the following two footnotes from Dell's 2006 Form 10-K (the annual report required by the Securities Exchange Act of 1934):

*Fiscal Year—Dell's fiscal year is the 52- or 53-week period ending on the Friday nearest January 31. The fiscal year ending February 3, 2006 included 53 weeks, and the fiscal years ending January 28, 2005 and January 30, 2004 included 52 weeks.*

*Shipping Costs—Dell's shipping and handling costs are included in cost of sales in the accompanying consolidated statement of income for all periods presented.*[2]

But other footnotes can be long and complex, such as the following footnote fragment from Tyco International's Form 10-K for the fiscal year ending September 29, 2006:

*Revenue Recognition—The Company recognizes revenue principally on four types of transactions—sales of products, sales of security systems, subscriber billings for monitoring services and contract sales.*

*Revenue from the sales of products is recognized at the time title and risks and rewards of ownership pass. This is generally when the products reach the free-on-board shipping point, the sales price is fixed and determinable and collection is reasonably assured.*

*Provisions for certain rebates, sales incentives, trade promotions, coupons, product returns and discounts to customers are accounted for as reductions in determining sales in the same period the related sales are recorded. These provisions are based on terms of arrangements with direct, indirect and other market participants. Rebates are estimated based on sales terms, historical experience and trend analysis.*[3]

This particular footnote goes on for five more paragraphs. Don't get us wrong: it's important that Tyco explains its approach to revenue recognition. Decisions about when revenue is recognized are a key element of the art of finance. And don't assume that Dell always has simple footnotes and Tyco always has complex ones. Our examples here are simply to illustrate the diversity of the types of footnotes you'll find relating to the income statement in an annual report. Sometimes you find out some very interesting things about companies by reading the footnotes, so have fun! (Did we just say that footnotes can be fun?)

Footnotes to the financial statements will often include information relevant to HR. For instance, companies must disclose current litigation, some of which may relate to HR issues such as alleged discrimination. The notes also present information about the financial impact of retirement benefits, incentive compensation, and reductions in force. Surprise: HR's financial effects are described right there in the footnotes. Incidentally, if you can't find the explanations you need in the notes, ask your CFO. He or she ought to have the answers.

## ONE BIG RULE

So those are the rules for reading. But don't forget the *one big rule* that should be in the forefront of your thinking whenever you confront an income statement. That rule says the following: *Remember that many numbers on the income statement reflect estimates and assumptions. Accountants have decided to include some transactions here and not there. They have decided to estimate one way and not another.* That is the art of finance. If you remember this one point, we assure you that your financial intelligence already exceeds that of many managers.

So let's plunge in for a more detailed look at some of the key categories. If you don't have another income statement handy, use the sample in appendix A for reference.

# 6

# Revenue

## The Issue Is Recognition

We'll begin at the top. We already noted that sales—the top line of an income statement—is also often called revenue. So far so good: only two words for the same thing isn't too bad, and we'll use both, just because they're so common. But watch out: some companies (and many people) call that top line income. In fact, the popular accounting software QuickBooks labels it income. That's really confusing because "income" more often means "profit," which is the *bottom* line. (Obviously, we have an uphill battle here. Where are the language police when you need them?)

In the past, many managers both inside and outside of HR have presumed that the human resource function had no impact on revenue. We don't believe it. Part of what HR does is create the "packaging" of the company—the attitudes of employees, the perceptions of the company in the industry and the marketplace, the organizational culture. Attitudes, perceptions, and culture have a huge impact on sales, and all are greatly influenced by how HR goes about its business. But even if you buy the traditional argument, you still need to understand revenue. If you're a businessperson first and an HR specialist second, you need to know where the money comes from and what the trend lines are. And if you're ever asked to participate in sales meetings, you should come armed with the relevant revenue data.

## Sales

Sales or revenue is the dollar value of all the products or services a company provided to its customers during a given period of time.

A company can record or recognize a sale when it delivers a product or service to a customer. That's a simple principle. But as we suggested earlier, putting it into practice immediately runs into complexity. In fact, the issue of when a sale can be recorded is one of the more artful aspects of the income statement. It's one that accountants have significant discretion with and that managers, therefore, must pay close attention to. So this is one place where your skills as an educated consumer of the financials will come in handy. If things don't seem right, ask questions—and if you can't get satisfactory answers, it might be time to be concerned. Revenue recognition is a common arena for financial fraud.

### MURKY GUIDELINES

The guideline that accountants use for recording or recognizing a sale is that the revenue must have been *earned*. A products company must have shipped the product. A service company must have performed the work. Fair enough—but what would you do about these situations?

- Your company does systems integration for large customers. A typical project requires about six months to design and gain approval from the customer and then another twelve months to implement. The customer gets no real value from the project until the whole thing is complete. So when have you earned the revenue that the project generates?

- Your company sells to retailers. Using a practice known as bill-and-hold, you allow your customers to buy product (say, a popular Christmas item) well in advance of the time they will actually need it. You warehouse it for them and ship it out later. When have you earned the revenue?

- You work for an architectural firm. The firm provides clients with plans for buildings, deals with the local building authorities, and supervises the construction or reconstruction. All these services are included in the firm's fee, which is generally figured as a percentage of construction costs. How do you figure out when the firm has earned its revenue?

- Your human resource department is one that has revenue. You charge the other parts of the organization for some of the services you provide, including training. The department earned revenue by providing a service but this is an internal transaction that doesn't show up in an external income statement. So how should it be accounted for?

We can't provide exact answers to these questions because accounting practices differ from one company to another. But that's precisely the point: there are no hard-and-fast answers. Project-based companies typically have rules that allow for partial revenue recognition when a project reaches certain milestones. Those rules, however, can vary. The "sales" figure on a company's top line always reflects the accountants' judgments about when they should recognize revenue. And where there is judgment, there is room for dispute—not to say manipulation.

## POSSIBILITIES FOR MANIPULATION

In fact, the pressures for manipulation can be intense. Let's take a software company, for example. And let's say that it sells software along with maintenance-and-upgrade contracts extending over a period of five years. So it has to make a judgment about when to recognize revenue from a sale.

Now suppose this software company is actually a division of a large corporation, one that makes earnings predictions to Wall Street. The folks in the corporate office want to keep Wall Street happy. This quarter, alas, it looks as if the parent company is going to miss its earnings-per-share estimate by one penny. If it does, Wall Street will not be happy. And when Wall Street isn't happy, the company's stock gets hammered.

Aha! (You can hear the folks in the corporate office thinking.) Here is this software division. Suppose we change how its revenue is recognized? Suppose we recognize 75 percent up front instead of 50 percent? The logic

## Earnings per Share

Earnings per share (EPS) is a company's net profit divided by the number of shares outstanding. It's one of the numbers that Wall Street watches most closely. Wall Street has "expectations" for many companies' EPS, and if the expectations aren't met, the share price is likely to drop.

might be that a sale in this business takes a lot of initial work, so the company should recognize the cost and effort of making the sale as well as the cost of providing the product and delivering the service. Make the change—recognize the extra revenue—and suddenly earnings per share are nudged up. Now they meet Wall Street's expectations.

Interestingly, such a change is not illegal. An explanation might appear in a footnote to the financial statements, but then again, it might not. Here is an example of a footnote from the 2007 Wal-Mart annual report explaining the change in how certain sales data is calculated:

> Comparable store sales is a measure which indicates the performance of our existing stores by measuring the growth in sales for such stores for a particular period over the corresponding period in the prior year. Beginning in fiscal 2007, we changed our method of calculating comparable store sales. We now include in our measure of comparable store sales all stores and clubs that have been open for at least the previous 12 months. Additionally, stores and clubs that are relocated, converted or expanded are excluded from comparable store sales for the first 12 months following the relocation, conversion or expansion. For fiscal 2006 and prior years, we considered comparable store sales to be sales at stores that were open as of February 1st of the prior fiscal year and had not been expanded, converted or relocated since that date. Stores that were expanded, converted or relocated during that period are not included in the calculation.[1]

In principle, any accounting change that is material to the bottom line should be footnoted in this manner. But who decides what is material and what isn't? You guessed it: the accountants. In fact, it could very well be that recognizing 75 percent up front presents a more accurate picture of the software division's reality. But was the change in accounting method a result of good financial analysis, or did it reflect the need to make the earnings forecast? Could there be a bias lurking in there? Remember, accounting is the art of using limited data to come as close as possible to an accurate description of how well a company is performing. Revenue on the income statement is an estimate, a best guess. This example shows how estimates can introduce bias.

It isn't just investors who have to be careful about bias—decisions like these can directly affect a manager's job. Say you are responsible for supporting the sales organization. You know that sales managers focus on the revenue numbers every month and use them in managing their direct reports, including performance reviews. You help the sales managers make decisions about hiring, firing, rewards, recognition, and so on—all according to the numbers. Now your company does what the software company did: to achieve some corporate goal, it changes the way it recognizes revenue. Suddenly, the sales staff seems to be doing great! Bonuses for everyone! But be careful: the underlying revenue figures might not look so good if they were recognized in the same way as before. If you didn't know the policy had changed and you and the sales manager began passing out bonuses, you'd be paying for no real improvement. Financial intelligence in this case means understanding how the revenue is recognized, analyzing the real variances in the sales figures, and paying bonuses (or not) based on true changes in performance.

Just as an aside, the most common source of accounting fraud has been and probably always will be in that top line: sales. Sunbeam, Cendant, Xerox, and Rite Aid all played with revenue recognition in questionable ways. The issue is particularly acute in the software industry. Many software companies sell their products to resellers, who then sell the products to end users. Manufacturers, often under pressure from Wall Street to make their numbers, are frequently tempted to ship unordered software to these distributors at the end of a quarter. (The practice is known as channel stuffing.) One company that took the high road in regard to this practice is Macromedia, creators of the Internet Flash player and other products. (Macromedia was eventually acquired by Adobe.) When channel stuffing was becoming a serious problem in the industry, Macromedia voluntarily reported estimates of inventory held by its distributors, thereby showing that the channels for its products were not artificially loaded up. The message was clear to shareholders and employees alike: Macromedia was not going to be dragged into this practice.

The next time you read about a financial scandal in the paper, check first to see whether somebody was messing around with the revenue numbers. Unfortunately, it is all too common.

# 7

# Costs and Expenses

## No Hard-and-Fast Rules

Most human resource managers have a lot of personal experience with expenses. But did you know that there are plenty of estimates and biases on those expense lines? Let's examine the major line items.

## COST OF GOODS SOLD OR COST OF SERVICES

As you probably know, expenses on the income statement fall into two basic categories. The first is cost of goods sold, or COGS. As usual, there are a couple of different names for this category—in a service company, for instance, it may be called cost of services (COS). We've also frequently seen cost of revenue and cost of sales. (For simplicity's sake, we'll use the acronyms COGS or COS.) At any rate, what matters isn't the label; it's what's included. The idea behind COGS is to measure all the costs directly associated with making the product or delivering the service—the materials, the labor, and so on. If you suspect that rule is open to a ton of interpretation, you're on the money. The accounting department has to make decisions about what to include in COGS and what to put somewhere else.

Some of these decisions are easy. In a manufacturing company, for instance, the following costs are definitely in:

- The wages of the people on the manufacturing line

- The cost of the materials that are used to make the product

And plenty of costs are definitely out, such as:

- The cost of supplies (like paper) used by the accounting department

- The salary of the IT manager in the corporate office

Ah, but then there's the gray area—and it's enormous. For example:

- What about the salary of the person who manages the plant where the product is manufactured?

- What about the salary of the human resource manager who works in the manufacturing facility and supports those people?

- What about the cost of the technical training needed by the manufacturing crew to do their job?

- What about the wages of the plant supervisors?

- What about sales commissions?

Are all these directly related to the manufacturing of the product? Or are they indirect expenses, like the cost of the IT manager? We know of one company that includes direct selling costs in their COGS. They believe that it is appropriate for their business. There's the same ambiguity in a service environment. COS in a service company typically includes the labor associated with delivering the service. But what about the group supervisor? You could argue that his salary is part of general operations and therefore shouldn't be included in the COS line. You could also argue that he is sup-

## Cost of Goods Sold and Cost of Services

Cost of goods sold or cost of services is one category of expenses. It includes all the costs directly involved in producing a product or delivering a service.

porting direct-service employees, so he should be included with them in that line. These are all judgment calls. There are no hard-and-fast rules.

The fact that there aren't any, frankly, is a little surprising. GAAP—the generally accepted accounting principles that govern how U.S. accountants keep their books—runs for some four thousand pages and spells out a lot of detailed rules. You'd think GAAP would say, "The plant manager is out" or "The supervisor is in." No such luck; GAAP only provides guidelines. Companies take those guidelines and apply a logic that makes sense for their particular situations. The key, as accountants like to say, is reasonableness and consistency. So long as a company's logic is reasonable, and so long as that logic is applied consistently, whatever it wants to do is OK.

Why should an HR manager care what's in and what's out? Consider the following scenarios:

• Let's say you support the engineering analysis department at an architectural firm, and in the past the staff's salaries have been included in COS. Now the finance folks are moving all those costs out of COS. It's perfectly reasonable—even though the department has a lot to do with completing an architectural design, a case can be made that it isn't directly related to any particular job. So does the change matter? You bet. The staff is no longer part of what's often called "above the line." That means staff salaries will show up differently on the corporate radar screen. If your company focuses on gross profit, for instance, management will be monitoring COS carefully and making sure that departments that affect COS have everything they need to

## GAAP

GAAP stands for "generally accepted accounting principles." GAAP defines the standard for creating financial reports in the United States. It helps ensure the statements' validity and reliability and allows for easy comparison between companies and across industries. But GAAP doesn't spell out everything; it allows for plenty of discretion and judgment calls.

hit their targets. Once you're outside of COS—"below the line"—the level of attention may be significantly less.

- Or let's look at the human resource department itself. Typically, HR is below the line, not included in COGS or COS. But suppose management has decided to reorganize and realign HR within the organization. Now there isn't any corporate HR department. Everyone in HR has moved to the field, and everyone is working in the division, unit, or department that he or she supports. Finance will need to decide whether each of those salaries is in COGS/COS or not. The attention placed on the cost of HR if it is above the line will be different than if it is below the line.

- Or consider the plant manager charged with making a gross profit of $1 million per month. This month she is $20,000 short. Then she realizes that $25,000 of her COGS is in a line item labeled "contract administration on plant orders." Does that really belong in COGS? She petitions the controller to move those costs to operating expenses. The controller agrees; the change is done. The plant manager hits her target, and everyone is happy. An outsider might even look at what's happening and think that gross margins are improving—all from a change the plant manager made because she was trying to hit a target. If you provide HR support to this plant and take part in regular manufacturing meetings, you should know exactly what happened and why.

Again, these changes are legal, so long as they meet the reasonable-and-consistent test. You can even take an expense out of COGS one month and

## Above the Line, Below the Line

The "line" generally refers to gross profit. Above that line on the income statement, typically, are sales and COGS or COS. Below the line are operating expenses, interest, and taxes. What's the difference? Items listed above the line tend to vary more (in the short term) than many of those below the line and so tend to get more managerial attention.

petition to put it back in next month. All you need is a reason good enough to convince the controller (and the auditor, if the changes are material to the company's financials). Of course, changing the rules constantly from one period to the next would be bad form. One thing we all need from our accountants is consistency.

## OPERATING EXPENSES: WHAT'S NECESSARY?

And where do costs go when they are taken out of COGS? Where is "below the line"? That's the other basic category of costs, namely operating expenses. Some companies refer to operating expenses as sales, general, and administrative expenses (SG&A, or just G&A); others treat G&A as one subcategory and give sales and marketing its own line. Often a company will make this distinction based on the relative size of each. Microsoft chooses to show sales and marketing on a separate line; sales and marketing are a significant portion of the company's expenses. By contrast, the biotech firm Genentech includes sales and marketing with G&A, the more typical approach. Both companies separate out R&D costs, most likely because of their relative importance. So pay attention to how your company organizes these expenses.

Operating expenses are often thought of and referred to as overhead. The category includes items such as rent, utilities, telephone, research, and marketing. It also includes management and staff salaries—corporate HR, accounting, IT, and so forth—plus everything else that the accountants have decided does not belong in COGS.

You can think of operating expenses as the cholesterol in a business. Good cholesterol makes you healthy, while bad cholesterol clogs your arteries.

### Operating Expenses (Once More)

Operating expenses are the other major category of expenses. The category includes costs that are not directly related to making the product or delivering a service.

Good operating expenses make your business strong, and bad operating expenses drag down your bottom line and prevent you from taking advantage of business opportunities. (Another name for bad operating expenses is "unnecessary bureaucracy." Or "lard." You can probably come up with others.) HR people know what it means to be part of operating expenses. Companies often want their SG&A expenses to be below a certain percentage of revenue—and if the expenses creep up above that level, the edict goes out to cut SG&A by so much. HR may not be responsible for the cost creep, but it may feel the pain nevertheless.

One more thing about COGS and operating expenses. You might think that COGS is the same as variable costs—costs that vary with the volume of production—and that operating expenses are fixed costs. Materials, for example, are a variable cost: the more you produce, the more material you have to buy. And materials are included in COGS. The salaries of the people in the accounting department are fixed costs, and they're included in operating expenses. Unfortunately, things aren't so simple here, either. For example, if supervisors' salaries are included in COGS, then that line item is fixed in the short run, whether you turn out one hundred thousand widgets or one hundred fifty thousand. Or take selling expenses, which are typically part of SG&A. If you have a commissioned sales force, sales expenses are to some extent variable, but they are included in operating expenses, rather than COGS.

## THE POWER OF DEPRECIATION AND AMORTIZATION

Another expense that is often buried in those COGS and SG&A lines is depreciation and amortization. How this expense is treated can greatly affect the profit on an income statement.

We described an example of depreciation earlier in this part—buying a delivery truck and then spreading the cost over the three-year period that we assume the truck will be used for. As we said, that's an example of the matching principle. In general, depreciation is the expensing of a physical asset, such as a truck or a machine, over its estimated useful life. All this means is that the accountants figure out how long the asset is likely to be in use, take the appropriate fraction of its total cost, and count that amount as an expense on the income statement.

In those few dry sentences, however, lurks a powerful tool that financial artists can put to work. It's worth going into some detail because you'll see exactly how assumptions about depreciation can affect any company's bottom line.

To keep things simple, let's assume we start a delivery company and line up a few customers. In the first full month of operation, we do $10,000 worth of business. At the start of that month, our company bought a $36,000 truck to make the deliveries. Since we're expecting the truck to last three years, we depreciate it at $1,000 a month (using the simple straight-line depreciation approach). So a greatly simplified income statement might look like this:

| | |
|---|---|
| Revenue | $10,000 |
| Cost of goods sold | 5,000 |
| Gross profit | 5,000 |
| Expenses | 3,000 |
| Depreciation | 1,000 |
| Net profit | $ 1,000 |

But our accountants don't have a crystal ball. They don't *know* that the truck will last exactly three years. They're making an assumption. Consider some alternative assumptions:

- They might assume the truck will last only one year, in which case they have to depreciate it at $3,000 a month. That takes $2,000 off the bottom line and moves the company from a net profit of $1,000 to a *loss* of $1,000.

- Or they could assume that it will last six years (seventy-two months). In that case, depreciation is only $500 a month, and net profit jumps to $1,500.

Hmm. In the former case, we're suddenly operating in the red. In the latter, we have increased net profit 50 percent—just by changing one assumption about depreciation. Accountants have to follow GAAP, of course, but GAAP allows plenty of flexibility. No matter what set of rules the accountants follow, estimating will be required whenever an asset lasts longer than a single accounting period. The job for the financially intelligent

HR manager is to understand those estimates and to know how they affect the financials.

If you think this is purely an academic exercise, consider the sorry example of Waste Management Inc. (WMI). WMI was one of the great corporate success stories of the 1970s and 1980s. So it came as a shock to everybody when the company announced in 1998 that it would take a pretax charge—a one-time write-off—of $3.54 *billion* against its earnings. Sometimes one-time charges are taken in advance of a restructuring, as we'll discuss later in this chapter. But this was different. In effect, WMI was admitting that it had been cooking its books on a previously unimaginable scale. It had actually earned $3.54 billion less in the previous several years than it had reported during that time.

What was going on? WMI had been a darling of Wall Street since the 1980s, when it began to grow rapidly by buying up other garbage companies. When the supply of garbage companies to buy began to dwindle, around 1992, it bought companies in other industries. But while it was pretty good at hauling trash, it didn't know how to run those other companies effectively. WMI's profit margins declined. Its share price plummeted. Desperate to prop up the stock, executives began looking for ways to increase earnings.

Their gaze fell first on their fleet of twenty thousand garbage trucks, for which they'd paid an average of $150,000 apiece. Up to that point, they had been depreciating the trucks over eight to ten years, which was the standard practice in the industry. That period wasn't long enough, the executives decided. A good truck could last twelve, thirteen, even fourteen years. When you add four years to your truck depreciation schedule, you can do wonderful things to your bottom line; it's like the preceding little example multiplied thousands of times over. But the executives didn't stop there. They realized that they had other assets they could do the same tricks with—about 1.5 million Dumpsters, for example. You could extend each Dumpster's depreciation period from the standard twelve years to, say, fifteen, eighteen, or twenty years, and you'd pick up another chunk of earnings per year. By fiddling with the depreciation numbers on the trucks and the Dumpsters, Waste Management's executives were able to pump up pretax earnings by a whopping $716 million. And this was just one of many tricks they used to make profits look larger than they were, which is why the end total was so huge.

Of course, the whole tangled web eventually came unraveled, as fraudulent schemes usually do. By then, however, it was too late to save the company. It was sold to a competitor, which kept the name but changed just about everything else. As for the perpetrators of the fraud, no criminal charges were ever filed against them, although some civil penalties were assessed.

Depreciation is a prime example of what accountants call a noncash expense. Right here, of course, is where they often lose the rest of us. How can an expense be other than cash? The key to that puzzling term is to remember that the cash has probably already been paid. The company already bought the truck. But the expense wasn't recorded that month, so it has to be recorded over the truck's life, a little at a time. No more money is going out the door; rather, it's just accountants' way of figuring that this month's revenues depend on using that truck, so the income statement better have something in it that reflects the truck's cost. Incidentally, you should know that there are many methods to determine how to depreciate an asset. You don't need to know what they are; you can leave that to the accountants. All you need to know is whether the use of the asset is matched appropriately to the revenue it is bringing in.

Amortization is the same basic idea as depreciation, but it applies to intangible assets. These days, intangible assets are often a big part of companies' balance sheets. Items such as patents, copyrights, and goodwill (to be explained in chapter 10) are all assets—they cost money to acquire, and

## Noncash Expense

A noncash expense is one that is charged to a period on the income statement but is not actually paid out in cash. An example is depreciation: accountants deduct a certain amount each month for the depreciation of equipment, but the company isn't obliged to pay out that amount because the equipment was acquired in a previous period.

they have value—but they aren't physical assets like real estate and equipment. Still, they must be accounted for in a similar way. Take a patent. Your company had to buy the patent, or it had to do the research and development itself and then apply for the patent. Now the patent is helping bring in revenue. So the company must match the expense of the patent with the revenue the patent helps bring in, a little bit at a time. When an asset is intangible, though, accountants call that process amortization rather than depreciation. We're not sure why—but whatever the reason, it's a source of confusion.

Incidentally, economic depreciation implies that an asset loses its value over time. And indeed, a truck used in a delivery business does lose its value as it gets older. But accounting depreciation and amortization are more about cost allocation than about loss of value. A truck, for example, may be depreciated over three years so that its accounting value at the end of that time is zero. But it may still have some value on the open market. A patent may be amortized over its useful life, but if technology has advanced beyond it, the patent's value may be close to zero after a couple of years, regardless of what the accountants say. So assets are rarely worth what the books say they are worth. (We'll discuss accounting or "book" value in greater detail in part 3.)

## ONE-TIME CHARGES: A YELLOW FLAG

Accounting is like life in at least one respect: there's a lot of stuff that doesn't fall neatly into categories. So every income statement has a big group of expenses that do not fall into COGS and are not operating expenses or overhead, either. Every statement is different, but typically you'll see lines for "other income/expense" (usually this is gain or loss from selling assets or from transactions unrelated to the actual operating of the business) and, of course, "taxes." Most of these you don't need to worry about. But there is one line that often turns up after COGS and operating expenses (though it is sometimes included under operating expenses)—a line you should definitely understand because it is often critical to profitability. The most common label for this line is "one-time charge." You are probably familiar with these one-time charges in HR because they often involve a reduction in force. You are probably painfully aware of your involvement in this process.

You may occasionally have seen the phrase "taking the big bath" or something similar in the *Wall Street Journal.* That's a reference to these one-time charges, which are also known as extraordinary items, write-offs, write-downs, or restructuring charges. Sometimes write-offs occur, as in Waste Management's case, when a company has been doing something wrong and wants to correct its books. More often, one-time charges occur when a new CEO takes over a company and wants to restructure, reorganize, close plants, and maybe lay off people. It's the CEO's attempt, right or wrong, to improve the company based on his or her assessment of what the company needs. Normally, such a restructuring entails a lot of costs—paying off leases, offering severance packages, disposing of facilities, selling off equipment, and so on.

Now, accountants always want to be conservative. In fact, they're required to be. GAAP recommends that accountants record expenses as soon as it is known that expenses will be incurred, even if they have to estimate exactly what the final figure will be. So when a restructuring occurs, accountants need to estimate those charges and record them.

Here is a real yellow flag—a truly terrific place for bias in the numbers to show up. After all, how do you really estimate the cost of restructuring? Accountants have a lot of discretion, and they're liable to be off the mark in one direction or another. If their estimate is too high—that is, if the actual costs are lower than expected—then part of that one-time charge has to be reversed. A reversed charge actually adds to profit in the new time period, so profits in that period wind up higher than they would otherwise have been—and all because an accounting estimate in a previous period was inaccurate! "Chainsaw Al" Dunlap, the notorious CEO of Sunbeam, was said to regard his accounting department as a profit center, and this example—adding to profits through reversing part of a previous estimate—may suggest why. (Incidentally, if you ever hear a senior executive refer to the accounting department in this manner, your company might have a problem.)

Of course, maybe the restructuring charge is too small. Then another charge has to be taken later. That clouds the numbers because the charge isn't really matched to any revenue in the new time period. This time around, profits are lower than they otherwise would be, again because the accountants made the wrong estimate in an earlier time frame. In the early 1990s, AT&T took a "one-time" restructuring charge every year for several years. The company kept saying that earnings before the restructuring charge were growing—but it didn't make much difference, because after all those restructuring charges, the company was in pretty rough shape financially. Besides, if a company takes extraordinary one-time restructuring charges for several years in a row, how extraordinary can those charges really be?

## PEOPLE COSTS IN THE SCHEME OF THINGS

HR people should understand the costs of the business and what they mean in order to support manufacturing, IT, marketing, and so on. In capital-intensive businesses such as oil companies, wages and benefits are a small percentage of total costs, and so HR's decisions about compensation might not have a big effect on the bottom line. In a people-intensive business such as retail, however, wages and benefits are a large percentage of total expenses, and decisions about these costs have a tremendous impact on financial results. You need to understand where the company's focus is likely to be and think strategically about its priorities and your own.

# 8

# The Many Forms of Profit

So far we have covered sales or revenue—the top line—and costs and expenses. Revenue minus costs and expenses equals profit.

Of course, it might also equal *earnings, net income,* or even *net margin.* Amazingly enough, some companies use all these different terms for *profit,* sometimes in the same document. An income statement might have items labeled "gross margin," "operating income," "net profit," and "earnings per share." All these are the different types of profit typically seen on an income statement—and the company could just as easily have said "gross profit," "operating profit," "net profit," and "profit per share." (And you thought you had a corner on the jargon market in HR.) When companies use different words right there in the same statement, it looks as if they are talking about different concepts. But they aren't.

So let's always use the term *profit* here and look at its various incarnations.

## GROSS PROFIT: HOW MUCH IS ENOUGH?

*Gross profit*—revenue minus COGS or COS—is a key number for most companies. It tells you the basic profitability of your product or service. If that part of your business is not profitable, your company is probably not going to survive long. After all, how can you expect to pay below-the-line expenses, including management salaries, if you aren't generating a healthy gross profit?

## Profit

Profit is the amount left over after expenses are subtracted from revenue. There are three basic types of profit: gross profit, operating profit, and net profit. Each one is determined by subtracting certain categories of expenses from revenue.

But what does *healthy* mean? How much gross profit is enough? That varies substantially by industry, and it's even likely to vary from one company to another in the same industry. In the grocery business, gross profit is typically a small percentage of sales. In the jewelry business, it's typically a much larger percentage. Other things being equal, a company with larger revenues can thrive with a lower gross profit percentage than a smaller one. (That's one reason why Wal-Mart can charge such low prices.) To gauge your company's gross profit, you can compare it with industry standards, particularly for companies of a similar size in your industry. You can also look at year-to-year trends, examining whether your gross profit is headed up or headed down. If it's headed down, you can ask why. Are production costs rising? Is your company discounting its sales? If gross profit is changing, understanding why helps managers figure out where to focus their attention.

Here too, however, you need to keep a sharp eye out for possible bias in the numbers. *Gross profit can be greatly affected by decisions about when to recognize revenue and by decisions about what to include in COGS.* Suppose you are the HR director of a market-research firm, and you find that gross profit is headed downward. You look into the numbers, and at first it appears that service costs have gone up. So you and your team begin anticipat-

## Gross Profit

Gross profit is sales minus cost of goods sold or cost of services. It is what is left over after a company has paid the direct costs incurred in making the product or delivering the service. Gross profit must be sufficient to cover a business's operating expenses, taxes, financing costs, and net profit.

ing cuts in service costs, perhaps even including some layoffs. But when you do some more digging, you find that salaries that were previously in operating expenses have been moved into COGS. So service costs did not go up, and laying off people would be a mistake. Now you have to talk with the people in accounting. Why did they move those salaries? Why didn't they tell you? If those salaries are to remain in COGS, then maybe the firm's gross profit targets need to be reduced. But nothing else needs to change.

## OPERATING PROFIT: A KEY TO HEALTH

*Operating profit*—gross profit minus operating expenses or SG&A, including depreciation and amortization—is also known by the peculiar acronym EBIT (pronounced EE-bit). EBIT stands for earnings before interest and taxes. (Remember, *earnings* is just another name for profit). What has not yet been subtracted from revenue is interest and taxes. Why not? Because operating profit is the profit a business earns from the business it is in—from operations. Taxes don't really have anything to do with how well you are running your company. And interest expenses depend on whether the company is financed with debt or equity (we'll explain this difference in chapter 11). But the financial structure of the company doesn't say anything about how well it is run from an operational perspective.

So operating profit, or EBIT, is a good gauge of how well a company is being managed. It's watched closely by all stakeholders because it measures both overall demand for the company's products or services (sales) and the company's efficiency in delivering those products or services (costs). Bankers and investors look at operating profit to see whether the company will be able to pay its debts and earn money for its shareholders. Vendors look at it to see whether the company will be able to pay its bills. (As we'll see later,

### Operating Profit, or EBIT

Operating profit is gross profit minus operating expenses, which include depreciation and amortization. In other words, it shows the profit made from running the business.

however, operating profit is not always the best gauge of this.) Large customers examine operating profit to ascertain whether the company is doing an efficient job and is likely to be around for a while.

Operating profit can be informative to employees as well. A healthy and growing operating profit suggests that the employees are going to be able to keep their jobs, maybe with opportunities for advancement. HR may need to shift its focus to employee development, recruitment, and so on. A declining operating profit will require a different focus. Whatever the case, human resources can be a real-time partner in the organization if its people pay attention to the numbers and understand their implications.

However, remember that potential biases in the numbers can impact operating profit as well. Are there any one-time charges? What is the depreciation line? As we have seen, depreciation can be altered to affect profits one way or another. For a while, Wall Street analysts were watching companies' operating profit, or EBIT, closely. But some of the companies that were later revealed to have committed fraud turned out to be playing games with depreciation (remember Waste Management), so their EBIT numbers were suspect. Before long, Wall Street began focusing on another number—EBITDA (pronounced EE-bid-dah), or earnings before interest, taxes, depreciation, and amortization. Some people think EBITDA is a better measure of a company's operating efficiency because it ignores noncash charges, such as depreciation, altogether.

## NET PROFIT AND HOW TO FIX IT

Now, finally, let's get to the bottom line: net profit. It is usually the last line on the income statement. *Net profit* is what is left over after everything is subtracted—cost of goods sold or cost of services, operating expenses, taxes, interest, one-time charges, and noncash expenses such as depreciation and amortization. When someone asks, "What's the bottom line?" he or she is almost always referring to net profit. Some of the key numbers used to measure a company, such as earnings per share and the price-earnings ratio, are based on net profit. Yes, it is strange that financial folks don't call it profit per share and price-profit ratio. But they don't.

What if a company's net profit is lower than it ought to be? Aside from monkeying with the books, there are only three possible fixes for low prof-

> ## Net Profit
>
> Net profit is the bottom line of the income statement: what's left after all costs and expenses are subtracted from revenue. It's operating profit minus interest expenses, taxes, one-time charges, and any other costs not included in operating profit.

itability. HR may be asked to advise on all three of these and will be heavily involved in at least one. Indeed, if HR people are paying attention to what is going on, they can help decide which fix to take, rather than being the ones to simply implement the fix.

So here are the three fixes. One, the company can increase profitable sales. This solution almost always requires a good deal of time. You have to find new markets or new prospects, work through the sales cycle, and so on. (In this case, HR might focus on the recruitment and development of salespeople.) Two, the company can figure out how to lower production costs and run more efficiently—that is, reduce COGS. (With this option, HR participates in the process improvement efforts.) This, too, takes time: you need to study the production process, find the inefficiencies, and implement changes. Three, it can cut operating expenses, which almost always means reducing the headcount. (We know what HR has to do in this case). This is usually the only short-term solution available. That's why so many CEOs who take over troubled companies start by cutting the payroll in the over-head expense areas. It makes profit look better fast.

Of course, layoffs can backfire. Even with the best human resource ef-forts, morale suffers. Good people whom the new CEO wants to keep may begin looking for jobs elsewhere. And that's not the only danger. For ex-ample, "Chainsaw Al" Dunlap used the lay-people-off strategy a number of times to pump up the profit of companies he took over, and Wall Street usually rewarded him for it. But the strategy didn't work when he got to Sunbeam. Yes, he slashed headcount, and yes, profit rose. In fact, Wall Street was so enthusiastic about the company's pumped-up profitability that it bid Sunbeam's shares way up. But Dunlap's strategy all along had been to sell the company at a profit—and now, with its shares selling at a premium, the company was too expensive for prospective buyers to consider. Without a buyer, Sunbeam was forced to limp along until its problems became apparent and Chainsaw Al was forced out by the board.

The moral? For most companies, it's better to manage for the long haul and to focus on increasing profitable sales and reducing costs. Sure, operating expenses may have to be trimmed. But if that's your only focus, you're probably just postponing the day of reckoning. HR has a role here, too. A financially intelligent HR manager can mediate the battle between those who say "costs walk" (we'd call them short-term thinkers) and those who focus on people's intrinsic value over time (we'd call them long-term thinkers).

## BUDGET RESULTS MEETINGS

At the end of the day, all managers are held accountable for their own bottom line. That shows up on their income statement, whether it is called their budget vs. actual results, their P&L results, or their cost center results. In many companies HR managers attend their business unit's monthly budget meetings, where variances are discussed and decisions are made. If you want to influence your organization, you need to take joint responsibility for all these measures of financial performance. "I had a pretty tight handle each week on what was shaking," says Michael Crist, now HR director at Colorado Energy Management, who regularly attended such meetings in a previous job. Crist learned what the financial issues were in manufacturing, in sales, and in marketing. As the HR guy, he could then focus on those HR issues most related to financial performance.

If you would like to try your hand at reading and analyzing a real income statement to practice what you have learned here—or if you just need a break from reading and you want to do something—please turn to the income-statement exercise in appendix B.

# Part Two
## TOOLBOX

### UNDERSTANDING VARIANCE

*Variance* just means difference. It might be the difference between budget and actual for the month or year, between actual this month and actual last month, and so on. It can be presented in dollars, percentages, or both. Percentages are usually more useful because they provide a quick and easy basis of comparison between the two numbers.

The only difficulty with variance comes with determining whether a variance is favorable or unfavorable. More revenue than expected, for instance, is favorable, but more expense than expected is unfavorable. Sometimes the folks in finance are helpful and let you know in a note that a variance enclosed in parentheses or a variance preceded by a minus sign is unfavorable. But often you have to figure it out on your own. We recommend doing a few calculations yourself, determining whether the indicated variances are bad or good, and then checking to see how they are displayed. Be sure to do the calculations for both a revenue line item and an expense line item. Sometimes parentheses or negative signs indicate the mathematical difference. In that case, parentheses for a revenue line item might mean favorable, and parentheses for an expense line item might mean unfavorable.

### CALCULATING PERCENT OF AND PERCENT CHANGE

When you're studying the income statement, there are two simple yet powerful tools that can help you understand the meaning behind the numbers.

The first is "percent of" calculations. *Percent of* determines what percent something is of something else. The basic formula is:

$$\text{percent of} = \frac{\text{part}}{\text{whole}}$$

For example, if you had $75 in your wallet and gave a friend $6, you've given him 8 percent of what you had:

$$\frac{\$6}{\$75} = .08$$

(Remember that to convert a decimal to a percentage, you move the decimal point over two places to the right, so that .08 becomes 8 percent.)

So, for example, if you wanted to analyze your budget from last year, you might wonder how much of your budget was spent on supplies. Assume that your department spent $600 on supplies last year and that its total budget was $5,000. So the calculation is as follows:

$$\frac{\$600}{\$5,000} = .12 = 12\%$$

The second tool is percent change. (The percent change formula is also the formula for percent variance—so once you have percent change down, you can also do percent variance.) Percent change is simply the percent something changed from one period to the next, from budget to actual, from forecast to actual, and so on (you get the idea).

The formula for percent change from one year to the next is as follows:

$$\frac{\text{current year} - \text{prior year}}{\text{prior year}}$$

For example, if prior year revenue was $3,000 and current year revenue was $3,750, then the percent change is as follows:

$$\frac{\$3,750 - \$3,000}{\$3,000} = .25 = 25\%$$

In general, the formula for percent change is as follows:

$$\frac{\text{final value} - \text{initial value}}{\text{initial value}}$$

You will find more opportunities to practice these percent of and percent change in the practice exercises in appendix B.

## LINE OF SIGHT

The income statement is the financial report in which it is easiest to see a line of sight. *Line of sight* is the connection between someone's job and that job's impact on the financials. Sales is easy—salespeople's line of sight is to revenue (and sales expenses). Human resources is not so straightforward, but it is still critical. Of course, the salaries of everyone in HR show up in the compensation expense line on the income statement. But HR also affects other lines, including travel, training, and office supplies. The fact that HR's direct line of sight is to expense items doesn't mean that HR should always be focused on expense reduction. For example, the investment in training might bring more value to the company than just cutting back on training expenses.

HR, because of its role in the organization, also needs to think about the line of sight of those it supports in the organization. HR's role is to help them improve the numbers that they affect.

# The Balance Sheet
# Reveals the Most

# 9

# Understanding Balance Sheet Basics

There's a puzzling fact about financial statements. Maybe you've noticed it.

Give a company's financials to an experienced manager in any part of the business, HR or otherwise, and the first thing he will turn to is the income statement. Most managers have—or aspire to have—"P&L responsibility." They're accountable for making the various forms of profit turn out right. They know that the income statement is where their performance is ultimately recorded. So that's what they look at first.

Now try giving the same set of financials to a banker, an experienced Wall Street investor, or maybe a veteran board member. The first statement this person will turn to is invariably the balance sheet. In fact, she's likely to pore over it for some time. Then she'll start flipping the pages, checking out the income statement and the cash flow statement—but always going back to the balance sheet.

Why don't managers do what the pros do? Why do they limit their attention to the income statement? We chalk it up to three factors:

- The balance sheet is a little harder to get your mind around than the income statement. The income statement, after all, is pretty intuitive. The balance sheet isn't—at least, not until you understand the basics.

- Most companies' budgeting processes focus on revenue and expenses. In other words, the budget categories more or less align with the income statement. You can't be a manager in human resources (or anywhere else for that matter) without knowing something about budgeting—which automatically means that you're familiar with many of the lines on the income statement. Balance sheet data, by contrast, rarely figures in a human resource manager's budgeting process (although the finance department certainly budgets the balance sheet accounts).

- Managing the balance sheet requires a deeper understanding of finance than managing an income statement. You not only have to know what the various categories refer to; you have to know how they fit together. You also have to understand how changes in the balance sheet impact the other financial statements, and vice versa.

Our guess is that you, too, are a bit wary of the balance sheet. But remember, what we're focusing on here is financial intelligence—understanding how financial results are measured and what you as a manager, an employee, or a leader can do to improve results. We won't get into the esoteric elements of the balance sheet, just the ones you need to appreciate the art of this statement and do the analyses that the statement makes possible.

## SHOWING WHERE THINGS STAND RIGHT NOW

So what is the balance sheet? *It's no more, and no less, than a statement of what a business owns and what it owes at a particular point in time.* The difference between what a company owns and what it owes represents *equity*. Just as one of a company's goals is to increase profitability, another is to increase equity. And as it happens, the two are intimately related.

What is this relationship? Consider an analogy. Profitability is sort of like the grade you receive for a course in college. You spend a semester writing papers and taking exams. At the end of the semester, the instructor tallies your performance and gives you an A– or a C+ or whatever. Equity is more like your overall grade point average (GPA). Your GPA always reflects your cumulative performance at one point in time. Any one grade affects it but doesn't determine it. When you as a manager evaluate a new

> ## Equity
>
> Equity is the shareholders' stake in the company as measured by accounting rules. It's also called the company's book value. In accounting terms, equity is always assets minus liabilities; it is also the sum of all capital paid in by shareholders plus any profits earned by the company since its inception minus dividends paid out to shareholders. That's the accounting formula, anyway; remember that what a company's shares are actually worth is whatever a buyer will pay for them.

graduate for a position in your company, what do you consider a better measure of that candidate's abilities—her GPA or her grades in the last semester? You would probably focus on the GPA. The income statement affects the balance sheet much the way an individual grade affects a GPA. Make a profit in any given period, and the equity on the balance sheet will show an increase. Lose money, and it will show a decrease. Over time, the equity section of the balance sheet shows the *accumulation* of profits or losses left in the business; the line is called retained earnings (losses) or sometimes accumulated earnings (deficit). It's one of the best measures of a company's long-term financial performance.

Here too, however, understanding the balance sheet means understanding all the assumptions, decisions, and estimates that go into it. Like the income statement, the balance sheet is in many respects a work of art, not just a work of calculation.

## INDIVIDUALS AND BUSINESSES

Since the balance sheet is so important, we want to begin with some simple lessons. Bear with us—it's important in this case to crawl before you walk.

Start by considering an individual's financial situation, or financial worth, at a given point in time. You add up what the person owns, subtract what she owes, and come up with her net worth:

owns – owes = net worth

Another way to state the same thing is this:

$$\text{owns} = \text{owes} + \text{net worth}$$

For an individual, the ownership category might include cash in the bank, big-ticket items like a house and a car, and all the other property the person can lay claim to. It also would include financial assets such as stocks and bonds or a 401(k) account. The "owing" category includes mortgages, car loans, credit card balances, and any other debt. Note that we're avoiding for the moment the question of how to calculate some of those numbers. What's the value of the house—what the person paid for it or what it might bring today? How about the car or the TV? You can see the art of finance peeking around the curtain here—but more on that in a moment.

Now move from an individual to a business. Same concepts, different language:

• What the company owns is called its *assets*.

• What it owes is called its *liabilities*.

• What it's worth is called *owners' equity* or *shareholders' equity*.

And the basic equation now looks like this:

$$\text{assets} - \text{liabilities} = \text{owners' equity}$$

or this:

$$\text{assets} = \text{liabilities} + \text{owners' equity}$$

If you took any sort of accounting course in school, you learned one of these formulas. The instructor probably called it the fundamental accounting equation. You also learned that the latter formulation reflects the two sides of the balance sheet: assets on the one side, liabilities and owners' equity on the other. The sum on one side has to equal the sum on the other side; the balance sheet has to balance. Before you finish this part of the book, you will understand why.

## READING A BALANCE SHEET

First, however, find a sample balance sheet, either your own company's or one in an annual report. Or just look at the sample in appendix A. Since

## Fiscal Year

A fiscal year is any twelve-month period that a company uses for accounting purposes. Many companies use the calendar year, but some use other periods (October 1 to September 30, for example). You must know the company's fiscal year to ascertain how recent the information you are looking at is.

the balance sheet shows the company's financial situation at a given point in time, there should be a specific date at the top. It's usually the end of a month, quarter, year, or fiscal year. When you're looking at financial statements together, you typically want to see an income statement for a month, quarter, or year, along with the balance sheet for the end of the period reported. Unlike income statements, balance sheets are almost always for an entire organization. Sometimes a large corporation creates subsidiary balance sheets for its operating divisions, but it rarely does so for a single facility. As we'll see, accounting professionals have to do some estimating on the balance sheet, just the way they do with the income statement. Remember the delivery business? The way we depreciate the truck affects not only the income statement but also the value of assets shown on the balance sheet. It turns out that the assumptions and biases in the income statement flow into the balance sheet one way or another.

Balance sheets come in two typical formats. The traditional model shows assets on the left-hand side of the page and liabilities and owners' equity on the right side, with liabilities at the top. The less traditional format puts assets on top, liabilities in the middle, and owners' equity on the bottom. Whatever the format, the balance remains the same: assets must equal liabilities plus owners' equity. (In the nonprofit world, owners' equity is sometimes called net assets.) Often a balance sheet shows comparative figures for, say, December 31 of the most recent year and December 31 of the previous year. Check the column headings to see what points in time are being compared.

As with income statements, some organizations have unusual line items on their balance sheets that you won't find discussed in this book.

Remember, many of these items may be clarified in the footnotes. In fact, balance sheets are notorious for their footnotes. Ford Motor Company's 2006 annual report contained a whopping fifty-one pages of notes, many of them pertaining to the balance sheet. Indeed, companies often include a standard disclaimer in the notes that makes the very point about the art of finance that we are making in this book. Ford, for instance, says:

### Use of Estimates

*The preparation of financial statements in accordance with GAAP requires us to make estimates and assumptions that affect our reported amounts of assets and liabilities, our disclosure of contingent assets and liabilities at the date of the financial statements, and our revenue and expenses during the periods reported. Estimates are used when accounting for certain items such as marketing accruals, warranty costs, employee benefit programs, etc. Estimates are based on historical experience, where applicable, and assumptions that we believe are reasonable under the circumstances. Due to the inherent uncertainty involved with estimates, actual results may differ.*[1]

If the notes don't provide the necessary enlightenment, you can leave the items to the financial professionals. (If something you're wondering about is significant, though, it makes sense to ask someone in your finance organization about the item and the number that goes with it.)

Since the balance sheet is new to most managers, we want to walk you through the most common line items. Some may look strange at first, but don't worry: just keep in mind that distinction between "owned" and "owed." As with the income statement, we'll pause along the way to see which lines are most easily monkeyed with.

# 10

# Assets

## More Estimates and Assumptions
## (Except for Cash)

**A**ssets are what the company owns: cash and securities, machinery and equipment, buildings and land, whatever. *Current assets*, which usually come first on the balance sheet, include anything that can be turned into cash in less than a year. *Long-term assets* are those that have a useful life of more than a year.

## TYPES OF ASSETS

Within those broad categories, of course, are many line items. We'll list the most common ones—those that appear on nearly every company's balance sheet.

### Cash and Cash Equivalents

Cash and cash equivalents are the hard stuff. Money in the bank. Money in money-market accounts. Publicly traded stocks and bonds—the kind you can turn into cash in a day or less if you need to. Another name for this category is *liquid assets*. This is one of the few line items that are not subject to accountants' discretion. When Microsoft says it has $56 billion in cash and short-term investments, or whatever the latest number is, it means it really has that much in banks, money funds, and publicly traded securities.

Of course, companies can lie. The giant Italian company Parmalat reported on its balance sheet that it had billions in an account with Bank of America. It didn't.

## Accounts Receivable

Accounts receivable, or A/R, is the amount customers owe the company. Remember, revenue is a promise to pay, so accounts receivable includes all the promises that haven't yet been collected. Why is this an asset? Because all or most of these commitments will convert to cash and soon *will* belong to the company. It's like a loan from the company to its customers—and the company owns the customers' obligations. Accounts receivable is one line item that every manager needs to watch closely, particularly since investors, analysts, and creditors are likely to be watching it as well. No matter who is looking, A/R provides valuable information about the company's future cash situation, about its customer base, and about its overall health.

Human resource managers can use A/R information as one gauge of what is coming down the pike, as a way to understand some of the financial issues the company will face in the future. Say that accounts receivable is rising as a percentage of sales, suggesting that customers are slow to pay their bills and that cash may be tight. HR people probably can anticipate a hold on new hires and maybe a slowdown in other activities requiring cash, such as outside training. HR people might consider being part of the

## "Smoothing" Earnings

You might think that Wall Street would like a big spike in a company's profits—more money for shareholders, right? But if the spike is unforeseen and unexplained—and especially if it catches Wall Street by surprise—investors are likely to react negatively, taking it as a sign that management isn't in control of the business. So companies like to "smooth" their earnings, maintaining steady and predictable growth.

team that investigates how customers can be persuaded to pay faster, perhaps through better customer service, a change in the invoicing process, or a focus on new customer segments. We'll say more on how to manage accounts receivable in part 7, on working capital.

Sometimes a balance sheet includes an item labeled "allowance for bad debt" that is subtracted from accounts receivable. This is the accountants' estimate—usually based on past experience—of the dollars owed by customers who don't pay their bills. In many companies, subtracting a bad-debt allowance provides a more accurate reflection of the value of those accounts receivable. But note well: estimates are already creeping in. In fact, many companies use the bad-debt reserve as a tool to "smooth" their earnings. When you increase the bad-debt reserve on the balance sheet, you have to record an expense against profit on the income statement. That lowers your reported earnings. When you decrease the bad-debt reserve, the adjustment increases profit on the income statement. Since the bad-debt reserve is always an estimate, there is room here for subjectivity.

## Inventory

Service companies typically don't have much in the way of inventory, but nearly every other company—manufacturers, wholesalers, retailers— does. One part of the inventory figure is the value of the products that are ready to be sold. That's called *finished-goods inventory*. A second part, usually relevant only to manufacturers, is the value of products that are under construction. Accountants dub that *work-in-process inventory*, or just WIP (pronounced "whip"). Then, of course, there's the inventory of raw materials that will be used to make products. That's called—stand back—*raw-materials inventory*.

Accountants can (and do!) spend days on end talking about ways of valuing inventory. We plan to spend no time at all on the subject because it doesn't really affect HR managers' jobs. However, different methods of inventory valuation can often alter the assets side of a balance sheet significantly. If the company changes its method of valuing inventory during a given year, that fact should appear in a footnote to the balance sheet. Many companies detail how they accounted for their inventories in the footnotes, as Barnes & Noble Inc. did in its 2006 annual report:

*Merchandise Inventories*

*Merchandise inventories are stated at the lower of cost or market. Cost is determined primarily by the retail inventory method on the first-in, first-out (FIFO) basis for 96% and 95% of the Company's merchandise inventories as of February 3, 2007 and January 28, 2006, respectively. The remaining merchandise inventories are recorded based on the average cost method.*[1]

What you do need to remember as an HR manager, however, is that all inventory costs money. It is created at the expense of cash. (Maybe you've heard the expression "All our cash is tied up in inventory," though we hope you don't hear it too often.) In fact, this is one way companies can improve their cash position. Decrease your inventory, other things being equal, and you raise your company's cash level. A company always wants to carry as little inventory as possible, provided that it still has materials ready for its manufacturing processes and products ready when customers come calling. We'll come back to this topic later in the book.

## Property, Plant, and Equipment

Another line on the balance sheet—property, plant, and equipment (PPE)—includes buildings, machinery, trucks, computers, and every other physical asset a company owns. The PPE figure is the total number of dollars it cost to buy all the facilities and equipment the company uses to operate the business. Note that the relevant cost here is the purchase price. Without constant appraisals, nobody really knows how much a company's real estate or equipment might be worth on the open market. So accountants, governed by the principle of conservatism, say in effect, "Let's use what we do know, which is the cost of acquiring those assets."

Another reason for using the purchase price is to avoid more opportunities to bias the numbers. Suppose an asset—land, for example—has actually increased in value. If we wanted to mark it up on the balance sheet to its current value, we would have to record a profit on the income statement. But that profit would be based simply on someone's opinion about what the land was worth today. This is not a good idea. Some companies—think Enron—go so far as to set up corporate shells, often owned by a company executive or other insider, and then sell assets to those shells. That allows them to record a profit, just the way they would if they were selling off assets. But it is not the kind of profit investors or the Securities and Exchange Commission likes to see.

The fact that companies must rely on purchase price to value their assets, of course, can create some striking anomalies. Maybe you work for an entertainment company that bought land around Los Angeles for $500,000 thirty years ago. The land could be worth $5 million today—but it will still be valued at $500,000 on the balance sheet. Sophisticated investors like to nose around in companies' balance sheets in hopes of finding such undervalued assets.

## Less: Accumulated Depreciation

Land doesn't wear out, so accountants don't record any depreciation each year. But buildings and equipment do. The point of accounting depreciation, however, isn't to estimate what the buildings and equipment are worth right now; the point is to allocate the investment in the asset over the time it is used to generate revenue and profits (remember the matching principle in chapter 4). The depreciation charge is a way of ensuring that the income statement accurately reflects the true cost of producing goods or delivering services. To calculate *accumulated* depreciation, accountants simply add up all the charges for depreciation they have taken since the day an asset was bought.

We showed you in a previous chapter how a company can magically go from unprofitable to profitable just by changing the way it depreciates its assets. That art-of-finance magic extends to the balance sheet as well. If a company decides its trucks can last six years rather than three, it will record a 50 percent smaller charge on its income statement year after year. That means less accumulated depreciation on the balance sheet, a higher figure for net PPE, and thus more assets. More assets, by the fundamental accounting equation, translate into more owners' equity.

## Goodwill

Goodwill is found on the balance sheets of companies that have acquired other companies. It's the difference between the price paid for the acquired company and the net assets the acquirer actually got. (Net assets, again, refers to the fair market value of the acquiree's assets minus the liabilities assumed by the acquirer.)

The idea isn't as complex as it sounds. Say you're the CEO of a company that is out shopping, and you spot a nice little warehousing business called MJQ Storage that fits your needs perfectly. You agree to buy MJQ for $5 million. By the rules of accounting, if you pay in cash, the asset called "cash" on your balance sheet will decrease by $5 million. That means other assets have to rise by $5 million. After all, the balance sheet still has to balance, and you haven't done anything so far that would change liabilities or owners' equity.

Now watch closely. Since you are buying a collection of physical assets (among other things), you will appraise those assets the way any buyer would. Maybe you decide that MJQ's buildings, shelving, forklifts, and computers are worth $2 million, after deducting whatever liabilities you are assuming. That doesn't mean you made a bad deal. You are buying a going concern with a name, a customer list, talented and knowledgeable employees, and so on, and these so-called intangibles can in some cases be much more valuable than the tangible assets. (How much would you pay for the brand name Coca-Cola or for Dell's customer list?) In our example, you're buying $3 million worth of intangibles. Accountants call that $3 million goodwill. The $3 million of goodwill and the $2 million of net physical assets add up to the $5 million you paid and the corresponding $5 million increase in assets on the balance sheet.

And now we want to tell a little story about goodwill that shows the art of finance at work.

In years past, goodwill was amortized. (Remember, amortization is the same idea as depreciation, except that it applies to intangible assets.) Other assets were typically depreciated over two to five years, but goodwill could be amortized over a maximum of forty years or the estimated useful life of the acquired business.

## Acquisitions

An acquisition occurs when one company buys another. Often you'll see in the newspaper the words *merger* or *consolidation*. Don't be fooled: one company still bought the other. The more neutral-sounding terms may make the deal sound better to the acquirees.

Then the rule changed. The people who write those generally accepted accounting principles—the Financial Accounting Standards Board, or FASB (pronounced faz-bee)—decided that if goodwill consists of the reputation, the customer base, and so on of the company you are buying, then all those assets don't lose value over time. They actually may become *more* valuable over time. In short, goodwill is more like land than it is like equipment. So not amortizing it helps accountants portray that accurate reflection of reality that they are always seeking.

But look at the effect. When you bought MJQ Storage, you wound up with $3 million worth of goodwill on your balance sheet, and let's say you estimated MJQ's useful life at thirty years. Before the rule change, you would have amortized the goodwill over thirty years at $100,000 per year. In other words, you would have deducted $100,000 a year from revenue, thereby reducing the profitability of your company by the same amount. Meanwhile, you're depreciating MJQ's physical assets over, say, a four-year period at $500,000 per year. Again, that $500,000 would be subtracted from revenue to determine profit.

So what happens? Before the rule change, other things being equal, you wanted to have *more* goodwill and *less* in physical assets, simply because goodwill is amortized over a longer period of time, so that the amount subtracted from revenue to determine profit is less (which keeps profits higher). You had an incentive to shop for companies where most of what you'd be buying was goodwill, and you had an incentive to *undervalue* the

## Intangibles

A company's intangible assets include anything that has value but that you can't touch or spend: employees, customer lists, proprietary knowledge, patents, brand names, reputation, strategic strengths, and so on. Most of these assets are not found on the balance sheet unless an acquiring company pays for them and records them as goodwill. The exception is intellectual property, such as patents and copyrights, which can be shown on the balance sheet and amortized over its useful life.

physical assets of the company you were buying. (Remember, it is your own people who are doing the appraisal of those assets!)

With the new rule, goodwill sits on the books and isn't amortized. Nothing at all is subtracted from revenue, and profitability is correspondingly higher. You now have even more of an incentive to look for companies without much in the way of physical assets, and even more of an incentive to undervalue those assets. Tyco was one company that was accused of taking advantage of this rule. In the go-go years of 2000 and 2001, as we noted earlier, Tyco was buying companies at breakneck speed—more than six hundred in those two years alone. Many analysts thought that Tyco regularly undervalued the assets of these companies. Doing so would increase the goodwill included in all those acquisitions and lower the depreciation Tyco had to take each year. That, in turn, would make profit higher and would drive up Tyco's share price.

But eventually, analysts and investors noticed a fact that we alluded to in part 1, namely that Tyco had so much goodwill on its books and so little (relatively speaking) in the way of physical assets, that if you took goodwill out of the balance sheet equation, the company's liabilities were actually higher than its assets. This is not a situation investors like to see.

## Intellectual Property, Patents, and Other Intangibles

How do you account for the cost of creating a new software program that you expect to generate revenue for years? What about the cost of developing a new wonder drug, which is protected by a twenty-year patent (from the date of application)? Obviously, it makes no sense to record the whole cost as an expense on the income statement in any given period, any more than you would record the whole cost of buying a truck. Like a truck, the software and the patent will help generate revenue in future accounting periods. So these investments are considered intangible assets and should be amortized over the life of the revenue stream they generate. By the same token, however, R&D expenses that do *not* result in an asset likely to generate revenue should be recorded as an expense on the income statement.

You can see the potential for subjectivity here. GAAP says that R&D can be amortized if the product under development is technologically feasible. But who determines technological feasibility? Again, we are back in the realm of art. If a company decides that its R&D projects are technologically feasible, it can amortize those sums over time and make its profits look higher. Otherwise, it must expense R&D costs as they are incurred—a more conservative approach. Computer Associates is one company that got itself into trouble for amortizing R&D on products that had a questionable future. Like depreciation, amortization decisions can often have a sizable effect on profitability and owners' equity.

Incidentally, management's attitude toward R&D budgets is often a function of how R&D is accounted for. R&D staffing and headcount decisions—decisions you might be involved in—may thus depend on the finance department's accounting policies.

## Accruals and Prepaid Assets

To explain accruals and prepaid assets, let's look at a hypothetical example. Say you start a bicycle manufacturing company, and you rent manufacturing space for the entire year for $60,000. Since your company is a lousy credit risk—nobody likes to do business with a start-up for just this reason—the landlord insists on payment up front.

Now, we know from the matching principle that it doesn't make sense to book the entire $60,000 in January as an expense on the income statement. It's rent for the whole year. It has to be spread out over the year, so that the cost of the rent is matched to the revenue that it helped bring in. So in January, you put $5,000 on the income statement for rent. But where does the other $55,000 go? You have to keep track of it somewhere. Well, prepaid rent is one example of a prepaid asset. You have bought something— you own the rights to that space for a year—so it is an asset. And you keep track of assets on the balance sheet.

Every month, of course, you'll have to move $5,000 out of the prepaid-asset line on the balance sheet and put it in the income statement as an expense for rent. That's called an *accrual*, and the account on the balance sheet that records what has not yet been expensed is called an *accrued asset account*. Though the terms are confusing, note that the practice is still conservative: we're keeping track of all our known expenses, and we're also tracking what we paid for in advance.

Human resource managers deal with accruals all the time, even if the word isn't familiar. Every month, for example, the accountants in your company probably ask you for certain data about project budgets. They want to know the expense commitments you've made for that big HRIS project. They want all your invoices submitted to their department by a certain date. They ask you to update your expense forecast for the department for the rest of the year. All these requests reflect the accountants' effort to create that accurate picture of reality—and a big part of financial reality is accruals.

If you work in compensation, you also deal with accruals, because you help finance calculate correct accruals for bonuses and profit sharing. In the case of profit-sharing plans, for instance, finance prepares the income statement, and you calculate projected payouts based on that income statement and the appropriate formulas. Finance then determines the accruals based on your numbers.

The art of finance can creep in here as well because there is room for judgment on what to accrue and what to charge in any given period. Say, for instance, your company has installed an HRIS with all the bells and whistles. The programming and installation is completed in January, and the total bill comes to $5 million. The accountants might decide that the system will benefit the company for five years, so they would book the $5 million as a prepaid asset and charge one-sixtieth of the cost each month on the income statement. A company facing a tough year is likely to decide that this is the best course—after all, it's better to deduct one-sixtieth of $5 million from profits than the whole $5 million. But what if the year is great? Could the accountants expense the entire system—charge it all against that year's revenue—because, well, they aren't sure that it will benefit the company beyond the first year? In that case, they would have an HRIS system that's all paid for, and profits in the months to come would be correspondingly higher. In a perfect world, our accounting friends would have a crystal ball to tell them exactly how long that HRIS will help generate revenue. Since they don't yet have such a device, they must rely on estimates.

So that's it for assets. Add them all up, along with whatever extraneous items you might find, and you get the "total assets" line at the bottom of the left side. Now it's time to move on to the other side—liabilities and owners' equity.

# 11

# On the Other Side

## Liabilities and Equity

**W**e said earlier that liabilities are what a company owes and that equity is its net worth. There's another—only slightly different—way to look at this side of the balance sheet, which is that *it shows how the assets were obtained*. If a company borrows funds in any way, shape, or form to obtain an asset, the borrowing is going to show up on one or another of the liabilities lines. If it sells stock to obtain an asset, that will be reflected on one of the lines under "owners' equity."

## TYPES OF LIABILITIES

But first things first, which on this side of the balance sheet means liabilities, the financial obligations a company owes to other entities. Liabilities are always divided into two main categories. *Current liabilities* are those that have to be paid off in less than a year. *Long-term liabilities* are those that come due over a longer time frame. Liabilities are usually listed on the balance sheet from shortest term to longest term, so the very layout tells you something about what's due when.

### Current Portion of Long-Term Debt

If your company owes $100,000 to a bank on a long-term loan, maybe $10,000 of it is due this year. So that's the amount that shows up in the current-liabilities section of the balance sheet. The line will be labeled "current portion of long-term debt" or something like that. The other $90,000 shows up under "long-term liabilities."

## Short-Term Loans

Short-term loans are lines of credit and short-term revolving loans. These lines are usually secured by current assets, such as accounts receivable and inventory. The entire balance outstanding is shown here.

## Accounts Payable

Accounts payable shows the amount the company owes its vendors. The company receives goods and services from suppliers every day and typically doesn't pay the bill for at least thirty days. The vendors, in effect, have loaned the company money. Accounts payable shows how much was owed on the date of the balance sheet. Any balance on a company's credit cards is usually included in accounts payable.

## Accrued Expenses and Other Short-Term Liabilities

This catchall category includes everything else the company owes. One example is payroll. Let's assume that you get paid on October 1. Does it make sense to charge your pay as an expense on the income statement in October? Probably not—your October paycheck is for work performed in September. So the accountants would figure out or estimate how much the company owes you on October 1 for work completed in September and then charge those expenses to September. This is an accrued liability. It's like an internal bill in September for a payment to be made in October. Accrued liabilities are part of the matching principle—we have matched expenses with the revenue they help bring in every month.

## Long-Term Liabilities

Most long-term liabilities are loans. But there are also other liabilities that you might see listed here. Examples include deferred bonuses or compensation, deferred taxes, and pension liabilities. If these other liabilities are substantial, this section of the balance sheet needs to be watched closely.

## OWNERS' EQUITY

Finally! Remember the equation? Owners' equity is what's left after we subtract liabilities from assets. Equity includes the capital provided by investors and the profits retained by the company over time. Owners' equity goes by many names, including shareholders' equity and stockholders' equity. The owners' equity line items listed in some companies' balance sheets can be quite detailed and confusing. They typically include the following categories.

### Preferred Shares

Preferred shares—also known as preference stock or shares—are a specific type of stock. People who hold preferred shares receive dividends on their investment before the holders of common stock get a nickel. But preferred shares typically carry a fixed dividend, so their price doesn't fluctuate as much as the price of common shares. Investors who hold preferred shares may not receive the full benefit of a company's growth in value. When the company issues preferred shares, it sells them to investors at a certain initial price. The value shown on the balance sheet reflects that price.

Most preferred shares do not carry voting rights. In a way, they're more like bonds than like common stock. The difference? With a bond, the owner gets a fixed coupon or interest payment; with preferred shares, the owner gets a fixed dividend. Companies use preferred stock to raise money because it does not carry the same legal implications as debt. If a company cannot

### Capital

The word *capital* means a number of things in business. *Physical capital* is plant, equipment, vehicles, and the like. *Financial capital* from an investor's point of view is the stocks and bonds he holds; from a company's point of view, it is the shareholders' equity investment plus whatever funds the company has borrowed. "Sources of capital" in an annual report shows where the company got its money. "Uses of capital" shows how the company used its money.

pay a coupon on a bond, bondholders can force it into bankruptcy. Holders of preferred shares normally can't.

## Common Shares or Common Stock

Unlike most preferred shares, common shares usually carry voting rights. People who hold them can vote for members of the board of directors (usually one vote per share) and on any other matter that may be put before the shareholders. Common shares may or may not pay dividends. The value shown on the balance sheet is typically shown at *par value*, which is the nominal dollar amount assigned to the stock by the issuer. Par value is usually a very small amount and has no relationship to the stock's market price. The balance sheet in appendix A shows the common stock with a par value of $1.

## Additional Paid-in Capital

This is the amount over the par value that investors initially paid for the stock. For example, if the stock is initially sold at $5 per share, and if the par value is $1 per share, the additional paid-in capital is $4 per share. It is summed up over time—so, for example, if a company issues additional shares, the additional paid-in capital is added to the existing amount.

## Retained Earnings

Retained earnings, or accumulated earnings, are the profits that have been reinvested in the business instead of being paid out in dividends. The number represents the *total* after-tax income that has been reinvested or retained over the life of the business. Sometimes a company that holds a lot of retained earnings in the form of cash—Microsoft is an example—comes under pressure to pay out some of the money to shareholders, in the form

## Dividends

Dividends are funds distributed to shareholders taken from a company's equity. In public companies dividends are typically distributed at the end of a quarter or year.

of dividends. After all, what shareholder wants to see his money just sitting there in the company's coffers, rather than being reinvested in productive assets? Of course, you may see an accumulated deficit—a negative number—which indicates that the company has lost money over time.

So owners' equity is what the shareholders would receive if the company were sold, right? Of course not! Remember all those rules, estimates, and assumptions that affect the balance sheet. Assets are recorded at their acquisition price less accumulated depreciation. Goodwill is piled up with every acquisition the company makes, and it is never amortized. And of course, the company has intangible assets of its own, such as its brand name and customer list, which don't show up on the balance sheet at all. The moral: the market value of a company almost never matches its equity or book value on the balance sheet. The actual market value of a company is what a willing buyer would pay for it. In the case of a public company, that value is estimated by calculating the company's market cap, or the number of shares outstanding multiplied by the share price on any given day. In the case of private companies, the market value can be estimated by one of the valuation methods described in part 1—at least, as a start.

# 12

# Why the Balance Sheet Balances

If you learned in school about the fundamental accounting equation, the instructor probably said something like this: "It's called the balance sheet because it balances. Assets always equal liabilities plus owners' equity." But even if you dutifully wrote down that answer on the exam, you may be less than 100 percent crystal clear on why the balance sheet balances. So here are three ways of understanding it.

## REASONS FOR BALANCE

First, let's go back to an individual. You can look at a company's balance sheet in the same way you'd look at a person's net worth. Net worth has to equal what she owns minus what she owes, because that's the way we define the term. The formulation of the equation for an individual, presented in chapter 9, is *owns − owes = net worth*. It's the same for a business. Owners' equity is defined as assets minus liabilities.

Second, look at what the balance sheet shows. On one side are the assets, which is what the company owns. On the other side are the liabilities and equity, which show how the company obtained what it owns. Since you can't get something for nothing, the "owns" side and the "how we obtained it" side will always be in balance. They have to be.

Third, consider what happens to the balance sheet over time. This approach should help you see why it always stays in balance.

Imagine a company that is just starting out. Its owner has invested $50,000 in the business, so he has $50,000 in cash on the assets side of the balance sheet. He has no liabilities yet, so he has $50,000 in owners' equity. The balance sheet balances.

Then the company buys a truck for $36,000 in cash. If nothing else changes—and if you constructed a balance sheet right after the truck transaction—the assets side of the balance sheet would look like this:

| Assets | |
| --- | --- |
| Cash | $14,000 |
| Property, plant, and equipment | 36,000 |

It still adds up to $50,000—and on the other side of the balance sheet, he still has $50,000 worth of owners' equity. The balance sheet still balances.

Next imagine that the owner decides he needs more cash. So he goes to the bank and borrows $10,000, raising his total cash to $24,000. Now the balance sheet looks like this:

| Assets | |
| --- | --- |
| Cash | $24,000 |
| Property, plant, and equipment | 36,000 |

Wow! It adds up to $60,000. He has increased his assets. But of course, he has increased his liabilities as well. So the other side of the balance sheet looks like this:

| Liabilities and Owners' Equity | |
| --- | --- |
| Bank loan | $10,000 |
| Owners' equity | $50,000 |

That, too, adds up to $60,000.

Note that owners' equity remains unchanged throughout all these transactions. Owners' equity is affected only when a company takes in funds from its owners, pays out money to its owners, or records a profit or loss.

In the meantime, *every transaction that affects one side of the balance sheet affects the other as well*. For example:

- A company uses $100,000 cash to pay off a loan. The cash line on the assets side decreases by $100,000, and the liabilities line on the other side decreases by the same amount. So the balance sheet stays in balance.

- A company buys a $100,000 machine, paying $50,000 down and owing the rest. Now the cash line is $50,000 less than it used to be— but the new machine shows up on the assets side at $100,000. So total assets increase by $50,000. Meanwhile, the $50,000 owed on the machine shows up on the liabilities side. Again, we're still in balance.

As long as you remember the fundamental fact that transactions affect both sides of the balance sheet, you'll be OK. That's why the balance sheet balances. Understanding this point is a basic building block of financial intelligence. Remember, if assets don't equal liabilities and equity, you do not have a balance sheet.

# 13

# The Income Statement Affects the Balance Sheet

**S**o far we have been considering the balance sheet by itself. But here's one of the best-kept secrets in the world of financial statements: *a change in one statement nearly always has an impact on the other statements*. So when you're managing the income statement, whether for the company as a whole or for HR as a cost center, you're also having an effect on the balance sheet. Part of developing your financial intelligence is understanding how human resources impacts the balance sheet.

## THE EFFECT OF PROFIT ON EQUITY

To see the relationship between profit, from the income statement, and equity, which appears on the balance sheet, we'll look at a couple of examples. Here's a highly simplified balance sheet for a brand-new (and very small!) company:

| Assets | |
| --- | --- |
| Cash | $25 |
| Accounts receivable | 0 |
| Total assets | $25 |

| **Liabilities and Owners' Equity** | |
| --- | --- |
| Accounts payable | $_0 |
| Owners' equity | $25 |

Say we operate this company for a month. We buy $50 worth of parts and materials, which we use to produce and sell $100 worth of finished product. We also incur $25 in other expenses. The income statement for the month looks like this:

| Sales | $100 |
| --- | --- |
| Cost of goods sold | 50 |
| Gross profit | 50 |
| All expenses | 25 |
| Net profit | $ 25 |

Now, what has changed on the balance sheet?

• First, we have spent all our cash to cover expenses.

• Second, we have $100 in receivables from our customers.

• Third, we have incurred $50 in obligations to our suppliers.

Thus, the balance sheet at the end of the month looks like this:

| **Assets** | |
| --- | --- |
| Cash | $  0 |
| Accounts receivable | 100 |
| Total assets | $100 |

| **Liabilities and Owners' Equity** | |
| --- | --- |
| Accounts payable | $ 50 |
| Owners' equity | $ 50 |
| Liabilities and owners' equity | $100 |

As you can see, that $25 of net profit becomes $25 of owners' equity. On a more detailed balance sheet, it would appear under "owners' equity" as retained earnings. That's true in any business: net profit adds to equity unless it is paid out in dividends. By the same token, a net loss decreases equity. If a business loses money every month, liabilities will eventually exceed assets, creating negative equity. Then it is a candidate for bankruptcy court.

Note something else about this simple example: the company wound up that month with no cash! It was making money, and equity was growing, but it had nothing in the bank. So a good manager needs to be aware of how both cash and profit interact on the balance sheet. This is a topic we'll return to in part 4, when we take up the cash flow statement.

## AND MANY OTHER EFFECTS

The relationship between profit and equity isn't the only link between changes in the income statement and changes on the balance sheet. Far from it. Think about the line items that human resources affects. Every payroll dollar recorded as COGS or operating expenses represents a dollar less on the cash line or a dollar more on the accrued-expenses line of the balance sheet. An incentive compensation payout is reflected on both the income statement and on the balance sheet, either as cash out or as an accrued expense (which, of course, will eventually be paid out in cash, thus changing the balance sheet again). The purchase of supplies, travel, and consulting services adds to accounts payable. And of course, all these changes have an effect on total assets or liabilities.

Overall, if a manager's job is to boost profitability, he or she can have a positive effect on the balance sheet, just because profits increase equity. But it isn't quite so simple, because it matters *how* those profits are achieved, and it matters what happens to the other assets and liabilities on the balance sheet itself. For example:

- A plant manager hears of a good deal on an important raw material and asks purchasing to buy a lot of it. Makes sense, right? Not necessarily. The inventory line on the balance sheet increases. The accounts payable line increases a corresponding amount. Eventually, the company will have to draw down its cash to cover the accounts payable—possibly long before the material is used to generate revenue. Meanwhile, the company has to pay to warehouse the inventory, and it may need to borrow money to cover the decrease in cash. Figuring out whether to take advantage of the deal requires detailed analysis; a manager must be sure to consider all the financial issues when making these kinds of decisions.

• A sales manager is looking to boost revenue and profit and decides to target smaller businesses as customers. Is it a good idea? Maybe not. Smaller customers may not be as good credit risks as larger ones. Accounts receivable may rise disproportionately because the customers are slower to pay. The accountants may need to increase that bad-debt allowance, which reduces profit, assets, and thus equity. The financially intelligent sales manager will need to investigate pricing possibilities: can he increase gross margin to compensate for the increased risk on sales to smaller customers?

• An HR manager makes a decision to buy a new computer system, believing that the new system will boost productivity and therefore contribute to profitability. But how is the new equipment going to be paid for? If a company is overleveraged—that is, if it has a heavy debt load compared with its equity—borrowing the money to pay for the system may not be a good idea. Perhaps it will need to issue new stock and therefore increase its equity investment. Making decisions about how to get the capital required to run a business is the job of the CFO and the treasurer, not HR. But an understanding of the company's cash and debt situation should inform the manager's decision about when to buy the new equipment.

Any manager, in short, may want to step back now and then and look at the big picture. So in addition to the line item or items on the income statement that you focus on, consider the balance sheet as a whole as well (and the cash flow statement, which we'll get to shortly). When you do, your thinking, your work, and your decisions will be deeper—that is, they will take into account more factors, and you'll be able to talk about the impact at a deeper level. Besides, imagine talking to your CFO about the impact of profit on equity: he's likely to be impressed (even shocked).

## ASSESSING A COMPANY'S HEALTH

Remember, we said at the beginning of this part that savvy investors typically pore over a company's balance sheet first. The reason is that the balance sheet answers a lot of questions—questions like the following:

• *Is the company solvent?* That is, do its assets outweigh its liabilities so that owners' equity is a positive number?

• *Can the company pay its bills?* Here the important numbers are current assets, particularly cash, compared with current liabilities. More on this in part 5, on ratios.

• *Has owners' equity been growing over time?* A comparison of balance sheets for a period of time will show whether the company has been moving in the right direction.

These are simple, basic questions, of course. But investors can learn much more from a detailed examination of the balance sheet and its footnotes, and from comparisons between the balance sheet and other statements. How important is goodwill to the company's "total assets" line? What assumptions have been used to determine depreciation, and how important is that? (Remember Waste Management.) Is the "cash" line increasing over time—usually a good sign—or is it decreasing? If owners' equity is rising, is that because the company has required an infusion of capital, or is it because the company has been making money?

The balance sheet, in short, helps show whether a company is financially healthy. All the statements help you make that judgment, but the balance sheet—a company's cumulative GPA—may be the most important of all.

Now it is time to try your hand at reading and analyzing a real balance sheet. To practice what you have learned here (or to give yourself another break from reading), turn to the balance sheet exercise in appendix B.

# Part Three
# TOOLBOX

## "EMPLOYEES ARE OUR MOST VALUABLE ASSET" (OR ARE THEY?)

You hear it all the time from CEOs: "Our people are our most valuable asset." But you see some CEOs acting as if employees aren't assets at all. Can you imagine a company downsizing or laying off any other asset—just putting it out on the street in hopes that it will walk away? When CEOs say they have to cut expenses, what they usually mean is that they are about to let people go.

How to reconcile these two views? From a commonsense perspective, employees *are* assets. Their knowledge and their work bring value to a company. When one company acquires another, the value of employees is recognized as part of the goodwill.

Otherwise, though, the value of employees doesn't show up on the balance sheet. There are two reasons:

- Outside of an acquisition, nobody has any idea how to value employees. What is the value of your knowledge? There isn't an accountant in the world who wants to tackle that one. And the Financial Accounting Standards Board isn't about to take it on by amending GAAP.

- Anyway, companies don't own employees, so employees can't be considered assets in accounting terms.

Employees *do* create an expense: payroll, in one form or another, is often one of the biggest items on the income statement. But what those CEOs are saying has more to do with a company's culture and attitudes than it does with accounting. Some organizations really do seem to regard employees as assets: they train them, they invest in them, and they take good care of them. HR in those companies has a lot to do with that. Other organizations focus on the expense angle, paying people as little as they can and squeezing as much work out of them as possible, sometimes frustrating HR. Is the former strategy worth it? Many people (including ourselves) believe that treating people right generally leads to higher morale, higher quality, and ultimately higher customer satisfaction. Other things being equal, it boosts the bottom line over the long term and thus increases a business's value. Of course, many other factors also influence whether a company succeeds or fails. So there's rarely a one-to-one correlation between a company's culture and attitudes and its financial performance.

One other note on this topic: human resources has always struggled with how to measure what it does. At one point, something called human resource accounting gained some popularity. The idea was to attempt to place a value on employees as assets in an organization and then to measure improvements or changes using standard accounting principles. In part, it was an extension of the matching principle, ensuring that all the assets used to create the product or deliver the service were included in the financials. The idea didn't take hold because of the difficulty of valuing people as assets, but it is nonetheless interesting.

## EXPENSE? OR CAPITAL EXPENDITURE?

When a company buys a piece of capital equipment, the cost doesn't show up on the income statement; rather, the new asset appears on the balance sheet, and only the depreciation appears on the income statement as a charge against profits. You might think the distinction between "expense" (showing up on the income statement) and "capital expenditure" (showing up on the balance sheet) would be clear and simple. But of course, it isn't. Indeed, it's a prime canvas for the art of finance.

Consider that taking a big item off the income statement and putting it on the balance sheet, so that only the depreciation shows up as a charge against profits, can have the effect of increasing profits considerably. WorldCom is a case in point. A large portion of this big telecom company's expenses consisted of so-called line costs. These were fees it paid to local phone companies to use their phone lines. Line costs were normally treated as ordinary operating expenses, but you could argue (albeit incorrectly) that some of them were actually investments in new markets and wouldn't start paying off for years. That was the logic pursued by CFO Scott Sullivan, anyway, who began "capitalizing" his company's line costs in the late 1990s. Bingo: these expenses disappeared off the income statement, and profits rose by billions of dollars. To Wall Street, it appeared that World-Com was suddenly generating profits in a down industry—and no one caught on until later, when the whole house of cards collapsed.

WorldCom took an overaggressive approach toward capitalizing its costs and wound up in hot water. But some companies will treat the occasional questionable item as a capital expenditure just to pump up their earnings a little. Does yours?

# Part Four

# Cash Is King

# 14

# Cash Is a Reality Check

"**C**ompanies hit the skids for all sorts of reasons," wrote Ram Charan and Jerry Useem in *Fortune* in May 2002, a time when a lot of companies were hitting the skids, "but it's one thing that ultimately kills them: they run out of cash." Most managers are too busy worrying about measures based on the income statement, such as EBITDA, to give cash much notice. Boards of directors and outside analysts sometimes focus too heavily on the income statement or the balance sheet. But, Charan and Useem noted, there is one investor who watches cash closely: Warren Buffett. The reason? "He knows cash is hard to fudge."[1]

Warren Buffett may be the single greatest investor of all time. His company, Berkshire Hathaway, has invested in scores of companies and achieved astonishing results. From January 1994 to January 2004, Berkshire Hathaway's Class A stock compiled an amazing compound annual growth rate of 17.9 percent; in other words, it rose an average of about 18 percent every year for ten years. How does Buffett do it? Many people have written books attempting to explain his investing philosophy and his analytical approach. But in our opinion, it all boils down to just three simple precepts. First, he evaluates a business based on its long-term rather than its short-term prospects. Second, he always looks for businesses he understands. (This led him to avoid dot-com investments.) And third, when he examines financial statements, he places the greatest emphasis on a measure of cash flow that he calls owner earnings. Warren Buffett has taken financial

## Owner Earnings

Owner earnings is a measure of the company's ability to generate cash over a period of time. We like to say it is the money an owner could take out of his business and spend at the grocery store for his own benefit. Owner earnings is an important measure because it allows for the continuing capital expenditures that are necessary to maintain a healthy business. Profit and even operating cash flow measures do not. More about owner earnings in the toolbox at the end of this part.

intelligence to a whole new level, and his net worth reflects it. How interesting that, to him, cash is king.

## WHY CASH IS KING

Let's look at that third element of the financial statements—cash—in more detail. Why target cash flow as a key measure of business performance? Why not just profit, as found on the income statement? Why not just a company's assets or owners' equity, as revealed by the balance sheet? We suspect Warren Buffett knows that the income statement and balance sheet, however useful, have all sorts of potential biases, a result of all the assumptions and estimates that are built into them. Cash is different. Look at a company's cash flow statement, and you are indirectly peering into its bank account. Today, after the dot-com bust and the financial-fraud revelations of the late 1990s and early 2000s, cash flow is once again the darling of Wall Street. It has become a prominent measure by which analysts evaluate companies. But Warren Buffett has been looking at cash all along because he knows that it's the number least affected by the art of finance.

So why don't managers—including HR managers—pay attention to cash? There are any number of reasons. In the past, nobody asked them to (though this is beginning to change). Some senior executives themselves may not worry about cash—at least, not until it's too late—so their direct reports don't think much about it, either. Folks in the finance organization often believe that cash is *their* concern and nobody else's. But often, the reason is simply a lack of financial intelligence. Managers don't understand the accounting rules that determine profit, so they assume that profit is pretty much the same as net cash coming in. Some don't believe that their actions affect their company's cash situation; others may believe it, but they don't understand how. For HR, of course, at least one connection should be clear: one of the largest expenses in many businesses is payroll, and people want to be paid in cash. If you have no cash, you will have no people.

There's another reason, too, which is that the language in the cash flow statement is a little arcane. Charan and Useem in their article were advocating a simple antidote to financial fraud: a "detailed, easily readable cash-flow report" required to be given to the board, to employees, and to investors. Unfortunately, no one, to our knowledge, has taken up the suggestion. So we are left with conventional cash flow statements. Most of these, however detailed, are hard for a nonfinancial person to read, let alone understand.

But talk about an investment that pays off: if you take the time to understand cash, you can cut right through a lot of the smoke and mirrors created by your company's financial artists. You can see how good a job your company is doing at turning profit into cash. You can spot early-warning signs of trouble, and you will know how to manage and how to work with your business partners so that cash flow is healthy. Cash is a reality check.

One of us, Joe, learned about the importance of cash when he was a financial analyst at a small company early in his career. The company was struggling, and everyone knew it. One day the CFO and the controller were both out golfing and were unreachable. (This was in the days before everybody had a cell phone, which shows you how old Joe is.) The banker called the office and talked with the CEO. Evidently, the CEO didn't like what he was hearing from the banker and felt he had better talk to someone in accounting or finance. So he passed the call to Joe. Joe learned from the banker that the company's credit line was maxed out. "Given that tomorrow is payday," the banker said, "we're curious about what your plan is to cover payroll." Thinking quickly (as always), Joe replied, "Um—can I call you back?" He then did some research and found that a big customer owed the company a good deal of money and that the check—really—was in the mail. He told the banker this, and the banker agreed to cover payroll, provided Joe brought the customer's check to the bank the minute it arrived.

In fact, the check arrived that same day, but after the bank closed. So first thing the next morning, Joe drove to the bank, check in hand. He arrived a few minutes before the bank opened and noticed that a line had already formed. In fact, he saw that several employees from his company were already there, holding their paychecks. One of them accosted him and said, "So you figured it out too, huh?" "Figured what out?" Joe asked. The guy looked at him with something resembling pity. "Figured it out. We've been taking our paychecks to the bank every Friday first break we get. We cash 'em and then deposit the cash in our own banks. That way, we can make sure the checks don't bounce—and if the bank won't cash them, we can spend the rest of the day looking for a job."

That was one day Joe's financial intelligence took a big leap upward. He realized what Warren Buffett already knew: cash keeps a company alive, and cash flow is a critical measure of its financial health. You need people to run the business—any business. You need a place of business, telephones, electricity, computers, supplies, and so on. And you can't pay for all these things with profits because profits aren't real money. Cash is.

# 15

# Profit ≠ Cash
# (and You Need Both)

**W**hy is profit not the same as cash coming in? Some reasons are pretty obvious: cash may be coming in from loans or from investors, and that cash isn't going to show up on the income statement at all. But even operating cash flow, which we'll explain in detail later, in chapter 16, is not at all the same as net profit. There are three essential reasons:

- *Revenue is booked at sale.* One reason is the fundamental fact that we explained in our discussion of the income statement. A sale is recorded whenever a company delivers a product or service. Ace Printing Company delivers $1,000 worth of brochures to a customer; Ace Printing Company records revenue of $1,000, and theoretically it could record a profit based on subtracting its costs and expenses from that revenue. But no cash has changed hands because Ace's customer typically has thirty days or more to pay. Since profit starts with revenue, it always reflects customers' promises to pay. Cash flow, by contrast, always reflects cash transactions.

- *Expenses are matched to revenue.* The purpose of the income statement is to tote up all the costs and expenses associated with generating revenue during a given time period. As we saw in part 2, however, those expenses may not be the ones that were actually paid during that time period. Some may have been paid earlier (remember the hypothetical bicycle company we mentioned in chapter 10, which was expected to pay a year's rent in advance). Most will be paid later, when vendors' bills come due. Payroll and vacation accruals are examples of this kind of expenses—they are charged to income as a liability, but they aren't paid out in cash until a later period. So the expenses on the income statement do not reflect cash going out. The cash flow statement, however, always measures cash in and out the door during a particular time period.

- *Capital expenditures don't count against profit.* Remember the toolbox at the end of part 3? A capital expenditure doesn't appear on the income statement when it occurs; only the depreciation is charged against revenue. So a company can buy trucks, machinery, computer systems, and so on, and the expense will appear on the income statement only gradually, over the useful life of each item. Cash, of course, is another story: all those items are often paid for long before they have been fully depreciated, and the cash used to pay for them will be reflected in the cash flow statement.

You may be thinking that in the long run cash flow will pretty much track net profit. Accounts receivable will be collected, so sales will turn into cash. Accounts payable will be paid, so expenses will more or less even out from one time period to the next. And capital expenditures will be depreciated, so the charges against revenue from depreciation, over time, will more or less equal the cash being spent on new assets. All this is true, to a degree, at least for a mature, well-managed company. But the difference between profit and cash can create all sorts of mischief in the meantime.

## PROFIT WITHOUT CASH

We'll illustrate this point by comparing two simple companies with two dramatically different profit and cash positions.

Sweet Dreams Bakery is a new cookies-and-cakes manufacturer that supplies specialty grocery stores. The founder has lined up orders based on her unique home-style recipes, and she's ready to launch on January 1. We'll assume she has $10,000 cash in the bank, and we'll also assume that in the first three months her sales are $20,000, $30,000, and $45,000. Cost of goods are 60 percent of sales, and her monthly operating expenses are $10,000.

Just by eyeballing those numbers, you can see she'll soon be making a profit. In fact, the simplified income statements for the first three months look like this:

| | January | February | March |
|---|---|---|---|
| Sales | $20,000 | $30,000 | $45,000 |
| COGS | 12,000 | 18,000 | 27,000 |
| Gross profit | 8,000 | 12,000 | 18,000 |
| Expenses | 10,000 | 10,000 | 10,000 |
| Net profit | ($ 2,000) | $ 2,000 | $ 8,000 |

A simplified cash flow statement, however, would tell a different story. Sweet Dreams Bakery has an agreement with its vendors to pay for the ingredients and other supplies it buys in thirty days. But those specialty grocery stores that the company sells to? They're kind of precarious, and they take sixty days to pay their bills. So here's what happens to Sweet Dreams' cash situation:

• In *January*, Sweet Dreams collects nothing from its customers. At the end of the month, all it has is $20,000 in receivables from its sales. Luckily, it does not have to pay anything out for the ingredients it uses, since its vendors expect to be paid in thirty days. (We'll assume that the COGS figure is all for ingredients, because the owner herself does all the baking.) But the company does have to pay expenses—rent, utilities, and so on. So *all* the initial $10,000 in cash goes out the door to pay expenses, and Sweet Dreams is left with no cash in the bank.

• In *February*, Sweet Dreams still hasn't collected anything. (Remember, its customers pay in sixty days.) At the end of the month, it has $50,000 in receivables—January's $20,000 plus February's $30,000—but still no cash. Meanwhile, Sweet Dreams now has to pay for the ingredients for January ($12,000), and it has another month's worth of expenses ($10,000). So it's now in the hole by $22,000.

Can the owner turn this around? Surely, in March those rising profits will improve the cash picture! Alas, no.

• In *March*, Sweet Dreams finally collects on its January sales, so it has $20,000 in cash coming in the door, leaving it only $2,000 short against its end-of-February cash position. But now it has to pay for February's COGS of $18,000 plus March's expenses of $10,000. So at the end of March, it ends up $30,000 in the hole—a worse position than at the end of February.

What's going on here? The answer is that Sweet Dreams is growing. Its sales increase every month, meaning that it must pay more each month for its ingredients. Eventually, its operating expenses will increase as well because the owner will have to hire more people. The other problem is the disparity between the fact that Sweet Dreams must pay its vendors in thirty days while waiting sixty days for receipts from its customers. In effect, it has to front the cash for thirty days—*and as long as sales are increasing, it will never be able to catch up unless it finds additional sources of cash.* As fictional and oversimplified as Sweet Dreams may be, this is precisely how profitable companies go out of business. It is one reason why so many small companies fail in their first year. They simply run out of cash.

## CASH WITHOUT PROFIT

But now let's look at another sort of profit/cash disparity.

Fine Cigar Shops is another start-up. It sells very expensive cigars, and it's located in a part of town frequented by businesspeople and well-to-do tourists. Its sales for the first three months are $50,000, $75,000, and $95,000—again, a healthy growth trend. Its cost of goods is 70 percent of sales, and its monthly operating expenses are $30,000 (high rent!). For the sake of comparison, we'll say it too begins the period with $10,000 in the bank.

So Fine Cigar's income statement for these months looks like this:

|  | January | February | March |
|---|---|---|---|
| Sales | $ 50,000 | $75,000 | $95,000 |
| COGS | 35,000 | 52,500 | 66,500 |
| Gross profit | 15,000 | 22,500 | 28,500 |
| Expenses | 30,000 | 30,000 | 30,000 |
| Net profit | ($ 15,000) | ($ 7,500) | ($ 1,500) |

Fine Cigar hasn't yet turned the corner on profitability, though it is losing less money each month. Meanwhile, what does its cash picture look like? As a retailer, of course, it collects the money on each sale immediately. And we'll assume that Fine Cigar was able to negotiate good terms with its vendors, paying them in sixty days.

- In *January*, it begins with $10,000 and adds $50,000 in cash sales. It doesn't have to pay for any cost of goods sold yet, so the only cash out the door is that $30,000 in expenses. End-of-the-month bank balance: $30,000.

- In *February*, it adds $75,000 in cash sales and still doesn't pay anything for cost of goods sold. So the month's net cash after the $30,000 in expenses is $45,000. Now the bank balance is $75,000!

- In *March*, it adds $95,000 in cash sales, pays for January's supplies ($35,000) and March's expenses ($30,000). Net cash in for the month is $30,000, and the bank balance is now $105,000.

Cash-based businesses—retailers, restaurants, and so on—can thus get an equally skewed picture of their situation. In this case Fine Cigar's bank balance is climbing every month even though the company is unprofitable. That's fine for a while, and it will continue to be fine so long as the company holds down expenses so that it can turn the corner on profitability. But the owner has to be careful: if he's lulled into thinking that his business is doing great and that he can increase those expenses, he's liable to continue on the unprofitable path. If he fails to attain profitability, eventually he will run out of cash.

Fine Cigar, too, has its real-world parallels. Every cash-based business, from tiny Main Street shops to giants such as Amazon.com and Dell, has the luxury of taking the customer's money before it must pay for its costs and expenses. It enjoys the float—and if it is growing, that float will grow ever larger. But ultimately, the company must be profitable by the standards of the income statement; cash flow in the long run is no protection against unprofitability. In the cigar-store example, the losses on the books will eventually lead to negative cash flow; just as profits eventually lead to cash, losses eventually use up cash. It's the *timing* of those cash flows that we are trying to understand here.

Understanding the difference between profit and cash is a key to increasing your financial intelligence. It is a foundational concept, one that many managers haven't had an opportunity to learn. And it opens a whole new window of opportunity for HR managers to ask questions and make smart decisions. For example:

- *Finding the right kind of expertise.* The two situations we described in this chapter require different skills. If a company is profitable but short on cash, then it needs financial expertise—someone capable of lining up additional financing. If a company has cash but is unprofitable, it needs operational expertise—someone capable of bringing down costs or generating additional revenue without adding costs. So financial statements tell you not only what is going on in the company but also what kind of expertise you need to hire. Can you imagine the look on your CEO's face if an HR manager analyzed the company's financial situation and made recommendations for the type of expertise needed to help turn things around?

- *Making good decisions about timing.* Informed decisions on when to take an action can increase a company's effectiveness. Take Setpoint as an example. When Joe isn't out training people in business literacy, he is CFO of Setpoint, a company that builds roller-coaster equipment and factory-automation systems. Managers at the company know that the first quarter of the year, when many orders for automation systems come in, is the most profitable for the business. But cash is always tight because Setpoint must pay out cash to buy components and pay contractors. The next quarter, Setpoint's cash flow typically improves because receivables from the prior quarter are collected, but profits slow down. Setpoint managers have learned that it's better to buy capital equipment for the business in the second quarter rather than the first, even though the second quarter is traditionally less profitable, just because there's more cash available to pay for it. When HR is supporting other business units or departments, this kind of understanding will help its managers make all sorts of decisions, including ones that relate to hiring, training, and timing incentive payouts.

The lessons here are twofold. One is that profit and cash are different, and a healthy business requires both. The other is that HR managers can use their understanding of cash flow as a tool in making strategic recommendations and decisions.

# 16

# The Language of Cash Flow

**Y**ou'd think a cash flow statement would be easy to read. Since cash is real money, there are no assumptions and estimates incorporated in the numbers. Cash coming in is a positive number, cash going out is a negative one, and net cash is simply the sum of the two. In fact, though, we find that nearly every nonfinancial manager takes a while to understand a cash flow statement. One reason is that it is always divided into categories, and the labels on the categories can be confusing. A second reason is that the positives and the negatives aren't always clear. For example, a typical line item might say, "(increase)/decrease in accounts receivable," followed by a positive or a negative number. Well, is it an increase or a decrease? A final reason is that it can be tough to see the relationship between the cash flow statement and the other two financial statements.

We'll take up the last issue in the following chapter. Right now, let's just sit down with a cash flow statement and learn the basic vocabulary.

## TYPES OF CASH FLOW

The statement shows the cash moving into a business, called the *inflows*, and the cash moving out of a business, called the *outflows*. These are divided into three main categories.

### Cash from or Used in Operating Activities

At times you'll see slight variations to the label, such as "cash provided by or used for operating activities." Whatever the specifics, it is more accountantspeak: too many accountants can't say, "operations"; they have to say, "operating activities." But whatever the exact language, this category includes all the cash flow, in and out, that is related to the actual operations of the business. It includes the cash customers send in when they pay their bills. It includes the cash the company pays out in salaries, to vendors, and to the landlord, along with all the other cash it must spend to keep the doors open and the business operating.

### Cash from or Used in Investing Activities

The second category is called "cash from or used in investing activities." Note that *investing activities* here refers to investments made by the company, not by its owners. The most important subcategory here is cash spent on capital investments—that is, the purchase of assets. If the company buys a truck or a machine, the cash it pays out shows up on this part of the statement. Conversely, if the company sells a truck or a machine (or any other asset), the cash it receives shows up here. When a company hires staff, it must usually spend a certain amount of capital to accommodate the new hires. For example, the new employees may need a computer, office furniture, and specialized tools or equipment. All these represent capital investments.

### Cash from or Used in Financing Activities

The final category is called "cash from or used in financing activities." *Financing* refers to borrowing and paying back loans, on the one hand, and transactions between a company and its shareholders, on the other. So if a company receives a loan, the proceeds show up in this category. If a company gets an equity investment from a shareholder, that too shows up here. Should the company pay off the principal on a loan, buy back its own stock, or pay a dividend to its shareholders, those expenditures of cash also would appear in this category.

You can see right away that there is a lot of useful information in the cash flow statement. The first category shows operating cash flow, which in many ways is the single most important number indicating the health of a business. A company with a consistently healthy operating cash flow is probably profitable, and it is probably doing a good job of turning its profits into cash. This information is important to HR. The HR partner who supports the accounting function, for instance, can guess that the A/R function is running smoothly. The HR partner who supports a manufacturing facility can deduce that production and sales are probably going well. A healthy operating cash flow, moreover, means that the company can finance more of its growth internally, without either borrowing more money or selling more stock. This is information HR people can use when they want to propose new initiatives.

The second category shows how much cash the company is spending on investments in its future. If the number is low, relative to the size of the company, it may not be investing much at all; management may be treating the business as a cash cow, milking it for the cash it can generate while not investing in future growth. If the number is high, relatively speaking, it may suggest that management has high hopes for the future of the company. Of course, what counts as high or low will depend on the type of company it is. A service company, for instance, typically invests less in assets than a manufacturing company. So your analysis has to reflect the big picture of the company you're assessing. This information, too, is relevant to HR. If management is treating the company as a cash cow, it is going to make different types of decisions about people than if it anticipates high growth.

The third category shows to what extent the company is dependent on outside financing. Look at this category over time, and you can see whether the company is a net borrower (borrowing more than it is paying off). You

## Financing a Company

How a company is financed refers to how it gets the cash it needs to start up or expand. Ordinarily, a company is financed through debt, equity, or both. Debt means borrowing money from banks, family members, or other creditors. Equity means getting people to buy stock in the company.

## Buying Back Stock

If a company has extra cash and believes that its stock is trading at a price that is lower than it ought to be, it may buy back some of its shares. The effect is to decrease the number of shares outstanding, so that each shareholder owns a larger piece of the company.

can also see whether it has been selling new shares to outside investors or buying back its own stock.

Finally, the cash flow statement allows you to calculate Warren Buffett's famous "owner earnings" metric (see the toolbox at the end of this part).

Wall Street in recent years has been focusing more and more on the cash flow statement. As Warren Buffett knows, there is much less room for manipulation of the numbers on this statement than on the others. To be sure, "less room" doesn't mean "no room." For example, if a company is trying to show good cash flow in a particular quarter, it may delay paying vendors or employee bonuses until the next quarter. Unless a company delays payments over and over, however—and, eventually, vendors who don't get paid will stop providing goods and services—the effects are significant only in the short term.

# 17

# How Cash Connects with Everything Else

Once you've learned to read the cash flow statement, you can simply take it the way it comes and inspect it for what it tells you about your company's cash situation. Then you can figure out how you affect it—how you as an HR manager can understand the implications of the company's cash situation and how you can help improve the business unit you support. We'll spell out some of these opportunities in the following chapter.

But if you're the type of person who enjoys a puzzle—who likes to understand the logic of what you're looking at—then stick with us through this chapter. Because we will show you an interesting fact: *you can calculate a cash flow statement just by looking at the income statement and two balance sheets.*

The calculations to do this aren't hard; they all require no more than adding and subtracting. But it's easy to get lost in the process. The reason is that accountants don't only have a special language and a special set of tools and techniques; they also have a certain way of thinking. They understand that profit as reported on the income statement is just the result of certain rules, assumptions, estimates, and calculations. They understand that assets as reported on the balance sheet aren't really worth what the balance sheet says, again because of the rules, assumptions, and estimates that go into valuing them.

But accountants also understand that the art of finance, as we have called it, doesn't exist in the abstract. Ultimately, all those rules, assumptions, and estimates have to provide us with useful information about the real world. And since in finance the real world is represented by cash, the balance sheet and the income statement must have some logical relationship to the cash flow statement.

You can see the connections in common transactions. For example, remember that a credit sale worth $100 shows up *both* as an increase of $100 in accounts receivable on the balance sheet and as an increase of $100 in sales on the income statement. When the customer pays the bill, accounts receivable decreases by $100 and cash increases by $100 on the balance sheet. And because cash is involved, that sale affects the cash flow statement as well.

Remember, too, that when the company buys $100 worth of inventory, the balance sheet records two changes: accounts payable, or A/P, rises by $100 and inventory rises by $100. When the company pays the bill, A/P decreases by $100 and cash decreases by $100—again, both on the balance sheet. When that inventory is sold (either intact by a retailer or incorporated into a product by a manufacturer), $100 worth of cost of goods sold will be recorded on the income statement. Again, the cash part of the transaction will show up on the cash flow statement.

So all these transactions ultimately have an effect on the income statement, the balance sheet, and the cash flow statement. In fact, most transactions eventually find their way onto all three. To show you more of the specific connections, let us walk you through how accountants use the income statement and the balance sheet to calculate cash flow.

## RECONCILING PROFIT AND CASH

The first exercise in this process is to reconcile profit to cash. The question you're trying to answer here is pretty simple: given that we have $X in net profit, what effect does that have on our cash flow?

We start with net profit for this reason: if every transaction were done in cash, and if there were no noncash expenses such as depreciation, net profit and operating cash flow would be identical. But since everything isn't a cash transaction, we need to determine which line items on the income statement and the balance sheet had the effect of increasing or

> ## Reconciliation
>
> In a financial context, reconciliation means getting the cash line on a company's balance sheet to match the actual cash the company has in the bank—sort of like balancing your checkbook, but on a larger scale.

decreasing cash—in other words, making operating cash flow *different* from net profit. As accountants put it, we need to find "adjustments" to net profit that, when they are added up, let us arrive at the changes in cash flow.

One such adjustment is in accounts receivable. We know that in any given time period, we're going to be taking in some cash from receivables, which will have the effect of decreasing the A/R line. We will also be making more credit sales, which will add to the A/R line. We can "net out" the cash figure from these two kinds of transactions by looking at the change in receivables from one balance sheet to the next. (Remember, the balance sheet is for a specific day, so changes can be seen when you compare two balance sheets.) Imagine, for example, we start with $100 in receivables on the balance sheet at the start of the month. We take in $75 in cash during the month, and we make $100 worth of credit sales. The new A/R line at the end of the month will be ($100 – $75 + $100) or $125. The change in receivables from the beginning of the period to the end is $25 ($100 – $125). It is also equal to new sales ($100) minus cash received ($75). Or to put it differently, cash received is equal to new sales minus the change in receivables.

Another adjustment is depreciation. Depreciation is deducted from operating profit on the way to calculating net profit. But depreciation is a noncash expense, as we have learned; it has no effect on cash flow. So you have to add it back in.

## A START-UP COMPANY

Clear? Probably not. So let's imagine a simple start-up company, with sales of $100 in the first month. The cost of goods sold is $50, other expenses are

$15, and depreciation is $10. You know that the income statement for the month will look like this:

| Income Statement | |
| --- | --- |
| Sales | $100 |
| COGS | 50 |
| Gross profit | 50 |
| Expenses | 15 |
| Depreciation | 10 |
| Net profit | $ 25 |

Let's assume that the sales are all receivables—no cash has come in yet—and COGS is all in payables. Using this information, we can construct two partial balance sheets:

| Assets | Beginning of month | End of month | Change |
| --- | --- | --- | --- |
| Accounts receivable | 0 | $100 | $100 |

| Liabilities | | | |
| --- | --- | --- | --- |
| Accounts payable | 0 | $50 | $50 |

Now we can take the first step in constructing a cash flow statement. The key rule here is that if an asset increases, cash decreases—so we subtract the increase from net income. With a liability, the opposite is true. If liabilities increase, cash increases, too—so we add the increase to net income.

Here are the calculations:

| | |
| --- | --- |
| Start with net profit | $ 25 |
| Subtract increase in A/R | (100) |
| Add increase in A/P | 50 |
| Add in depreciation | 10 |
| Equals: net change in cash | ($ 15) |

You can see that this is true because the only cash expense the company had during the period was $15 in expenses. With a real business, however, you can't confirm your results just by eyeballing them, so you need to calculate the cash flow statement scrupulously according to the same rules.

## A REALISTIC COMPANY

Let's try it with a more complex example. Here (for easy reference) are the income statement and balance sheets for the imaginary company whose financials appear in appendix A.

### Income Statement *(in millions)*

|  | Year ended Dec. 31, 2007 |
|---|---|
| Sales | $8,689 |
| Cost of goods sold | 6,756 |
| **Gross profit** | **$1,933** |
| Selling, general, and admin. (SG&A) | 1,061 |
| Depreciation | 239 |
| Other income | 19 |
| **EBIT** | **$ 652** |
| Interest expense | 191 |
| Taxes | 213 |
| **Net profit** | **$ 248** |

### Balance Sheet *(in millions)*

|  | Dec. 31, 2007 | Dec. 31, 2006 |
|---|---|---|
| **Assets** | | |
| Cash and cash equivalents | $ 83 | $ 72 |
| Accounts receivable | 1,312 | 1,204 |
| Inventory | 1,270 | 1,514 |
| Other current assets and accruals | 85 | 67 |
| Total current assets | 2,750 | 2,857 |
| Property, plant, and equipment | 2,230 | 2,264 |
| Other long-term assets | 213 | 233 |
| **Total assets** | **$5,193** | **$5,354** |
| **Liabilities** | | |
| Accounts payable | $1,022 | $1,129 |
| Credit line | 100 | 150 |
| Current portion of long-term debt | 52 | 51 |
| Total current liabilities | 1,174 | 1,330 |
| Long-term debt | 1,037 | 1,158 |
| Other long-term liabilities | 525 | 491 |
| **Total liabilities** | **$2,736** | **$2,979** |

**Shareholders' equity**

| | | |
|---|---|---|
| Common stock, $1 par value (100,000,000 authorized, 74,000,000 outstanding in 2007 and 2006) | $ 74 | $ 74 |
| Additional paid-in capital | 1,110 | 1,110 |
| Retained earnings | 1,273 | 1,191 |
| **Total shareholders' equity** | **$2,457** | **$2,375** |
| **Total liabilities and shareholders' equity** | **$5,193** | **$5,354** |

| *2007 footnotes:* | |
|---|---|
| *Depreciation* | *$239* |
| *Number of common shares (mil)* | *74* |
| *Earnings per share* | *$3.35* |
| *Dividend per share* | *$2.24* |

The same logic applies as in the simple example we gave earlier:

- Look at every change from one balance sheet to the next.

- Determine whether the change resulted in an increase or a decrease in cash.

- Then add or subtract the amount to or from net income.

Here are the steps:

| Observation | Action |
|---|---|
| Start with net profit, $248 | |
| Depreciation was $239 | Add that noncash expense to net profit |
| Accounts receivable increased by $108 | Subtract that increase from net profit |
| Inventory declined by $244 | Add that decrease to net profit |
| Other current assets rose by $18 | Subtract that increase from net profit |
| PPE rose by $205 (after adjusting for depreciation of $239—see note 1) | Subtract that increase from net profit |
| Other long-term assets decreased by $20 | Add that decrease to net profit |

*(continued)*

| Observation | Action |
| --- | --- |
| Accounts payable decreased by $107 | Subtract that decrease from net profit |
| Credit line decreased by $50 | Subtract that decrease from net profit |
| Current portion of long-term debt rose by $1 | Add that increase to net profit |
| Long-term debt decreased by $121 | Subtract that decrease from net profit |
| Other long-term liabilities increased by $34 | Add that increase to net profit |
| Dividends paid—$166 (see note 2) | Subtract that payment from net profit |

Note 1: Why do we need to adjust for depreciation when looking at the change in PPE? Remember that every year PPE on the balance sheet is lowered by the amount of depreciation charged to the assets in the account. So if you had a fleet of trucks that were acquired for $100,000, the balance sheet immediately after the acquisition would include $100,000 for trucks on the PPE line. If depreciation on the trucks was $10,000 for the year, then at the end of twelve months, the line in PPE for trucks would be $90,000. But depreciation is a noncash expense, and since we're trying to arrive at a cash number, we have to "factor out" depreciation by adding it back in.

Note 2: Notice the dividends footnoted on the balance sheet? Multiply the dividend by the number of shares outstanding and you get roughly $166 million (which we're representing as just $166). Net income of $248 minus the dividend of $166 equals $82—the precise amount by which shareholders' equity increased. This is the amount of profit that stayed in the company as retained earnings. If there is no dividend paid out or no new stock sold, then the cash provided or used by equity financing would be zero. Equity would simply increase or decrease by the amount of profit or loss in the period.

Now we can construct a cash flow statement based on all these steps (see the facing page). Of course, with a full balance sheet like this one, you have to put the change in cash in the right categories as well. The words in the right-hand column show where each number comes from. The "cash at end," of course, equals the cash balance on the ending balance sheet.

This is a complicated exercise! But you can see that there's a good deal of beauty and subtlety in all the connections (OK, maybe only if you are an accountant). Go beneath the surface a little—or, to mix metaphors, read between the lines—and you can see how all the numbers relate to one another. Your financial intelligence is on the way up, as is your appreciation of the art of finance.

**Cash Flow Statement** *(in millions)*

### Year ended Dec. 31, 2007

**Cash from operating activities**

| | | |
|---|---|---|
| Net profit | $ 248 | net profit on income statement |
| Depreciation | 239 | depreciation from income statement |
| Accounts receivable | (108) | change in A/R from 2006 to 2007 |
| Inventory | 244 | change in inventory |
| Other current assets | (18) | change in other current assets |
| Accounts payable | (107) | change in A/P |
| **Cash from operations** | **$ 498** | |

**Cash from investing activities**

| | | |
|---|---|---|
| Property, plant, and equipment | $(205) | PPE change adjusted for depreciation |
| Other long-term assets | 20 | change from balance sheet |
| **Cash from investing** | **($185)** | |

**Cash from financing activities**

| | | |
|---|---|---|
| Credit line | (50) | change in short-term credit |
| Current portion of long-term debt | 1 | change in current long-term debt |
| Long-term debt | (121) | change from balance sheet |
| Other long-term liabilities | 34 | change from balance sheet |
| Dividends paid | (166) | dividends paid to shareholders |
| **Cash from financing** | **($302)** | |

| | | |
|---|---|---|
| Change in cash | 11 | add the three sections together |
| Cash at beginning | 72 | from 2006 balance sheet |
| **Cash at end** | **$ 83** | change in cash + beginning cash |

# 18

# Why Cash Matters

**O**f course, by now you may be saying to yourself, "So what? All this is cumbersome to figure out, and why do I care?"

For starters, let's see what our sample company's cash flow statement reveals (that is, the cash flow statement for the imaginary company whose financials appear in the previous chapter and in appendix A). In terms of operations, it is certainly doing a good job of generating cash. Operating cash flow is considerably higher than net income. Inventory declined, so it's reasonable to suppose that the company is tightening up its operations. All this makes for a stronger cash position.

We can also see, however, that there is not a lot of new investment going on. Depreciation outweighed new investment, which makes us wonder whether management believes that the company has much of a future. Meanwhile, it is paying its shareholders a healthy dividend, which may suggest that they value it more for its cash-generating potential than for its future. (Many growing companies don't pay large dividends because they retain the earnings to invest in the business. Many, indeed, pay no dividends at all.)

Of course, these are all suppositions; to really know the truth, you'd have to know a lot more about the company, what business it's in, and so on—the big-picture part of financial intelligence. But if you did know all those things, the cash flow statement would be extraordinarily revealing.

That brings us to your own situation as an HR manager and to your own company's cash flow. We think there are three big reasons for looking at and trying to understand the cash flow statement.

## THE POWER OF UNDERSTANDING CASH FLOW

First, knowing your company's cash situation will help you understand what is going on now, where the business is headed, and what senior management's priorities are likely to be. You need to know not just whether the overall cash position is healthy but specifically where the cash is coming from. Is it from operations? That's a good thing—it means the business is generating cash. Is investing cash flow a sizable negative number? If it isn't, it may mean that the company isn't investing in its future. And what about financing cash flow? If investment money is coming in, that may be an optimistic sign for the future, or it may mean that the company is desperately selling stock to stay afloat. Looking at the cash flow statement may generate a lot of questions, but they are the right ones to be asking. Are we paying off loans? Why or why not? Are we buying equipment? The answers to those questions will reveal a lot about senior management's plans for the company. The cash flow statement will also give you some insight into the timing of major investments in the business, including hiring. Often it makes sense to add staff when cash flow is strong. During periods of rapid growth, cash may be tight even though the business is profitable. That will make it more difficult to hire new people.

Second, you *affect* cash. So does everyone whom you support. As we've said before, most managers focus on profit when they should be focusing on both profit and cash. Of course, their impact is usually limited to operating cash flow—but that's one of the most important measures. For instance:

- *Accounts receivable.* Do you support the sales function? Where is sales focusing its efforts? Are salespeople selling to customers who pay their bills on time? Does the sales team have a close enough relationship with customers to talk with them about payment terms? Think about how HR can support improvement in that area. If you support customer service, does that unit offer customers the kind of service that will encourage them to pay their bills on time? Is the product free of defects? Are the invoices accurate? Does the mail room send invoices on a timely basis? Is the receptionist helpful? Such factors help determine how customers feel about your company and indirectly influence how fast they are likely to pay their bills. And HR can influence each of those factors. Disgruntled customers are not known for prompt payments—they like to wait until any dispute is resolved.

- *Inventory.* If you support engineering, you affect inventory, which has a big impact on cash. For example, engineers may request special products all the time, creating an inventory nightmare. Have you offered them the training they need to understand the cost of such a practice? If people in operations like to have lots in stock—just in case—they may be creating a situation where cash is sitting on the shelves when it could be used for something else. Manufacturing and warehouse managers can often reduce inventory hugely by studying and applying the principles of "lean" enterprise, pioneered at Toyota. A lean initiative is something that HR might lead—and if there's a chance for that to happen, HR leaders need to understand the financial requirements and implications of such an initiative.

- *Expenses.* Do you defer expenses when you can? Do you consider the timing of cash flow when adding new hires, making purchases, or proposing a training rollout? Obviously, we're not saying it's always wise to hold up hiring needed employees, to defer expenses, or to cut back on training. But it is wise to understand the cash impact of deciding to spend money and to take that into account.

The list goes on. Maybe you support the manufacturing part of the business, and the plant manager always recommends buying more equipment. Or perhaps IT thinks that the company always needs the latest upgrades to its computer systems. All these decisions affect cash flow, and senior management usually understands that very well. If you want to support your business units in making an effective request, you need to familiarize yourself with the company's current cash situation (along with the other results). Then you can take part in the discussions examining both the financial and the operational needs of the unit and the company.

Third, managers who understand cash flow tend to be given more responsibilities, and thus tend to advance more quickly, than those who focus purely on the income statement. In the following part, for instance, you'll learn to calculate ratios such as days sales outstanding (DSO), which is a key measure of the company's efficiency in collecting receivables. The faster receivables are collected, the better a company's cash position. You could go to someone in finance and say, "Say, I notice our DSO has been heading in the wrong direction over the past few months—how can I help turn that around?" Alternatively, you might learn the precepts of lean enterprise, which focuses on (among other things) keeping inventories to a minimum. A manager who leads a company in converting to lean thereby frees up huge quantities of cash.

But our general point here is that cash flow is a key indicator of a company's financial health, along with profitability and shareholders' equity. It's the final link in the triad, and you need all three to assess a company's financial health. It's also the final link in the first level of financial intelligence. You now have a good understanding of all three financial statements, so it's time to move on to the next level—to put that information to work.

Do you want to try reading and analyzing a cash flow statement? If you do—and we promise it is pretty straightforward—turn to the cash flow statement exercise in appendix B.

# Part Four
# TOOLBOX

## FREE CASH FLOW

EBITDA, as we noted earlier, is no longer Wall Street's favorite measure to watch. Now the hot metric is free cash flow. Some companies have looked at free cash flow for years. Warren Buffett's Berkshire Hathaway is the best-known example, though Buffett calls it *owner earnings*.

How to calculate free cash flow? First, get the company's cash flow statement. Next take net cash from operations, and deduct the amount invested in capital equipment. That's all there is to it—free cash flow is simply the cash generated by operating the business less the money invested to keep it running. Once you think about it, it makes perfect sense as a performance measure. If you're trying to evaluate the cash generated by the company, what you really want to know is the cash from the business itself minus the cash required to keep it healthy over the longer term.

Publicly traded companies are not required to disclose free cash flow, but many do report it, especially with Wall Street's new focus on cash. It might have helped us all back in the dot-com craze, when so many new companies had negative operating cash and huge capital investments. Their free cash flow was a big negative number, and their cash needs were covered only because investors were throwing lots of dollars into the pot. Buffett, who was nearly alone back then in relying on free cash flow, never invested in any of those companies. What a surprise!

At any rate, if your company's free cash flow is healthy and increasing, you know at least the following:

- Our company has options. It can use free cash flow to pay down debt, buy a competitor, or pay dividends to owners.

- You and your colleagues can focus on the business, not on making payroll or on raising additional funds.

- Wall Street is likely to look favorably on the company's stock.

As an HR manager, you may know that a low level of free cash flow is likely to present a real challenge—that's when senior executives are most likely to begin talking about layoffs.

## COMPENSATION, BONUS, AND PROFIT-SHARING PLANS

Human resources is likely to be involved in the development of all sorts of compensation programs, including incentive pay, such as bonus and profit-sharing plans. Every such plan, no matter what type it is, must be based on an understanding of the financial needs of the company and the financial implications of the plan. (Of course, the plan must also meet the financial needs of the target population.)

Many bonus plans, for instance, are based on hitting some particular target. If you help set the targets or track progress, you'll need to understand what the key metrics are, how they affect the health of the company, and how they are calculated (so you can understand the progress). We've seen plans based on sales, operating profit, inventory levels, return on assets, and cash, just to name a few.

This book isn't about developing compensation, bonus, or profit-sharing plans, but we will outline some of the financial considerations in developing them. As Connie Haney, vice president of compensation and benefits of Mentor Graphics Corporation says, "It's important to understand the financials so that we can provide guidance to the business as leaders set their human capital strategy around what it is going to cost."

First, the financial needs of the company:

- What are the company's financial goals? For example, if its focus is cash (rather than profit), then you might want to tie sales bonuses to collected sales rather than to top-line revenue.

- What life-cycle stage is the company in? If it is in a growth phase, then profit-sharing plans might be focused on gross profit rather than net profit, because profitable sales of product might be more important than the efficiency of the business as a whole. (However, it might be wise to factor in net profit, too, so that ball doesn't get dropped completely.)

• What is the competition doing? If you want to attract good people, you'll need to consider what others are offering. Ultimately, the plan should help keep your company on its chosen path, but knowing what the competition is offering can help you ensure that your plan is attractive to prospective hires.

Now the financial implications of the plan:

• How will the plan affect profitability, cash, and other key measures if the company does really well? What will it cost? You'll need to make some assumptions and then see how the numbers play out. If sales are above forecast, for example, you'll want to know what the impact on the bottom line will be.

• How will the plan affect those same measures if the company does poorly? This is the other side of the coin, and it's equally important to determine.

• What are the long-term implications of plan outcomes? For example, if the company needs lots of cash for an acquisition but the incentive plans end up using all the cash, then you have a problem.

You'll also probably have to work closely with the accounting and finance folks. They'll need to determine the appropriate accruals for any incentive plans in place. Remember, expenses that have been incurred but have not yet been paid out must be accrued on the balance sheet. So someone needs to look at the plans every month or every quarter and determine how much in incentive compensation was earned in the period being reported for the accruals. All that must happen before the final financials for that time period are released because those numbers are needed to put together accurate financials.

Finally, your role in HR is also to explain the compensation plan. To explain it clearly means you need to understand it completely. To do that, you need to understand the measures it is based on. But if you do your job well, you'll help encourage behavior in employees that makes the company more successful.

# Ratios:
# Learning What the
# Numbers Are Really
# Telling You

# 19

# The Power of Ratios

**T**he eyes may or may not be a window into the soul, as Immanuel Kant suggested, but ratios are definitely a window into a company's financial statements. They offer a quick shortcut to understanding what the financials are saying. A Paine Webber analyst named Andrew Shore knew this and used his skill at analyzing ratios to tell the public about a fraudulently managed company—Sunbeam, when it was run by the notorious CEO "Chainsaw Al" Dunlap. We've mentioned Sunbeam before in this book, but now we want to relate a few more of the sorry details.

Dunlap had arrived at Sunbeam in early 1997. By the time he got there, he already had a great reputation on Wall Street and a standard modus operandi. He would show up at a troubled company, fire the management team, bring in his own people, and immediately start slashing expenses by closing down or selling factories and laying off thousands of employees. Soon the company would be showing a profit because of all those cuts, even though it might not be well positioned for the longer term. Dunlap would then arrange for it to be sold, usually at a premium—which means that he was often hailed as a champion of shareholder value. Sunbeam's stock jumped more than 50 percent on the news that he'd been hired as CEO.

At Sunbeam, everything went according to plan until Dunlap began readying the company for sale in the fourth quarter of 1997. By then, he'd cut the workforce in half, from twelve thousand to six thousand, and was reporting strong profits. Wall Street was so impressed that Sunbeam's stock price had gone through the roof—which, as we noted earlier, turned out to be a major problem. When the investment bankers went out to sell the company, the price was so high that they had trouble identifying prospective buyers. Dunlap's only hope was to boost sales and earnings to a level that could justify the kind of premium a buyer would have to offer for Sunbeam's stock.

## ACCOUNTING TRICKS

We now know that Dunlap and his CFO, Russ Kersh, used a whole bag of accounting tricks in that fourth quarter to make Sunbeam look far stronger and more profitable than it actually was. One of the tricks was a perversion of a technique called bill-and-hold.

*Bill-and-hold* is essentially a way of accommodating retailers who want to buy large quantities of products for sale in the future but put off paying for them until the products are actually being sold. Say that you have a chain of toy stores, and you want to ensure that you have an adequate supply of Barbie dolls for the Christmas season. Sometime in the spring, you might go to Mattel and propose a deal whereby you'll buy a certain number of Barbies, take delivery of them, and even allow Mattel to bill you for them—but you won't pay for the dolls until the Christmas season rolls around and you start selling them. Meanwhile, you'll keep them in a warehouse. It's a good deal for you because you can count on having the Barbies when you need them and hold off paying for them until you have decent cash flow. It's also a good deal for Mattel, which can make the sale and record it immediately, even though it has to wait a few more months to collect the cash.

Dunlap figured that a variation on bill-and-hold was one answer to his problem. The fourth quarter was not a particularly strong period for Sunbeam, which makes a lot of products geared toward summer—gas grills, for example. So Sunbeam went to major retailers such as Wal-Mart and Kmart and offered to guarantee that they'd have all the grills they wanted for the following summer provided they did their buying in the middle of winter. They'd be billed immediately, but they wouldn't have to pay until spring, when they actually put the goods in the stores. The retailers were cool to the idea. They didn't have anywhere to keep all that stuff, nor did they want to bear the cost of storing the inventory through the winter. "No problem," said Sunbeam. "We'll take care of that for you. We'll lease space near your facilities and cover all the storage costs ourselves."

Supposedly, the retailers agreed to those terms, although an audit conducted after Dunlap was fired failed to turn up a complete paper trail. In any case, Sunbeam went ahead and reported an additional $36 million in sales for the fourth quarter based on the bill-and-hold deals it had initiated. The scam worked well enough to fool most analysts, investors, and even Sunbeam's board of directors, which in early 1998 rewarded Dunlap and other members of the executive team with lucrative new employment contracts. Although they had been on the job for less than a year, they received some $38 million in stock grants, based largely on the mistaken belief that the company had just had a stellar fourth quarter.

But Andrew Shore, an analyst who specialized in consumer products companies, had been following Sunbeam since Dunlap arrived and now was scrutinizing its financials. He noticed some oddities, like higher-than-normal sales in the fourth quarter. Then he calculated a ratio called days sales outstanding (DSO) and found that it was huge, far above what it ought to have been. In effect, it indicated that the company's accounts receivable had gone through the roof. That was a bad sign, so he called a Sunbeam accountant to ask what was going on. The accountant told Shore about the bill-and-hold strategy. Shore realized that Sunbeam, in effect, had already recorded a hefty chunk of sales that would normally appear in the first and second quarters. After discovering this bill-and-hold game and other questionable practices, he promptly downgraded the stock.

The rest, as they say, is history. Dunlap tried to hang on, but the stock plummeted and investors grew wary of what Sunbeam's financials were telling them. Eventually, he was forced out—and it all started because Andrew Shore knew enough to dig beneath the surface and find out what was really going on. Ratios such as DSO were a useful tool for Shore, as they can be for you.

## ANALYZING RATIOS

Ratios indicate the relationship of one number to another. People use them every day. A baseball player's batting average of .333 shows the relationship between hits and official at bats—one hit for every three at bats. The odds of winning a lottery jackpot, say 1 in 6 million, show the relationship between winning tickets sold (1) and total tickets sold (6 million). Ratios don't require any complex calculations. To figure a ratio, usually you just divide one number by another and then express the result as a decimal or as a percentage.

Different people use different kinds of financial ratios in assessing a business. For example:

- Bankers and other lenders examine ratios such as debt-to-equity, which gives them an idea of whether a company will be able to pay back a loan.

- Senior managers watch ratios such as gross margin, which helps them be aware of rising costs or inappropriate discounting.

- Credit managers assess potential customers' financial health by inspecting the quick ratio, which gives them an indication of the customer's supply of ready cash compared with its current liabilities.

- Potential and current shareholders look at ratios such as price-to-earnings, which helps them decide whether a company is valued high or low in comparison with other stocks (and with its own value in previous years).

In this part we'll show you how to calculate many such ratios. The ability to calculate them—to read between the lines of the financials, so to speak—is a mark of financial intelligence. Learning about ratios will give you a host of intelligent questions to ask your boss or CFO. And of course, we'll show you how to use them to boost your company's performance.

*The power of ratios lies in the fact that the numbers in the financial statements by themselves don't reveal the whole story.* Is net profit of $10 million a healthy bottom line for a company? Who knows? It depends on the size of the company, on what net profit was last year, on what net profit was expected to be this year, and on many other variables. If you ask whether a $10 million profit is good or bad, the only possible answer is the one given by the woman in the old joke. Asked how her husband was, she replied,

"Compared to what?" As a leader in human resources, you need to identify the ratios that indicate how good a job you are doing. You also need to understand the ratios that can help assess the position of the business you support.

Ratios offer points of comparison and thus tell you more than the raw numbers alone. Profit, for example, can be compared with sales, or with total assets, or with the amount of equity shareholders have invested in the company. A different ratio expresses each relationship, and each gives you a way of gauging whether a $10 million profit is good news or bad news. As we'll see, many of the different line items on the financials are incorporated into ratios. Those ratios help you understand whether the numbers you're looking at are favorable or unfavorable.

What's more, the ratios themselves can be compared. For instance:

- *You can compare ratios with themselves over time.* Is profit relative to sales up or down this year? This level of analysis can reveal some powerful trend lines—and some big warning flags if the ratios are headed in the wrong direction.

- *You can also compare ratios with what was projected.* To pick just one of the ratios we'll be examining in this part, if your inventory turnover is worse than you expected it to be, you need to find out why.

- *You can compare ratios with industry averages.* If you find that your company's key ratios are worse than those of your competitors, you definitely want to figure out the reason. To be sure, not all the ratio results we discuss will be similar from one company to another, even in the same industry. For most, there's a reasonable range. It's when the ratios get outside of that range, as Sunbeam's DSO did, that it's worth your attention.

There are four categories of ratios that managers and other stakeholders in a business typically use to analyze the company's performance: profitability, leverage, liquidity, and efficiency. We will give you examples in each category. Note, however, that many of these formulas can be tinkered with by the financial folks to address specific approaches or concerns. Tinkering of this sort doesn't mean that people are cooking the books, only that they are using their expertise to obtain the most useful information for particular situations (yes, there is art even in formulas). What we will provide are the foundational formulas, the ones you need to learn first. Each provides a different view—like looking into a house through windows on all four sides.

# 20

# Profitability Ratios

## The Higher the Better (Mostly)

Profitability ratios help you evaluate a company's ability to generate profits. There are dozens of them, a fact that helps keep the financial folks busy. But here we are going to focus on just five. These are really the only ones most HR managers need to understand and use. Profitability ratios are the most common of ratios. If you get these, you'll be off to a good start in financial statement analysis.

Before we plunge in, however, do remember the artful aspects of what we're looking at. Profitability is a measure of a company's ability to generate sales and to control its expenses. None of these numbers is wholly objective. Sales are subject to rules about when the revenue can be recorded. Expenses are often a matter of estimation, if not guesswork. Assumptions are built into both sets of numbers. So profit as reported on the income statement is a product of the art of finance, and any ratio based on those numbers will itself reflect all those estimates and assumptions. We don't propose throwing out the baby with the bathwater—the ratios are still useful—only that you keep in mind that estimates and assumptions can always change.

Now on to the five profitability ratios that we promised you.

## GROSS PROFIT MARGIN PERCENTAGE

Gross profit, you'll recall, is revenue minus cost of goods sold. *Gross profit margin percentage*, often called gross margin, is simply gross profit divided by revenue, with the result expressed as a percentage. Look at the sample income statement in appendix A, which we'll use to calculate examples of all these ratios. In this case the calculation is as follows:

$$\text{gross margin} = \frac{\text{gross profit}}{\text{revenue}} = \frac{\$1,933}{\$8,689} = 22.2\%$$

Gross margin shows the basic profitability of the product or service itself, before expenses or overhead are added in. It tells you how much of every sales dollar you get to use in the business—22.2 cents in this example—and (indirectly) how much you must pay out in direct costs (COGS or COS), just to get the product produced or the service delivered. (COGS or COS is 77.8 cents per sales dollar in this example.) It's thus a key measure of a company's financial health. After all, if you can't deliver your products or services at a price that is sufficiently above cost to support the rest of your company, you don't have a chance of earning a net profit.

Trend lines in gross margin are equally important because they indicate potential problems. IBM not long ago announced great sales numbers in one quarter—better than expected—but the stock actually dropped. Why? Analysts noted that gross margin percentage was heading downward and assumed that IBM must have been doing considerable discounting to record the sales it did. In general, a negative trend in gross margin indicates one of two things (sometimes both). Either the company is under severe price pressure and salespeople are being forced to discount, or else materials and labor costs are rising, driving up COGS or COS. Gross margin thus can be a kind of early-warning light, indicating favorable or unfavorable trends in the marketplace. If HR keeps abreast of these trends, it can respond by proposing initiatives to support the appropriate efforts.

## OPERATING PROFIT MARGIN PERCENTAGE

*Operating profit margin percentage*, or operating margin, is a more comprehensive measure of a company's ability to generate profit. operating profit, or EBIT, remember, is gross profit minus operating expenses, so the level of operating profit indicates how well a company is running its entire business from an operational standpoint. Operating margin is just operating profit divided by revenue, with the result expressed as a percentage:

$$\text{operating margin} = \frac{\text{operating profit (EBIT)}}{\text{revenue}} = \frac{\$652}{\$8,689} = 7.5\%$$

Operating margin can be a key ratio for HR managers to watch. Many companies tie bonus payments to operating-margin targets—so if you're involved in developing or operating a bonus plan, you will want to pay close attention to this number. In addition, HR managers don't have much control over the other items—interest and taxes—that are ultimately subtracted to get net profit. So operating margin is a good indicator of how well all managers as a group are doing their jobs. A downward trend line in operating margin should be a flashing yellow light. It shows that costs and expenses are rising faster than sales, which is rarely a healthy sign. Remember, as with gross margin, it's easier to see the trends in operating results when you're looking at percentages rather than at raw numbers. A percentage change shows not only the direction of the change but also how great a change it is.

HR often comes under scrutiny when expenses need to be cut. But if you've studied the numbers and know what they mean, you will be well positioned to propose alternatives. You will be acting like a true strategic business partner.

## NET PROFIT MARGIN PERCENTAGE

*Net profit margin percentage*, or net margin, tells a company how much out of every sales dollar it gets to keep after everything else has been paid for—people, vendors, lenders, the government, and so on. It is also known as return on sales, or ROS. Again, it's just net profit divided by revenue, expressed as a percentage:

$$\text{net margin} = \frac{\text{net profit}}{\text{revenue}} = \frac{\$248}{\$8,689} = 2.9\%$$

Net profit is the proverbial bottom line, so net margin is a bottom-line ratio. But it's highly variable from one industry to another. Net margin is low in most kinds of retailing, for example. In some kinds of manufacturing, it can be relatively high. The best point of comparison for net margin is a company's performance in previous time periods and its performance relative to similar companies in the same industry.

All the ratios we have looked at so far use numbers from the income statement alone. Now we want to introduce two different profitability metrics, which draw from both the income statement and the balance sheet.

## RETURN ON ASSETS

*Return on assets*, or ROA, tells you what percentage of every dollar invested in the business was returned to you as profit. This measure isn't quite as intuitive as the ones we already mentioned, but the fundamental idea isn't complex. Every business puts assets to work: cash, facilities, machinery, equipment, vehicles, inventory, whatever. A manufacturing company may have a lot of capital tied up in plant and equipment. A service business may have expensive computer and telecommunications systems. Retailers may have a lot of inventory. All these assets show up on the balance sheet. The total assets figure shows how many dollars, in whatever form, are being utilized in the business to generate profit. ROA simply shows how effective the company is at using those assets to generate profit. It's a measure that can be used in any industry to compare the performance of companies of different size.

The formula (and sample calculation) is simply this:

$$\text{return on assets} = \frac{\text{net profit}}{\text{total assets}} = \frac{\$248}{\$5,193} = 4.8\%$$

ROA has another idiosyncrasy by comparison with the income statement ratios mentioned earlier. It's hard for gross margin or net margin to be too high; you generally want to see them as high as possible. But ROA can be too high. An ROA that is considerably above the industry norm may suggest that the company isn't renewing its asset base for the future—that is, it isn't investing in new machinery and equipment. If that's true, its long-term prospects will be compromised, however good its ROA may look at the moment. (In assessing ROA, however, remember that norms vary widely from one industry to another. Service and retail businesses re-

## Return on Investment

Why isn't ROI included in our list of profitability ratios? The reason is that the term has a number of different meanings. Traditionally, ROI was the same as ROA: return on assets. But these days it can also mean return on a particular investment. What's the ROI on our training program? What is the ROI from that initiative you are proposing? What is the ROI on that machine? What's the ROI on our new computer system? These calculations will be different depending on how people are measuring costs and returns. We'll return to ROI calculations of this sort in the following part.

quire less in terms of assets than manufacturing companies; then again, they usually generate lower margins.)

Another possibility if ROA is very high is that executives are playing fast and loose with the balance sheet, using various accounting tricks to reduce the asset base and therefore making the ROA look better than it otherwise would. Enron, for instance, set up a host of partnerships partially owned by CFO Andrew Fastow and other executives and then "sold" assets to the partnerships. The company's share of the partnerships' profits appeared on its income statement, but the assets were nowhere to be found on its balance sheet. Enron's ROA was great, but Enron wasn't a healthy company.

## RETURN ON EQUITY

*Return on equity*, or ROE, is a little different: it tells us what percentage of profit we make for every dollar of equity invested in the company. Remember the difference between assets and equity: *assets* refers to what the company owns, and *equity* refers to its net worth as determined by accounting rules.

As with the other profitability ratios, ROE can be used to compare a company with its competitors (and, indeed, with companies in other industries). Still, the comparison isn't always simple. For instance, Company A may have a higher ROE than Company B because it has borrowed more money—that is, it has greater liabilities and proportionately less equity invested in the company. Is this good or bad? The answer depends on whether Company A is taking on too much risk or whether, by contrast, it is using borrowed money judiciously to enhance its return. That gets us into ratios such as debt-to-equity, which we'll take up in the following chapter.

At any rate, here are the formula and sample calculation for ROE:

$$\text{return on equity} = \frac{\text{net profit}}{\text{shareholders' equity}} = \frac{\$248}{\$2,457} = 10.1\%$$

From an investor's perspective, ROE is a key ratio. Depending on interest rates, an investor can probably earn 3 percent or 4 percent on a treasury bond, which is essentially a risk-free investment. So if someone is going to put money into a company, he'll want a substantially higher return on his equity. ROE doesn't specify how much cash he'll ultimately get out of the company, since that depends on the company's decision about dividend payments and on how much the stock price appreciates until he sells. But it's a good indication of whether the company is even capable of generating a return that is worth whatever risk the investment may entail.

Again, note one thing about all these ratios: the numerator is some form of profit, which is always an estimate. The denominators, too, are based on assumptions and estimates. The ratios are useful, particularly when they are tracked over time to establish trend lines. But we shouldn't be lulled into thinking that they are impervious to artistic effort.

# 21

# Leverage Ratios
## The Balancing Act

Leverage ratios let you peer into how—and how extensively—a company uses debt. *Debt* is a loaded word for many people: it conjures up images of credit cards, interest payments, an enterprise in hock to the bank. But consider the analogy with home ownership. As long as a family takes on a mortgage it can afford, debt allows them to live in a house that they might otherwise never be able to own. What's more, homeowners can deduct the interest paid on the debt from their taxable income, making it even cheaper to own that house. So it is with a business: debt allows a company to grow beyond what its invested capital alone would allow and, indeed, to earn profits that expand its equity base. A business can also deduct interest payments on debt from its taxable income. The financial analyst's word for debt is *leverage*. The implication of this term is that a business can use a modest amount of capital to build up a larger amount of assets through debt to run the business, just the way a person using a lever can move a larger weight than she otherwise could.

The term *leverage* is actually defined in two ways in business—operating leverage and financial leverage. The ideas are related but different. *Operating leverage* is the ratio between fixed costs and variable costs; increasing your operating leverage means adding to fixed costs with the objective of reducing variable costs. A retailer that occupies a bigger, more efficient store and a manufacturer that builds a bigger, more productive factory are both increasing their fixed costs. But they hope to reduce their variable costs, because the new collection of assets is more efficient than the old. These are examples of operating leverage. *Financial leverage*, by contrast, simply means the extent to which a company's asset base is financed by debt.

Leverage of either kind can help a company make more money, but it also increases risk. The airline industry is an example of a business with high operating leverage (all those airplanes!) and high financial leverage (since most of the planes are financed through debt). The combination creates enormous risk, because if revenue drops off for any reason, the companies are not easily able to cut those fixed costs. That's pretty much what happened after September 11, 2001. The airlines were forced to shut down for a couple of weeks, and the industry lost billions of dollars in a short amount of time. (Some of them haven't done too well in the years since then, either.)

Here we will focus only on financial leverage, and we'll look at just two ratios: debt-to-equity and interest coverage.

## DEBT-TO-EQUITY

The debt-to-equity ratio is simple and straightforward: it tells how much debt the company has for every dollar of shareholders' equity. The formula and sample calculation (again, based on the financials of the imaginary company in appendix A) look like this:

$$\text{debt-to-equity ratio} = \frac{\text{total liabilities}}{\text{shareholders' equity}} = \frac{\$2,736}{\$2,457} = 1.11$$

(Note that this ratio isn't usually expressed in percentage terms.) Both of these numbers come from the balance sheet.

What's a good debt-to-equity ratio? As with most ratios, the answer depends on the industry. But many, many companies have a debt-to-equity ratio considerably larger than 1—that is, they have more debt than equity. Since the interest on debt is deductible from a company's taxable income, plenty of companies use debt to finance at least a part of their business. In fact, companies with particularly low debt-to-equity ratios may be targets for a leveraged buyout, in which management or other investors use debt to buy up the stock.

Bankers love the debt-to-equity ratio. They use it to determine whether to offer a company a loan. They know from experience what a reasonable debt-to-equity ratio is for a company of a given size in a particular industry (and, of course, they check out profitability, cash flow, and other measures as well). For an HR manager, knowing the debt-to-equity ratio and how it compares with those of competitors is a handy gauge of how senior management is likely to feel about taking on more debt. If the ratio is high, raising more cash through borrowing could be difficult, so expansion could require more equity investment. Also, a high debt-to-equity ratio may have an effect on the workforce. Higher debt means higher risk, which can affect employee turnover and morale.

## INTEREST COVERAGE

Bankers love interest coverage, too. It's a measure of the company's interest exposure—how much interest it has to pay every year—relative to how much it's making. The formula and calculation look like this:

$$\text{interest coverage} = \frac{\text{operating profit}}{\text{annual interest charges}} = \frac{\$652}{\$191} = 3.41$$

In other words, the ratio shows how easy it will be for the company to pay its interest. A ratio that gets too close to 1 is obviously a bad sign: most of a company's profit is going to pay off interest! A high ratio is generally a sign that the company can afford to take on more debt—or at least that it can make the payments.

What happens when either of these ratios heads too far in the wrong direction—that is, too high for debt-to-equity and too low for interest coverage? We'd like to think that senior management's response is always to focus on paying off debt, to get both ratios back into a reasonable range. But financial artists often have different ideas. There's a wonderful little invention called an operating lease, for instance, which is widely used in the airline industry and others. Rather than buying equipment such as an airplane outright, a company leases it from an investor. The lease payments count as an expense on the income statement, but there is no asset and no debt related to that asset on the company's books. Some companies that are already overleveraged are willing to pay a premium to lease equipment just to keep these two ratios in the area that bankers and investors like to see. If you want to get a complete sense of your company's indebtedness, by all means calculate the ratios—but ask someone in finance if the company uses any debt-like instruments such as operating leases as well.

Debt-to-equity and interest coverage provide HR people with information about a part of the company they aren't used to being involved in. But it doesn't mean they can't ask questions and participate in the discussions and decisions that will ultimately affect everyone HR supports.

# 22

# Liquidity Ratios

## Can We Pay Our Bills?

Liquidity ratios tell you about a company's ability to meet all its financial obligations—not just debt, but payroll, payments to vendors, taxes, and so on. These ratios are particularly important to small businesses—the ones that are often in danger of running out of cash—but they become important whenever a larger company encounters financial trouble as well. Not to harp on the airlines too much, but again they are a case in point. You can bet that in the years right after 2001, professional investors and bondholders were carefully watching the liquidity ratios of some of the larger airlines.

Again, we'll limit ourselves to two of the most common ratios.

## CURRENT RATIO

The current ratio measures a company's current assets against its current liabilities. Remember from the balance sheet chapters (part 3) that *current* in accountantese generally means a period of less than a year. So *current assets* are those that can be converted into cash in less than a year; the figure normally includes accounts receivable and inventory as well as cash. *Current liabilities* are those that will have to be paid off in less than a year, mostly accounts payable and short-term loans.

The formula and sample calculation (for the imaginary company in appendix A) for the current ratio are as follows:

$$\text{current ratio} = \frac{\text{current assets}}{\text{current liabilities}} = \frac{\$2{,}750}{\$1{,}174} = 2.34$$

This is another ratio that can be both too low and too high. In most industries a current ratio is too low when it is getting close to 1. At that point, you are just barely able to cover the liabilities that will come due with the cash you'll have coming in. This is a stressful time for the whole business. Most bankers aren't going to lend money to a company with a current ratio anywhere near 1. Less than 1, of course, is way too low, regardless of how much cash you have in the bank. With a current ratio of less than 1, you know you're going to run short of cash sometime during the next year unless you can find a way of generating more cash or attracting more from investors. That is important information for all managers, including those in HR.

A current ratio is too high when it suggests to shareholders that the company is sitting on its cash. Microsoft, for example, had amassed a cash hoard of nearly $60 billion (yes, billion) until 2004, when it announced a one-time dividend of $32 billion to its shareholders. You can imagine what its current ratio was before the dividend! (And it was probably pretty darn good after the dividend, too.)

## QUICK RATIO

The quick ratio is also known as the acid test, which gives you an idea of its importance. Here are the formula and calculation:

$$\text{quick ratio} = \frac{\text{current assets} - \text{inventory}}{\text{current liabilities}} = \frac{\$2{,}750 - \$1{,}270}{\$1{,}174} = 1.26$$

Notice that the quick ratio is the current ratio with inventory removed from the calculation. What's the significance of subtracting inventory? Nearly everything else in the current assets category is cash or is easily transformed into cash. Most receivables, for example, will be paid in a month or two, so they're almost as good as cash. The quick ratio shows how easy it would be for a company to pay off its short-term debt without waiting to sell off inventory or convert it into product. Any business that has a lot of cash tied up in inventory has to know that lenders and vendors will be looking at its quick ratio—and that they will be expecting it (in most cases) to be above 1.

# 23

# Efficiency Ratios

## Making the Most of Your Assets

Efficiency ratios help you evaluate how efficiently you manage certain key balance sheet assets and liabilities.

The phrase *managing the balance sheet* may have a peculiar ring, especially since most managers are accustomed to focusing only on the income statement. But think about it: the balance sheet lists assets and liabilities, and these assets and liabilities are always in flux. If you can reduce inventory or speed up collection of receivables, you will have a direct and immediate impact on your company's cash position. The efficiency ratios let you know how you're doing on just such measures of performance. (We'll have more to say on managing the balance sheet in part 7.)

### INVENTORY DAYS AND INVENTORY TURNOVER

Inventory days and inventory turnover ratios can be a little confusing. They're based on the fact that inventory flows through a company, and it can flow at a greater or lesser speed. Moreover, how fast it flows matters a lot. If you look at inventory as frozen cash, then the faster you can get it out the door and collect the actual cash, the better off you will be.

So let's begin with a ratio sporting the catchy name *days in inventory*, or DII. (It's also called *inventory days*.) Essentially, it measures the number of days inventory stays in the system. The numerator is average inventory, which is the beginning inventory plus ending inventory (found on the balance sheet for each date) divided by 2. (Some companies use just the ending inventory number.) The denominator is cost of goods sold (COGS) per day, which is a measure of how much inventory is actually used in each day. Here are the formula and sample calculation.

$$DII = \frac{\text{average inventory}}{\text{COGS/day}} = \frac{(\$1,270 + \$1,514)/2}{\$6,756/360} = 74.2$$

(Financial folks tend to use 360 as the number of days in a year, just because it's a round number.) In this example, inventory stayed in the system for 74.2 days. Whether that's good or bad, of course, depends on the product, the industry, the competition, and so on.

*Inventory turns*, the other inventory measure, is a measure of how many times inventory turns over in a year. If every item of inventory was processed at exactly the same rate, inventory turns would be the number of times per year you sold out your stock and had to replenish it. The formula and sample calculation are simple:

$$\text{inventory turns} = \frac{360}{DII} = \frac{360}{74.2} = 4.85$$

In the example, inventory turns over 4.85 times a year. But what are we actually measuring here? Both ratios are a measure of how efficiently a company uses its inventory. The higher the number of inventory turns—or the lower the inventory days—the tighter your management of inventory and the better your cash position. So long as you have enough inventory on hand to meet customer demands, the more efficient you can be, the better. In 2006 Target had inventory turns of 6.30—a pretty good number for a big retailer. But Wal-Mart's turns were 7.84—even better. In the retail business, a difference in the inventory turnover ratio can spell the difference between success and failure; both Target and Wal-Mart are successful, though Wal-Mart is certainly in the lead. People whose responsibilities are anywhere near inventory management need to track this ratio carefully. (Even if yours aren't, there's nothing to stop you from raising the issue: "Hey, Sally, how come there's been an uptick in our DII recently?") For HR managers, knowing where your organization is on these ratios helps you understand how it is doing and where you might want to focus your efforts. For all financially intelligent managers, HR or otherwise, these two ratios are key levers that can be used to create a more efficient organization.

## DAYS SALES OUTSTANDING

*Days sales outstanding*, or DSO, is also known as *average collection period* and *receivable days*. It's a measure of the average time it takes to collect the cash from sales—in other words, how fast customers pay their bills.

The numerator of this ratio is ending accounts receivable, taken from the balance sheet at the end of the period you're looking at. The denominator is revenue per day—just the annual sales figure divided by 360. The formula and sample calculation look like this:

$$\text{days sales outstanding} = \frac{\text{ending A/R}}{\text{revenue/day}} = \frac{\$1,312}{\$8,689/360} = 54.4$$

In other words, it takes this company's customers an average of about fifty-four days to pay their bills.

Right there, of course, is an avenue for rapid improvement in a company's cash position. Why is it taking so long? Are customers unhappy because of product defects or poor service? Are salespeople too lax in negotiating terms? Are the receivables clerks demoralized or inefficient? Is everybody laboring with outdated financial management software? Some of these questions can be addressed by HR, but the first step HR people need to take is to calculate the ratios and understand their meaning. Perhaps then, after you've analyzed why DSO is increasing, you can propose an initiative that focuses on the appropriate issue.

DSO does tend to vary a good deal by industry, region, economy, and seasonality, but still, if this company could get the ratio down to forty-five or even forty days, it would improve its cash position considerably. This is a prime example of a significant phenomenon, namely that careful management can improve a business's financial picture even with no change in its revenue or costs.

DSO is also a key ratio for the folks who are doing due diligence on a potential acquisition. A high DSO may be a red flag. Maybe the customers themselves are in financial trouble. Maybe the target company's operations and financial management are poor. Maybe, as was the case at Sunbeam, there is some fast-and-loose financial artistry going on. We'll come back to DSO in part 7, on the management of working capital; for the moment, note only that it is by definition a weighted average. So it's important that the due diligence folks look at the aging of receivables—that is, how old specific invoices are and how many there are. It may be that a couple of un-usually large, unusually late invoices are skewing the DSO number.

## DAYS PAYABLE OUTSTANDING

The *days payable outstanding* (DPO) ratio shows the average number of days it takes a company to pay its own outstanding invoices. It's sort of the flip side of DSO. The formula is similar: take ending accounts payable, and divide by COGS per day:

$$\text{days payable outstanding} = \frac{\text{ending A/P}}{\text{COGS/day}} = \frac{\$1,022}{\$6,756/360} = 54.5$$

In other words, this company's suppliers are waiting a long time to get paid—about as long as the company is taking to collect its receivables.

So what? Isn't that the vendors' problem to worry about, rather than this company's managers? Well, yes and no. The higher the DPO, the better a com-pany's cash position, but the less happy its vendors are likely to be. A company with a reputation for slow payments may find that top-of-the-line vendors don't compete for its business quite as aggressively as they otherwise might. Prices might be a little higher, terms a little stiffer. A company with a repu-tation for prompt thirty-day payment will find the exact opposite. Watching DPO is a way of ensuring that the company is sticking to whatever balance it wants to strike between preserving its cash and keeping vendors happy.

## PROPERTY, PLANT, AND EQUIPMENT TURNOVER

The next ratio tells you how many dollars of sales your company gets for each dollar invested in property, plant, and equipment (PPE). It's a mea-sure of how efficient you are at generating revenue from fixed assets such as buildings, vehicles, and machinery. The calculation is simply total rev-enue (from the income statement) divided by ending PPE (from the bal-ance sheet):

$$\text{PPE turnover} = \frac{\text{revenue}}{\text{PPE}} = \frac{\$8,689}{\$2,230} = 3.90$$

By itself, $3.90 of sales for every dollar of PPE doesn't mean much, but it may mean a lot when compared with past performance and with competitors' performance. A company that generates a lower PPE turnover, other things being equal, isn't using its assets as efficiently as a company with a higher one. So check the trend lines and the industry averages to see how your company stacks up.

But please note that sneaky little qualifier, "other things being equal." The fact is, this is one ratio where the art of finance can affect the numbers dramatically. If a company leases much of its equipment rather than owning it, for instance, the leased assets may not show up on its balance sheet. Its apparent asset base will be that much lower and its PPE turnover that much higher. Some companies pay bonuses pegged to this ratio, which gives managers an incentive to lease equipment rather than buy it. Leasing may or may not make strategic sense for any individual enterprise. But whatever the bonus or incentive plan at your company, you should determine the financial implications (and possible artistry) that may come along with the plan. Incidentally, a lease must meet specific requirements to qualify as an operating lease (which may not show up on the balance sheet) as opposed to a capital lease (which does). Check with your finance department before entering into any kind of lease.

## TOTAL ASSET TURNOVER

*Total asset turnover* is the same idea as the previous ratio, but it compares revenue with total assets, not just fixed assets. (Total assets, remember, includes cash, receivables, and inventory as well as PPE and other long-term assets.) The formula and calculation:

$$\text{total asset turnover} = \frac{\text{revenue}}{\text{total assets}} = \frac{\$8,689}{\$5,193} = 1.67$$

Total asset turnover gauges not just efficiency in the use of fixed assets; it gauges efficiency in the use of *all* assets. If you can reduce inventory, total asset turnover rises. If you can cut average receivables, total asset turnover rises. If you can increase sales while holding assets constant (or increasing at a slower rate), total asset turnover rises. Any of these managing-the-balance-sheet moves improves efficiency. Watching the trends in total asset turnover shows you how you're doing. If HR managers can support an improvement in efficiency as measured by this ratio, they are demonstrating their concern for (and intelligence about) the overall financial welfare of the company.

## REVENUE PER EMPLOYEE

One ratio that is fairly common in many labor-intensive businesses is revenue per employee. This is a good benchmark of how efficient and productive the workforce is. This ratio must be computed internally, since actual headcount numbers are not usually reported publicly. And there is no good or bad level for the ratio that can be applied to all industries; "good" is purely a function of best practices in your own industry. Still, the number can be a key indicator for HR about how the staffing level matches the workload. HR can use it to measure staff and department productivity and changes in that productivity over time. The formula is quite straightforward:

$$\frac{\text{Revenue}}{\text{Full-time equivalents}}$$

Full-time equivalents is the denominator in this ratio because the total number of employees can be a bit misleading if the organization has many part-timers. So just add up the number of hours worked by part-timers, figure out how many full-timers that equates to, and add that figure to the number of full-time employees.

There are many more ratios than these, of course. Financial professionals of all sorts use a lot of them. Investment analysts do, too. (A familiar one to investors is the price-to-earnings ratio, which shows the relationship between a company's stock price and its earnings or profits.) Your own organization is likely to have specific ratios that are appropriate for the company, the industry, or both. You'll want to learn how to calculate them, how to use them, and how you affect them.

But the ratios we have outlined here are the most common for most working managers. Although understanding the financial statements is important, it is just a start on the journey to financial intelligence. Ratios take you to the next level; they give you a way to read between (or maybe underneath) the lines, so that you can really see what is going on. They are a useful tool for analyzing your company and for telling its financial story.

Are you ready to practice pulling the three statements together and calculating some ratios? You'll learn a lot by doing it, rather than just reading about it. Please turn to the ratio exercise in appendix B.

# Part Five
## TOOLBOX

### WHICH RATIOS ARE MOST IMPORTANT TO YOUR BUSINESS?

Certain ratios are generally seen as critical in certain industries. Retailers, for instance, watch inventory turnover closely. The faster they can turn their stock, the more efficient use they are making of their other assets, such as the store itself. But individual companies typically like to create their own key ratios, depending on their circumstances and competitive situation. For example, Joe's company, Setpoint, is a small, project-based business that must keep a careful eye on both operating expenses and cash. So which ratios do Setpoint's managers watch most closely? One is home-grown: gross profit divided by operating expenses. Keeping an eye on that ratio ensures that operating expenses don't get out of line by comparison with the gross profit dollars the company is generating. The other is the current ratio, which compares current assets with current liabilities. The current ratio is usually a good indication of whether a company has enough cash to meet its obligations.

You may already know your company's key ratios. If not, try asking the CFO or people on her staff. We bet they'll be able to answer the question pretty easily.

### WHICH RATIOS ARE MOST IMPORTANT TO HUMAN RESOURCES?

There are many ratios that can provide human resource managers with information about their part of the business. To be sure, we believe you are first a businessperson, and so the first ratios for you to understand are those that are important to the business as a whole. But there are some HR measures that you will want to understand and use, depending on your company's situation. Here are a few:

- Revenue per employee

- Total expenses per employee

- Compensation as a percent of revenue

- Compensation as a percent of total expenses

- Cost per hire (at different levels of the company)

- Benefit cost as a percent of revenue

- Benefit cost as a percent of total expenses

- Benefit cost as a percent of compensation

- HR department expense as a percent of total expenses

- Employee turnover

- Ratio of offers made to number of applicants

- Training hours per employee

- Frequency/severity ratio of accidents

- Absenteeism rate

## THE POWER OF PERCENT OF SALES

You'll often see one kind of ratio built right into a company's income statement: each line item will be expressed not only in dollars but as a percent of sales. For instance, COGS might be 68 percent of sales, operating expenses 20 percent, and so on. The percent-of-sales figure itself will be tracked over time to establish trend lines. Companies can pursue this analysis in some detail—for example, tracking what percent of sales each product line accounts for or what percent of sales each store or region in a retail chain accounts for. The power here is that percent-of-sales calculations give a manager much more information than the raw numbers alone. Percent of sales allows an HR manager, for instance, to track his expenses in relationship to sales. Otherwise, it's tough for the manager to know whether he is in line as sales increase and decrease.

If your company doesn't break out percent of sales, try this exercise: locate the last three income statements, and calculate percent of sales for each major line item. Then track the results over time. If you see certain items creep up while others creep down, ask yourself why that happened—and if you don't know, try to find someone who does. The exercise can teach you a lot about the competitive (or other) pressures your company has been under.

## RATIO RELATIONSHIPS

Like the financial statements themselves, ratios fit together mathematically. We won't go into enormous detail here because this book isn't aimed at financial professionals. But one relationship among ratios is worth spelling out because it shows so clearly what we have been saying, namely that managers can affect a business's performance in a variety of ways.

Start with the fact that one of a business's key profitability objectives is return on assets, or ROA. That's a critical metric because investment capital is a business's fuel, and if a company can't deliver a satisfactory ROA, its flow of capital will dry up. We know from this part that ROA is equal to net income divided by total assets.

But another way to express ROA is through two different factors that, multiplied together, equal net income divided by total assets. Here they are:

$$\frac{\text{net income}}{\text{revenue}} \times \frac{\text{revenue}}{\text{assets}} = \frac{\text{net income}}{\text{assets}} = \text{ROA}$$

The first term, net income divided by revenue, is of course net profit margin percentage, or return on sales (ROS). The second term, revenue divided by assets, is asset turnover, discussed in chapter 23. So net profit margin multiplied by asset turnover equals ROA.

The equation shows explicitly that there are two moves to the hoop, where the hoop is higher ROA. One is to increase net profit margin, either by raising prices or by delivering goods or services more efficiently. That can be tough if the marketplace you operate in is highly competitive. A second is to increase the asset turnover ratio. That opens up another set of possible actions: reducing average inventory, reducing days sales outstanding, and reducing the purchase of property, plant, and equipment. If you can't improve your net profit margin, working on those ratios—that is, managing the balance sheet—may be your best path to beating the competition and improving your ROA.

When HR understands these options, it can truly support its business partners. For example, if the company has chosen the first move to the hoop, then one of the things you may be doing is helping find ways to cut back on operating expenses. If the company increasingly focuses on the asset turnover ratio (the second move to the hoop), then you may be involved in process improvement initiatives. Either way, understanding the business need of those actions takes your job to a higher level.

# How to Calculate
# (and Really Understand)
# Return on Investment

# 24

# The Building Blocks of ROI

Financial intelligence is all about understanding how the financial side of business works and how financial decisions are made. The principles discussed in this chapter are the foundation of how some decisions—those relating to capital investment—are made in corporate America.

Before we get into this concept called return on investment, or ROI, we need to stop and talk about HR's relationship to ROI. ROI calculations have traditionally been used by the finance department to analyze capital investments—expenditures on big, long-lasting, tangible assets—and determine whether they will benefit the company. Over the past several years, however, ROI has turned up in every manager's lexicon, including managers in HR. What is the ROI of that training program? Did you determine the ROI of that new hire? What are the ROI results of that lean-manufacturing initiative? There are lots of books and articles about ROI in HR, and plenty of controversy regarding its value. We aren't going to get into that here, but we would like you to consider the following.

The traditional ROI analysis is meant for things that can be quantified (although we know now that estimates and assumptions crop up in every quantification). The problem with many HR initiatives is that the results may not really be measurable. For example, how do you measure the financial impact of a training program? To be sure, you need to build a business case for it—but HR as a discipline doesn't have one best way to measure the return a company gets from such initiatives. The HR gurus have some good books on HR measurement, so take a look at the discussions and decide the best approach for your organization.

What we'll do here is teach the traditional finance approach to ROI that your CFO and others are using to evaluate capital expenditures in your organization. This applies to that HRIS system your department might be buying and to capital investments made by the departments or units you are supporting. Once again, an understanding of the basics will ensure that you are a strategic business partner. We'll also briefly review how ROI might be calculated for some HR activities, and we'll look at the pros and cons of the resulting number.

## TIME VALUE OF MONEY

Most of us need little introduction to the fundamental principle of finance known as the *time value of money*. The reason is that we take advantage of it every day in our personal finances. We take out home mortgages and car loans. We run up big balances on our credit cards. When the debt gets too high, we refinance. Meanwhile, we're putting our own savings into interest-bearing checking or savings accounts, money-market funds, treasury bills, stocks and bonds, and probably half a dozen other kinds of investments. We are a nation of borrowers, but we are also a nation of savers, lenders, and investors. Since all these activities reflect the time value of money, it's a safe bet that most of us have a gut-level understanding of the idea. Those who don't are likely to wind up on the losing end of the principle, which can be expensive indeed.

At its simplest, the principle of the time value of money says this: a dollar in your hand today is worth more than a dollar you expect to collect tomorrow—and it's worth a whole lot more than a dollar you hope to collect ten years from now. The reasons are obvious. You know you have today's dollar, whereas a dollar you expect to get tomorrow (let alone in ten years) is a little iffy. There's risk involved. What's more, you can buy something today with the dollar you have. If you want to spend the dollar you hope to have, you have to wait until you have it. Given the time value of money, anyone who lends money to somebody else expects to be paid interest, and anybody who borrows money expects to pay interest. The longer the time period and the higher the risk, the larger the interest charges are likely to be.

The principle is the same, of course, even if *interest* isn't the term used and even if there is no fixed expectation about what the return will be. Say you buy stock in a high-tech start-up. You're not going to get any interest, and you probably will never receive a dividend—but you hope you can sell the stock for more than you paid for it. In effect, you're lending the company your money with the expectation of a return on your investment. When and if the return materializes, you can calculate it in percentage terms just as if it were really interest.

This is the basic principle that underlies a business's decisions about capital investments, which we will discuss in this part. The business has to spend cash that it has now in hopes of realizing a return at some future date. If you are charged with preparing a financial proposal for buying a new learning software program, adding HR-related functions to your ERP system, or opening a new branch office —tasks that we'll show you how to do in these pages—you will be relying on calculations that involve the time value of money. (The typical ROI methodology used in HR does not take into account time value of money, which is one of its downfalls. More on this shortly.)

## FUTURE VALUE AND PRESENT VALUE

While the time value of money is the basic principle, the three key concepts you'll be using in analyzing capital expenditures are future value, present value, and required rate of return. You may find them confusing at first, but none of them is too complicated. They're simply ways to calculate the time value of money. If you can understand these concepts and use them in your decision making, you'll find yourself thinking more creatively—maybe we should say more artistically—about financial matters, just the way the pros do.

### Future Value

*Future value* is what a given amount of cash will be worth in the future if it is loaned out or invested. In personal finance, it's a concept often used in retirement planning. Perhaps you have $50,000 in the bank at age thirty-five, and you want to know what that $50,000 will be worth at age sixty-five. That's the future value of the $50,000. In business, an investment analyst might project the value of a company's stock in two years if earnings grow at some given percent a year. That future-value calculation can help her advise clients about whether the company is a good investment.

Figuring future value offers a broad canvas for financial artists. Look at that retirement plan, for example. Do you assume an average 3 percent return over the next thirty years, or do you assume an average 6 percent? The difference is substantial: at 3 percent your $50,000 will grow to slightly more than $121,000 (and never mind what inflation will have done to the value of a dollar in the meantime). At 6 percent it will grow to more than $287,000. It's tough to decide what's the right interest rate to use: how on earth can anyone know what interest rates will prevail over the next thirty years? At best, calculating future value that far out is educated guesswork—an exercise in artistry.

The stock analyst is in a somewhat better position because she is looking out only two years. Still, she has more variables to contend with. Why does she think earnings might grow at 3 percent or 5 percent or 7 percent or some other rate entirely? And what happens if they do? If earnings grow at only 3 percent, for instance, investors might lose interest and sell their shares, and the stock's price-to-earnings ratio might decline. If earnings grow at 7 percent, investors might get excited, buy more stock, and push up that ratio. And of course, the market itself will have an effect on the stock's price, and nobody can reliably predict the market's overall direction. Again, we're back to educated guesswork.

In fact, every calculation of future value involves a series of assumptions about what will happen between now and the time that you're looking at. Change the assumptions, and you get a different future value. The variance in return rates is a form of financial risk. The longer the investment outlook, the more estimating is required, hence the higher the risk.

## Present Value

*Present value* is the concept used most often in capital expenditure analysis. It's the reverse of future value. Say you believe that a particular investment will generate $100,000 in cash flow per year over the next three years. If you want to know whether the investment is worth spending money on, you need to know what that $300,000 would be worth right now. Just as you use a particular interest rate to figure future value, you also use an interest rate to "discount" a future value and bring it back to present value. To take a simple example, the present value of $106,000 one year from now at 6 percent interest is $100,000. We are back to the notion that a dollar today is worth more than a dollar tomorrow. In this example, $106,000 next year is worth $100,000 today.

Present-value concepts are widely used to evaluate investments in equipment, real estate, business opportunities, and even mergers and acquisitions. But you can see the art of finance clearly here as well. To figure present value, you have to make assumptions both about the cash the investment will generate in the future and about what kind of an interest rate can reasonably be used to discount that future value. And you can probably start to see the difficulty in using the traditional ROI method for HR. How do you determine the cash your HR investment will generate in the future?

## Required Rate of Return

When you're figuring what interest rate to use in calculating present value, remember that you're working backward. You are assuming your investment will pay off a certain amount in the future, and you want to know how much is worth investing now to get that amount at a future date. So your decision about the interest or discount rate is essentially a decision about what interest rate you need to make the investment at all. You might not invest $100,000 now to get $102,000 in a year (a 2 percent rate), but you might very well invest $100,000 now to get $120,000 in a year (a 20 percent rate). Different companies set the bar, or "hurdle," at different points, and they typically set it higher for riskier projects than for less risky ones. The rate that they require before they will make an investment is called the *required rate of return*, or the "hurdle rate."

There is always some judgment involved in establishing a hurdle rate, but the judgment isn't wholly arbitrary. One factor is the opportunity cost involved. The company has only so much cash, and it has to make judgments about how best to use its funds. That 2 percent return is unattractive because the company could do better just by buying a treasury bill, which might pay 4 percent or 5 percent with almost no risk. The 20 percent return may well be attractive—it's hard to make 20 percent on most investments—but it obviously depends on how risky the venture is. A second factor is the company's own cost of capital. If it borrows money, it has

## Opportunity Cost

In everyday language, this phrase denotes what you had to give up to follow a certain course of action. If you spend all your money on a fancy vacation, the opportunity cost is that you can't buy a car. In business, opportunity cost often means the potential benefit forgone from not following the financially optimal course of action.

to pay interest. If it uses shareholders' capital, the shareholders expect a return. The proposed investment has to add enough value to the company that debtholders can be repaid and shareholders kept happy. An investment that returns less than the company's cost of capital won't meet these two objectives—so the required rate of return should always be higher than the cost of capital.

That said, decisions about hurdle rates are rarely a matter of following a formula. The company's CFO or treasurer will evaluate how risky a given investment is, how it is likely to be financed, and what the company's overall situation is. He knows that shareholders expect the company to invest for the future. He knows, too, that shareholders expect those investments to generate a return at least comparable to what they can get elsewhere at a similar level of risk. He knows—or, at least, you hope he does—how tight the company's cash position is, how much risk the CEO and the board are comfortable with, and what's going on in the marketplace the company operates in. Then he makes judgments—assumptions—about what kind of hurdle rates make sense. High-growth companies typically use a high hurdle rate because they must invest their money where they think it will generate the level of growth they need. More stable, low-growth companies typically use a lower hurdle rate. If you don't already know it, someone in your finance organization can tell you what hurdle rate your company uses for the kind of projects you're likely to be involved in.

A word on the calculations involving these concepts: in the following chapter, we'll show you a formula or two. But you don't need to work it all out by hand; you can use a financial calculator, find a book of tables, or just go online. For instance, type "future-value calculator" into Google, and

## Cost of Capital

Financial analysts figure a company's cost of capital by (1) figuring the cost of its debt (the interest rate), (2) estimating the return expected by shareholders, and (3) taking a weighted average of the two. Say a company can borrow at 4 percent (after taking into account the fact that it can deduct interest payments from its taxes), and its shareholders expect a 16 percent return. Say it's financed 25 percent by debt and 75 percent by equity. The cost of capital is simply $(25\%)(4\%) + (75\%)(16\%) = 13\%$. If an investment isn't projected to return more than 13 percent, it isn't likely to be funded.

you'll get several sites where you can figure simple future values. To be sure, real-world calculations aren't always so easy. Maybe you think the investment you're considering will generate $100,000 in cash in the first year and 3 percent more in each of the subsequent years. Now you have to figure the increase, make assumptions about whether the appropriate discount rate should change from one year to the next, and so forth. Nonfinancial managers generally don't have to worry about actually doing these more complex calculations; the finance folks will do them for you. Usually, the finance staff or business analysts will have a spreadsheet or template with the appropriate formulas embedded, so that you or they can just plug in the numbers. But you do have to be aware of the concepts and assumptions that they'll use in the process. If you're just plugging in numbers without understanding the logic, you won't understand why the results turn out as they do, and you won't know how to make them turn out differently by starting with different assumptions.

Now let's put these concepts to work.

# 25

# Figuring ROI

## The Nitty-Gritty

**C**apital expenditures. Cap-ex. Capital investments. Capital budgeting. And of course, return on investment, or ROI. Many companies use these terms loosely or even interchangeably, but they're usually referring to the same thing, namely the process of deciding what capital investments to make to improve the value of the company. This chapter will teach you about traditional ROI analysis. Every HR manager should understand the approach. Not only does it inform your analysis of HR activities, but it also gives you the knowledge you need to participate in discussions with business partners about the proposals they are working on. Whenever capital expenditures are the topic of conversation, you will have the knowledge you need to ask good questions.

### ANALYZING CAPITAL EXPENDITURES

*Capital expenditures* are large projects that require a significant investment of cash. Every organization defines *significant* differently; some draw the line at $1,000, others at $5,000 or more. Capital projects are typically expected to help generate revenue or reduce costs for more than a year. The category is broad. It includes equipment purchases, business expansions, acquisitions, and the development of new products. A new marketing campaign can be considered a capital expenditure. So can the renovation of a building, the upgrade of a computer system, and the purchase of a new company car.

Expenditures like these are treated differently from ordinary purchases of inventory, supplies, utilities, and so on, for at least three reasons. One is simply that they require the company to commit large (and sometimes indeterminate) amounts of cash. A second is that they are typically expected to provide returns for several years, so the time value of money comes into play. A third is that they always entail some degree of risk. A company may not know whether the expenditure will work—that is, whether it will deliver the expected results. Even if it does work as planned, the company can't know exactly how much cash the investment will help generate. We will outline the basic steps of analyzing capital expenditures and then teach you the three methods finance people generally use for calculating whether a given expenditure is worth making.

But please, remember that this, too, is an exercise in the art of finance. It's actually kind of amazing: financial professionals can and do analyze proposed projects and make recommendations using a host of assumptions and estimates, and the results turn out well. They even enjoy the challenge of taking these unknowns and quantifying them in a way that makes their company more successful. With a little financial intelligence, you can contribute your own specialized knowledge to this process. We know of a company where the CFO makes a point of involving engineers and technicians in the capital budgeting process, precisely because they are likely to know more about what an investment in a steel-fabricating plant, say, will actually produce. The CFO likes to say that he'd rather teach those people a little finance than learn metallurgy himself. As an HR professional, you will have expertise of your own that can add to the quality of this analysis.

So here's how to go about it:

- Step 1 in analyzing a capital expenditure is to *determine the initial cash outlay*. Even this step involves estimates and assumptions: you must make judgments about what a machine or project is likely to cost before it begins to generate revenue. The costs may include purchasing equipment, installing it, allowing people time to learn to use it, and so on. Typically, most of the costs are incurred during the first year, but some may spill over into year two or even year three. All these calculations should be done in terms of cash out the door, not in terms of decreased profits.

- Step 2 is to *project future cash flows* from the investment. (Again, you want to know cash inflows, not profit.) This is a tricky step—definitely an example of the art of finance—both because it is so difficult to predict the future and because there are many factors that need to be taken into account. (See the toolbox at the end of this part.) Managers need to be conservative, even cautious, in projecting future cash flows from an investment. If the investment returns more than projected, everybody will be happy. If it returns significantly less, no one will be happy, and the company may well have wasted its money.

- Step 3, finally, is to *evaluate the future cash flows*—to figure the return on investment. Are they substantial enough so that the investment is worth making? On what basis can we make that determination? Finance professionals typically use three different methods—alone or in combination—for deciding whether a given expenditure is worth it: the payback method, the net present value (NPV) method, and the internal rate of return (IRR) method. Each provides different information, and each has its characteristic strengths and weaknesses.

You can see right away that most of the work and intelligence in good capital budgeting involves the estimates of costs and returns. A lot of data must be collected and analyzed—a tough job in and of itself. Then the data has to be translated into projections about the future. Financially savvy managers will understand that both of these are difficult processes and will ask questions and challenge assumptions.

## LEARNING THE THREE METHODS

To help you see these steps in action and understand how they work, we'll take a simple example. Your company is considering buying a $3,000 piece of equipment—a specialized computer, say. It's expected to last three years. At the end of each of the three years, the cash flow from this piece of equipment is estimated at $1,300. Your company's required rate of return—the hurdle rate—is 8 percent. Do you buy this computer or not?

## Payback Method

The payback method is probably the simplest way to evaluate the future cash flow from a capital expenditure. It measures the time required for the cash flow from the project to return the original investment—in other words, it tells you how long it will take to get your money back. The payback period obviously has to be shorter than the life of the project; otherwise, there's no reason to make the investment at all. In our example, you just take the initial investment of $3,000 and divide by the cash flow per year to get the payback period:

$$\frac{\$3,000}{\$1,300/year} = 2.31 \text{ years}$$

Since we know the machine will last three years, the payback period meets the first test: it is shorter than the life of the project. What we have not yet calculated is how much cash the project will return over its entire life.

Right there you can see both the strengths and the weaknesses of the payback method. On the plus side, it is simple to calculate and explain. It provides a quick and easy reality check. If a project you are considering has a payback period that is obviously longer than the life of the project, you probably need to look no further. If it has a quicker payback period, you're probably justified in doing some more investigation. This is the method often used in meetings to quickly determine whether a project is worth exploring.

On the minus side, the payback method doesn't tell you much. A company doesn't want just to break even on an investment, after all; it wants to generate a return. This method doesn't consider the cash flow beyond breakeven, and it doesn't give you an overall return. Nor does the method consider the time value of money. The method compares the cash outlay today with projected cash flows tomorrow, but it is really comparing apples to oranges, because dollars today have a different value than dollars down the road.

For these reasons, payback should be used only to compare projects (so that you know which will return the initial investment sooner) or to reject projects (those that will never cover their initial investment). But remember, both numbers used in the calculation are estimates. The art in this is pulling the numbers together—how close can you come to quantifying an unknown?

So the payback method is a rough rule of thumb, not strong financial analysis. If your results with payback look promising, go on to the next method to see whether the investment is really worth making.

### Net Present Value Method

The net present value method is more complex than payback, but it's also more powerful; indeed, it's usually the finance professional's first choice for analyzing capital expenditures. The reasons? One, it takes into account the time value of money, discounting future cash flows to obtain their value right now. Two, it considers a business's cost of capital or other hurdle rate. Three, it provides an answer in today's dollars, thus allowing you to compare the initial cash outlay with the present value of the return.

How to compute present value? As we mentioned, the actual calculation is usually part of a spreadsheet or template developed by your finance department. You can also use a financial calculator, online tools, or the tables found in finance textbooks. But we'll show you what the actual formula—it's called the discounting equation—looks like, so you can look "underneath" the result and really know what it means.

The discounting equation looks like this:

$$PV = \frac{FV_1}{(1+i)} + \frac{FV_2}{(1+i)^2} + \cdots \frac{FV_n}{(1+i)^n}$$

where:

PV = present value
FV = projected cash flow for each time period
i = discount or hurdle rate
n = number of time periods you're looking at

*Net present value* is simply equal to present value minus the initial cash outlay.

For the example we mentioned, the calculations would look like this:

$$PV = \frac{\$1,300}{1.08} + \frac{\$1,300}{(1.08)^2} + \frac{\$1,300}{(1.08)^3} = \$3,350$$

$$NPV = \$3,350 - \$3,000 = \$350$$

In words, the total expected cash flow of $3,900 is worth only $3,350 in today's dollars when discounted at 8 percent. Subtract the initial cash outlay of $3,000, and you get a net present value of $350.

How should you interpret this? If the net present value of a project is greater than zero, it should be accepted, because the return is greater than the company's hurdle rate. Here the return of $350 shows you that the project has a return greater than 8 percent.

Some companies may expect you to run an NPV calculation using more than one discount rate. If you do, you'll see the following relationship:

• As the interest rate increases, NPV decreases.

• As the interest rate decreases, NPV increases.

This relationship holds because higher interest rates mean a higher opportunity cost for funds. If a treasurer sets the hurdle rate at 20 percent, it means she's pretty confident she can get almost that much elsewhere for similar levels of risk. The new investment will have to be pretty darn good to pry loose any funds. By contrast, if she can get only 4 percent elsewhere, many new investments may start to look good. Just as the Federal Reserve stimulates the national economy by lowering interest rates, a company can stimulate internal investment by lowering its hurdle rate. (Of course, it may not be wise policy to do so.)

One drawback of the net present value method is that it can be hard to explain and present to others. Payback is easy to understand, but net present value is a number that's based on the *discounted value of future cash flows*—not a phrase that trips easily off the nonfinancial tongue. Still, an HR manager who wants to make an NPV presentation should persist. Assuming that the hurdle rate is equal to or greater than the company's cost of capital, any investment that passes the net present value test will increase shareholder value, and any investment that fails will (if carried out anyway) actually hurt the company and its shareholders.

Another potential drawback—the art of finance, again—is simply that NPV calculations are based on so many estimates and assumptions. The cash flow projections can only be estimated. The initial cost of a project may be hard to pin down. And different discount rates, of course, can give you radically different NPV results. Still, the more you understand about the method, the more you can question somebody else's assumptions—and the easier it will be to prepare your own proposals, using assumptions that you can defend. Your financial intelligence also will be clear to others— your boss, your CEO, whomever—when you present and explain NPV in a meeting to discuss a capital expenditure. Your understanding of the analysis will allow you to confidently explain why, or why not, the investment should be made.

### Internal Rate of Return Method

Calculating internal rate of return is similar to calculating net present value, but the variable is different. Rather than assuming a particular discount rate and then inspecting the present value of the investment, IRR calculates the actual return provided by the projected cash flows. That rate of return can then be compared with the company's hurdle rate to see whether the investment passes the test.

In our example, the company is proposing to invest $3,000, and it will receive $1,300 in cash flow at the end of each of the following three years. You can't just use the gross total cash flow of $3,900 to figure the rate of return because the return is spread out over three years, so we need to do some calculations.

First, here's another way of looking at IRR: it's the hurdle rate that makes net present value equal to zero. Remember, we said that as discount rates increase, NPV decreases. If you did NPV calculations using a higher and higher interest rate, you'd find NPV getting smaller and smaller until it finally turned negative, meaning the project no longer passed the hurdle rate. In the preceding example, if you tried 10 percent as the hurdle rate, you'd get an NPV of about $233. If you tried 20 percent, your NPV would be negative, at –$262. So the inflection point, where NPV equals zero, is somewhere between 10 percent and 20 percent. In theory, you could keep narrowing in until you found it. In practice, you can just use a financial calculator or a Web tool, and you will find that the point where NPV equals zero is 14.36 percent. That is the investment's internal rate of return.

IRR is an easy method to explain and present because it allows for a quick comparison of the project's return to the hurdle rate. On the downside, it does not quantify the project's contribution to the overall value of the company, as NPV does. It also does not quantify the effects of an important variable, namely how long the company expects to enjoy the given rate of return. When competing projects have different durations, using IRR exclusively can lead you to favor a quick-payback project with a high-percentage return when you should be investing in longer-payback projects with lower-percentage returns. IRR also does not address the issue of *scale*. For example, an IRR of 20 percent does not tell you anything about the dollar size of the return. It could be 20 percent of one dollar or 20 percent of one million dollars. NPV, by contrast, does tell you the dollar amount. When the stakes are high, in short, it may make sense to use both IRR and NPV.

## COMPARING THE THREE METHODS

We've been hinting at two lessons here. One is that the three methods we have reviewed may lead you to make different decisions, depending on which one you rely on. The other is that the net present value method is the best choice when the methods conflict. Let's take another example and see how the differences play out.

Assume again that your company has $3,000 to invest. (Keeping the numbers small makes the calculations easier to follow.) It also has three different possible investments in different types of computer systems, as follows:

- Investment A: returns cash flow of $1,000 per year for three years

- Investment B: returns cash flow of $3,600 at the end of year one

- Investment C: returns cash flow of $4,600 at the end of year three

The required rate of return—the hurdle rate—in your company is 9 percent, and all three investments carry similar levels of risk. If you could select only one of these investments, which would it be?

The payback method tells us how long it will take to get back the initial investment. Assuming the payback occurs at the end of each year, here is how it turns out:

- Investment A: three years

- Investment B: one year

• Investment C: three years

By this method alone, investment B is the clear winner. But if we run the calculations for net present value, here is how they turn out:

• Investment A: −$469 (negative!)

• Investment B: $303

• Investment C: $552

Now investment A is out, and investment C looks like the best choice. What does the internal rate of return method say?

• Investment A: 0 percent

• Investment B: 20 percent

• Investment C: 15.3 percent

Interesting. If we went by IRR alone, we would choose investment B. But the NPV calculation favors C—and that would be the correct decision. As NPV shows us, investment C is worth more in today's dollars than investment B.

The explanation? While B pays a higher return than C, it only pays that return for one year. With C we get a lower return, but we get it for three years. And three years at 15.3 percent is better than one year at 20 percent. Of course, if you assume you could keep on investing the money at 20 percent, then B would be better—but NPV can't take into account hypothetical future investments. What it does assume is that the company can go on earning 9 percent on its cash. But even so, if we take the $3,600 that investment B gives us at the end of year one and reinvest it at 9 percent, we still end up with less at the end of year three than we would get from investment C.

So it always makes sense to use NPV calculations for your investment decisions, even if you sometimes decide to use one of the other methods for discussion and presentation. But again, the most important step any manager can take when analyzing capital expenditures is to revisit the cash flow estimates themselves. They are where the art of finance really comes into play and where companies make their biggest mistakes. Often it makes sense to do a *sensitivity analysis*—that is, to check the calculations using future cash flows that are 80 percent or 90 percent of the original projections and see whether the investment still makes sense. If it does, you can be more confident that your calculations are leading you to the right decision.

This chapter, we know, has involved a lot of calculating. But sometimes you'd be surprised at how intuitive the whole process can be. Not long ago, Joe was running a financial review meeting at Setpoint. A senior manager in the company was suggesting that Setpoint invest $80,000 in a new machining center so that it could produce certain parts in-house rather than relying on an outside vendor. Joe wasn't wild about the proposal for several reasons, but before he could speak up, a shop assembly technician asked the manager the following questions:

- Did you figure out the monthly cash flow return we will get on this new equipment? Eighty thousand dollars is a lot of money!

- Do you realize that we are in the spring—and that the business is typically slow, and cash is tight, during the summer?

- Have you figured in the cost of labor to run the machine? We are all pretty busy in the shop; you will probably have to hire someone to run this equipment.

- Are there better ways we could spend that cash to grow the business?

After this grilling, the manager dropped the proposal. The assembly technician might not have been an expert in net present value calculations, but he sure understood the concepts.

## ROI IN HR

Jack J. Phillips, Dave Ulrich, and Jac Fitz-enz—to name a few—are all well-respected authors who have addressed the issue of return on investment in human resources. We are not the HR experts they are, so what we'll do here is briefly look at ROI in HR.

Jack J. Phillips lists nine evaluation myths in his book *Accountability in Human Resource Management*. The eighth one is "unless a return on investment (ROI) is calculated, evaluation will be useless. Some HR managers have the mistaken belief that when a program is evaluated, a benefit/cost ratio or ROI must be developed. ROI is only one approach to evaluation. It is not only difficult to produce, but in some cases it is impossible."[1] Later on in the same book, he states, "An ROI calculation should be used when the program benefits can be clearly documented and substantiated, even if they are subjective."[2] (He, too, is acknowledging the art of finance.) For example, according to Phillips, ROI is not particularly useful for measuring recruitment and selection efforts, but it is useful for safety and health initiatives. Not so useful for employee relations, but very useful for productivity improvements. We too are not so sure that ROI is the best measure to use in HR. However, because the term is thrown around so much, let's look at the calculation used by some:

$$\text{ROI} = \frac{\text{program benefits} - \text{program costs}}{\text{program costs}} \times 100$$

Program benefits include cost savings from the program (e.g., cost savings from a lean initiative) and increased revenue as a result of the program (e.g., increase in revenue from a new sales support program). Program costs include all costs—development costs, implementation costs, and operating costs. The time of the people working on the project should be included in the costs as well.

What does the result tell us? It tells us the return (we use that term very loosely here) we earned on our program costs. But what is wrong with this approach? Clearly, the time value of money needs to be considered and compared to the cost of capital. If we changed the ROI formula as follows, we could use the company's cost of capital as the discount rate on costs and benefits for the HR program. This would give us the program's NPV:

$$\text{NPV} = \text{PV of program benefits} - \text{PV of program costs}$$

Let us repeat here that there are helpful books out there in HR measurement. That's good—because as Marcia Conner, an education executive who writes for Learnativity.com about ROI for learning programs, says, "One thing is certain: many smart people are completely befuddled by the topic."[3]

# Part Six
## TOOLBOX

### A STEP-BY-STEP GUIDE TO ANALYZING CAPITAL EXPENDITURES

You've been talking with your boss about developing a new labor-hour tracking system. He ends the meeting abruptly. "Sounds good," he says. "Write me up a proposal with the ROI and have it on my desk by Monday." Don't panic: here's a step-by-step guide to preparing your proposal.

1. Remember that ROI means return on investment—just another way of saying, "Prepare an analysis of this capital expenditure." The boss wants to know whether the investment is worth it, and he wants calculations to back it up.

2. Collect all the data you can about the cost of the investment. In the case of a new tracking system, total costs would include any necessary hardware, software purchase or development, installation, debugging, training, and so on. Note where you must make estimates. Treat the total as your initial cash outlay. You will also need to determine the system's useful life, not an easy task (but part of the art we enjoy so much!). You might talk to others who have developed or purchased similar systems to help you answer the question.

3. Determine the benefits of the new investment, in terms of what it will save the company or what it will help the company earn. A calculation for a new system should include any cost savings from greater labor efficiency, a reduction in the number of hours required to track labor hours, and so on. The tricky part here is that you need to figure out how all these factors translate into an estimate of cash flow. Don't be

afraid to ask for help from your finance department—those folks are trained in this kind of thing and should be willing to help.

4. Find out the company's hurdle rate for this kind of investment.

5. Calculate the net present value of the project using this hurdle rate.

6. Calculate payback and internal rate of return as well. You'll probably get questions about what they are from your boss, so you need to have the answers ready.

7. Write up the proposal. Keep it brief. Describe the project, outline the costs and benefits (both financial and otherwise), and describe the risks. Discuss how it fits with the company's strategy or competitive situation. Then give your recommendations. Include your NPV, payback, and IRR calculations in case there are questions about how you arrived at your results.

Managers sometimes go overboard in writing up capital expenditure proposals. It's probably human nature: we all like new things, and it's usually pretty easy to make the numbers turn out so that the investment looks good. But we advise conservatism and caution. Explain exactly where you think the estimates are good and where you think they may be shaky. Do a sensitivity analysis, and show (if you can) that the estimate makes sense even if cash flows don't materialize at quite the level you hope. A conservative proposal is one that is likely to be funded—and one that is likely to add the most to the company's value in the long run.

## A BIG HR DECISION

One of the biggest decisions that HR is involved in making these days is whether to outsource all or part of HR itself. It may be scary to think about, but it's a reality. HR outsourcing can include just transactional activities (such as payroll) or the HR function in its entirety.

Some see this as a promising development. Future HR departments, they argue, will focus only on strategic activities, with a small staff of HR business-people and all the rest outsourced. (Better keep improving your financial intelligence!) On the other side are those who believe that outsourcing any

HR activity is counterproductive. To them, it's like saying that the employer doesn't want in-house staff to develop and lead the people in the organization.

The issues are complex. Demographers predict a tightening of the U.S. labor market, which will put pressure on HR departments across the country to find innovative ways of attracting talent. Yet every company's ongoing focus on reducing costs means that HR must learn to provide more value at a lower price. Also, the complexity of the legal environment for HR makes it tough for HR managers in smaller companies to keep up. In the case of mergers and acquisitions, the challenges can be so daunting and the needs so specialized that outsourcing the work to specialists may be the only option. Finally, the technological changes in HR may help make it easier to outsource, as certain functions can now more easily be split off.

The risks are not negligible. Outsourcing may mean a decrease in service quality. It may mean that the company has less control over the HR function. Costs could be much higher than anticipated. Then there is a vital question that every company needs to ask about outsourcing: in the long term, does it create or destroy value? Companies with a strong culture usually need a strong HR department to build and reinforce the culture. Southwest Airlines, for example, has made the decision not to outsource any HR activity.

Whatever the specifics of your company's situation, you need to be able to think like an HR businessperson to participate in these discussions, do the analysis, and help make the decisions.

# Applied Financial Intelligence: Working Capital Management

# 26

# The Magic of Managing the Balance Sheet

**W**e've mentioned the phrase *managing the balance sheet* a couple of times in this book. Right now, we want to go into greater detail about how to do it. The reason? Astute management of the balance sheet is like financial magic. It allows a company to improve its financial performance even without boosting sales or lowering costs. Better balance sheet management makes a business more efficient at converting inputs to outputs and ultimately to cash. It speeds up the cash conversion cycle, a concept that we'll take up later in this part. Companies that can generate more cash in less time have greater freedom of action; they aren't so dependent on outside investors or lenders.

To be sure, the finance organization in your company is ultimately responsible for managing most of the balance sheet. They're the ones responsible for figuring out how much to borrow and on what terms, for lining up equity investment when necessary, and for generally keeping an eye on the company's overall assets and liabilities. But HR and other nonfinancial managers have a huge impact on certain key line items from the balance sheet, which, taken together, are known as working capital. Working capital is a prime arena for the development and application of financial intelligence. Once you grasp the concepts, you'll become a valuable partner to the finance organization and senior managers. Learn to manage working capital better, and you can have a powerful effect on both your company's profitability and its cash position.

## THE ELEMENTS OF WORKING CAPITAL

*Working capital* is a category of resources that includes cash, inventory, and receivables, minus whatever a company owes in the short term. It comes straight from the balance sheet, and it's often calculated according to the following formula:

$$\text{working capital} = \text{current assets} - \text{current liabilities}$$

Of course, this equation can be broken down further. Current assets, as we have seen, includes items such as cash, receivables, and inventory. Current liabilities includes payables and other short-term obligations. But these aren't isolated line items on the balance sheet; they represent different stages of the production cycle and different forms of working capital.

To understand this, imagine a small manufacturing company. Every production cycle begins with cash, which is the first component of working capital. The company takes the cash and buys some raw materials. That creates raw-materials inventory, a second component of working capital. Then the raw materials are used in production, creating work-in-process inventory and eventually finished-goods inventory, also part of the "inventory" component of working capital. Finally, the company sells the goods to customers, creating receivables, which are the third and last component of working capital (figure 26-1). In a service business, the cycle is similar but simpler. For example, our own company—the Business Literacy Institute—is partly a training business. Its operating cycle involves the time required to go from the initial development of training materials, to completion of training classes, and finally to collection of the bill. The more efficient we are in finishing a project and following up on collections, the healthier our profitability and cash flow will be. In fact, the best way to make money in a service business is to provide the service quickly and well, and then to collect as soon as possible. Throughout this cycle, the form taken by working capital changes. But the amount doesn't change unless more cash enters the system—for example, from loans or from equity investments.

FIGURE 26-1

**Working capital and the production cycle**

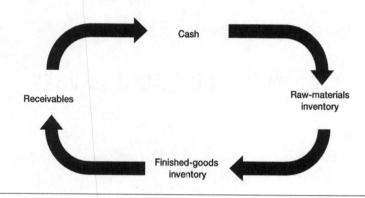

Of course, if the company buys on credit, then some of the cash re-mains intact—but a corresponding "payables" line is created on the liabili-ties side of the balance sheet. So that must be deducted from the three other components to get an accurate picture of the company's working capital.

Overall, how much working capital is appropriate for a company? This question doesn't allow for an easy answer. Every company needs enough cash and inventory to do its job. The larger it is and the faster it is growing, the more working capital it is likely to need. But the real challenge is to use working capital efficiently. The three working capital accounts that nonfi-nancial managers can truly affect are accounts receivable, inventory, and (to a lesser extent) accounts payable. We'll take up each one in turn.

Before we do, though, it's worth asking once again how much art is in-volved in all these calculations. In this case, the best answer might be "some." Cash is a hard number, not easily subject to manipulation. Receivables and payables are relatively hard as well. Inventory isn't quite so hard. Various accounting techniques and assumptions allow a company to value inven-tory in different ways. So a company's calculation of working capital will depend to an extent on the rules the company follows. Still, you can gener-ally assume that working capital figures aren't subject to as much discre-tion and judgment as many of the numbers we learned about earlier.

# 27

# Your Balance Sheet Levers

Most companies use their cash to finance customers' purchase of products or services. That's the "accounts receivable" line on the balance sheet—the amount of money customers owe at a given point in time, based on the value of what they have purchased before that date.

The key ratio that measures accounts receivable, as we saw in part 5, is days sales outstanding, or DSO—that is, the average number of days it takes to collect on these receivables. *The longer a company's DSO, the more working capital is required to run the business.* Customers have more of the company's cash in the form of products or services not yet paid for, so that cash isn't available to buy inventory, deliver more services, and so on. Conversely, the shorter a company's DSO, the less working capital is required to run the business. It follows that the more people who understand DSO and work to bring it down, the more cash the company will have at its disposal.

## MANAGING DSO

The first step in managing DSO is to understand what it is and in which direction it has been heading. If it's higher than it ought to be, and particularly if it's trending upward (which it nearly always seems to be), managers need to begin asking questions. As an HR manager, you have two roles. One is to help the managers you support ask the questions that apply to them. The other is this: HR may be in a good position to be part of the team *answering* these questions. As you'll see, the answers may involve many departments and multiple issues.

Operations and R&D managers, for example, must ask themselves whether there are any problems with the products that might make customers less willing to pay their bills. Is the company selling what customers want and expect? Is there a problem with delivery? Quality problems and late deliveries often provoke late payment, just because customers are not pleased with the products they're receiving and decide that they will take their own sweet time about payment. Managers in quality assurance, market research, product development, and so on thus have an effect on receivables, as do managers in production and shipping. In a service company, people who are out delivering the service need to ask themselves the same questions. If service customers aren't satisfied with what they're getting, they too will take their time about paying.

Customer-facing managers—those in sales and customer service—have to ask a similar set of questions. Are our customers healthy? What is the standard in their industry for paying bills? Are they in a region of the world that pays fast or slow? Salespeople typically have the first contact with a customer, so it is up to them to flag any concerns about the customer's financial health. Once the sale is made, customer-service reps need to pick up the ball and learn what's going on. What's happening at the customer's shop? Are employees working overtime? Is the company laying people off? Meanwhile, salespeople need to work with the folks in credit and customer service so that everybody understands the terms up front and will notice when a customer is late. At one company we worked with, the delivery people knew the most about customers' situations because they were at the customers' facilities every day. They would alert sales and accounting if there seemed to be issues cropping up in a customer's business. Developing a mechanism in your organization whereby line employees can communicate such insights to the right people is critical. HR can play a key role in creating these lines of communication.

Credit managers need to ask whether the terms offered are good for the company and whether they fit the credit histories of the customers. They need to make judgments about whether the company is giving credit too easily or whether it is too tough in its credit policies. There's always a trade-off between increasing sales on the one hand and issuing credit to poorer credit risks on the other. Credit managers need to set the precise terms they're willing to offer. Is net thirty days satisfactory—or should we allow net sixty? They need to determine strategies such as offering discounts for early pay. For example, "2/10 net 30" means that customers get a discount of 2 percent if they pay their bill in ten days and no discount if they wait thirty days. Sometimes a 1 percent or 2 percent discount can help a struggling company collect its receivables and thereby lower its DSO—but, of course, it does so by eating into profitability.

We know of a small company that has a simple homegrown approach to the issue of giving credit to customers. The company has identified the traits it wants in its customers and has even named its ideal customer Bob. Bob's qualities include the following:

- He works for a large company.

- His company is known for paying its bills on time.

- He can maintain and understand the product provided (this company makes complex technology-intensive products).

- He is looking for an ongoing relationship.

If a new customer meets these criteria, it will get credit from this small manufacturer. Otherwise, it won't. As a result of this policy, the company has been able to keep its DSO quite low and to grow without additional equity investment.

All these decisions greatly affect accounts receivable and thus working capital. And the fact is, they can have a huge impact. Reducing DSO even by one day can save a large company millions of dollars per day. For example, check back to the DSO calculation in chapter 23, and you'll note that one day of sales in our sample company is just over $24 million. Reducing DSO from 55 days to 54 in this company would thus increase cash by $24 million. That's cash that can be used for other things in the business.

## MANAGING INVENTORY

Many managers (and consultants!) these days are focusing on inventory. They work to reduce inventory wherever possible. They use buzzwords such as *lean manufacturing, just-in-time inventory management,* and *economic order quantity.* The reason for all this attention is exactly what we're talking about here. Managing inventory efficiently reduces working capital requirements by freeing up large amounts of cash.

The challenge for inventory management, of course, isn't to reduce inventory to zero, which would probably leave a lot of customers unsatisfied. The challenge is to reduce it to a minimum level while still ensuring that every raw material and every part will be available when needed and that every product will be ready for sale when a customer wants it. A manufacturer needs to be constantly ordering raw materials, making things, and holding those finished products for delivery to customers. Wholesalers and retailers need to replenish their stocks regularly and to avoid the dreaded stockout—an item that isn't available when a customer wants it. Yet every item in inventory can be regarded as frozen cash, which is to say cash that the company cannot use for other purposes. Exactly how much inventory is required to satisfy customers while minimizing that frozen cash, well, that's the million-dollar question (and the reason for all those consultants).

The techniques for managing inventory are beyond the scope of this book. But we do want to emphasize that many different kinds of managers affect a company's use of inventory—which means that all these managers can have an impact on reducing working capital requirements. Here again is HR's opportunity to partner with the departments or units it supports. For example:

- Salespeople love to tell customers they can have exactly what they want. ("Have it *your* way," as the old Burger King jingle put it.) Custom paint job? No problem. Bells and whistles? No problem. Every variation, however, requires a little more inventory, meaning a little more cash. Obviously, customers must be satisfied. But that common-sense requirement has to be balanced against the fact that inventory costs money. The more that salespeople can sell standard products with limited variations, the less inventory their company will have to carry.

- Engineers love those same bells and whistles. In fact, they're constantly working to improve the company's products, replacing version 2.54

with version 2.55 and so on. Again, this is a laudable business objective, but it's one that has to be balanced against inventory requirements. A proliferation of product versions adds to frozen cash and puts a burden on inventory management. When a product line is kept simple with a few easily interchangeable options, the amount of inventory needed is likely to be less and therefore less cash is tied up.

• Production departments greatly affect inventory. For instance, what's the percentage of machine downtime? Frequent breakdowns require the company to carry more work-in-process inventory and more finished-goods inventory. And what's the average time between change-overs? Decisions about how much to build of a particular part have an enormous impact on inventory requirements. Even the layout of a plant affects inventory: an efficiently designed production flow in an efficient plant minimizes the need for inventory.

Along these lines, it's worth noting that many U.S. plants operate on a principle that eats up tremendous amounts of working capital. When business is slow, they nevertheless keep on churning out product, with the goal of maintaining factory efficiency. Plant managers focus on keeping unit costs down, often because that goal has been pounded into their heads for so long that they no longer question it. They have been trained to do it, told to do it, and paid (with bonuses) for achieving it.

When business is good, the goal makes perfect sense: keeping unit costs down is simply a way of managing all the costs of production in an efficient manner. (This is the old approach of focusing only on the income statement, which is fine as far as it goes.) When demand is slow, however, the plant manager must consider the company's cash as well as its unit costs. A plant that continues to turn out product in these circumstances is just creating more inventory that will sit on a shelf taking up space and cash. Coming to work and reading a book might be better than building product that is not ready to be sold.

How much can a company save through astute inventory management? Look again at our sample company: cutting *just one day* out of the DII number—reducing it from 74 days to 73—would increase cash by nearly $19 million. Any large company can save millions of dollars of cash, and thereby reduce working capital requirements—just by making modest improvements in its inventory management.

You may think that all these questions aren't in HR's purview. But if you expect to be a businessperson—and if part of your job is to help your business succeed financially—you should be involved in figuring out what it would take to improve these numbers.

# Homing In on Cash Conversion

In this chapter we'll take up the cash conversion cycle, which measures how effectively a company collects its cash. But there's one little wrinkle we have to consider first—how fast a company decides to pay the money it owes its vendors.

Accounts payable is a tough number to get right. It's an area where finance meets philosophy. Financial considerations alone would encourage managers to maximize days payable outstanding (DPO), thus conserving the company's cash. A change in this ratio is as powerful as a change in the other ratios we've been discussing. In our sample company, for instance, increasing DPO by just one day would add about $19 million to the company's cash balance.

But there are other considerations, as we mentioned in chapter 23. What kind of a relationship does a company want with its vendors? What kind of reputation does it want? In practical terms, how much leverage does it have with vendors—will they even continue doing business with a late payer? Another practical consideration is the Dun & Bradstreet rating. D&B bases its scores, in part, on a company's payment history. An organization that consistently pays late may find that it has trouble getting a loan later on.

A personal story may illustrate the point. Joe's company, Setpoint, never lets an invoice go beyond thirty days. The company's philosophy is that slow pay simply isn't good business. Where did that philosophy come from? When Joe's partners, both engineers, started Setpoint, they had recently left another company. There they had been project managers, designing custom products for the company's customers. But when they sent their designs out to be fabricated, nobody would build parts for them. When they asked why not, they found that their employer regularly took more than one hundred days to pay its bills. In effect, the engineers had to become negotiators just to get their projects built! When they started their own business, they vowed they would never put their new company's engineers in that position. While the philosophy puts constraints on cash flow, Setpoint's leaders believe that it positively affects the company's reputation and relationship with its vendors—and in the long term helps Setpoint build a stronger community of businesses around itself. When a company is developing its philosophy, mission, and vision, why not include this type of discussion? The philosophy of finance! It's an approach everyone can be proud of and—who knows?—it may even contribute to higher morale and lower turnover.

HR managers don't usually have much direct impact on payables, so we won't go into any more detail. But in general, if you notice that your company's DPO is climbing—and particularly if it is higher than your DSO—you might want to ask the finance folks a few questions. After all, HR's work depends on good relationships with vendors, and you don't want the finance department to mess up those relationships unnecessarily.

## THE CASH CONVERSION CYCLE

Another way to understand working capital is to study the cash conversion cycle. It's essentially a timeline relating the stages of production (the operating cycle) to the company's investment in working capital. The timeline has three levels, and you can see how the levels are linked in figure 28-1. Understanding these three levels and their measures provides a powerful way of understanding the business and should help you make financially intelligent decisions.

Starting at the left, the company purchases raw materials. That begins the accounts payable period and the inventory period. In the next phase, the company has to pay for those raw materials. That begins the cash con-

FIGURE 28-1

## The operating cycle

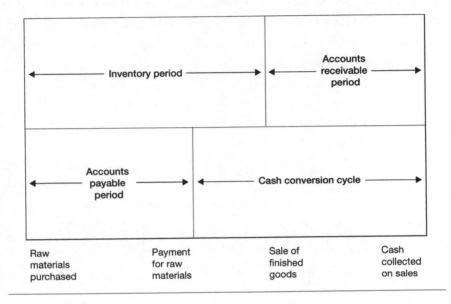

version cycle itself—that is, the cash has now been paid out, and the job is to see how fast it can come back. Yet the company is still in its inventory period; it hasn't actually sold any finished goods yet.

Eventually, the company does sell its finished goods, ending the inventory period. But it is just entering the accounts receivable period; it still hasn't received any cash. Finally, it does collect the cash on its sales, which ends both the accounts receivable period and the cash conversion cycle.

Why is this important? Because with it, we can determine how many days all this takes and then understand how many days a company's cash is tied up. That's an important number for managers and leaders to know. Armed with the information, managers can potentially find ways to "save" lots of cash for their company. To figure it out, use the following formula:

$$\text{cash conversion cycle} = \text{DSO} + \text{DII} - \text{DPO}$$

In other words, take days sales outstanding, add days in inventory, and subtract the number of days payable outstanding. That tells you, in days, how fast the company recovers its cash, from the moment it pays its payables to the moment it collects its receivables.

The cash conversion cycle gives you a way of calculating how much cash it takes to finance the business: you just take sales per day and multiply it by the number of days in the cash conversion cycle. Here are the calculations for our sample company:

$$54 \text{ days} + 74 \text{ days} - 55 \text{ days} = 73 \text{ days}$$

$$73 \text{ days} \times \$24,136,000 \text{ sales/day} = \$1,761,928,000$$

This business requires working capital of around $1.8 billion just to finance its operations. That isn't unusual for a large corporation. Even small companies require a lot of working capital relative to their sales if their cash conversion cycle is as long as sixty days. Companies of any size can get themselves into trouble on this score. Tyco International—mentioned earlier in this book—was famous for acquiring six hundred companies in two years. All those acquisitions entailed a lot of challenges, but one serious challenge involved huge increases in the cash conversion cycle. The reason? Tyco often was acquiring companies in the same industry, and competing products were added to its product list. With several very similar products in inventory, the inventory didn't move as fast as it once had—and inventory days began to spiral out of control, increasing in some parts of the business by more than ten days. In a multinational company with more than $30 billion in revenue, increases on that scale can deplete cash by several hundred million dollars! (This is an issue that Tyco has addressed in recent years by closing down the acquisition pipeline and focusing on the operations of the business.)

The cash conversion cycle can be shortened by all the techniques discussed in this part: decreasing DSO, decreasing inventory, and increasing DPO. Find out what your company's cycle is and which direction it's heading in. You may want to discuss it with the folks in finance. Who knows? They might even be impressed that you know what it is and what levers can affect it. More important, you might start a conversation that will result in a faster cash conversion cycle, lower working capital requirements, and more cash. That will benefit everybody in the business.

# Part Seven
## TOOLBOX

### ACCOUNTS RECEIVABLE AGING

Accounts receivable is a major cash lever. So even though HR hasn't traditionally paid much attention to accounts receivable, you may want to do so now that you've built up your financial intelligence. There is a way to manage accounts receivable more effectively. We've talked about one measure, DSO, but it isn't the only measure to look at. Another is what's called the aging of receivables. Often, reviewing aging is the key to understanding the true situation in your company's receivables.

Here's why. As we mentioned earlier, DSO is by definition an average. For example, if you have $1 million in receivables that are under ten days and $1 million that are more than ninety days, your overall DSO is about fifty days. That doesn't sound too bad—but, in fact, your company may be in substantial trouble because half of its customers don't seem to be paying their bills. Another business of the same size might have a DSO figure of fifty days with only $250,000 over ninety days. That business isn't in the same sort of trouble.

An aging analysis will present you with just these kinds of figures: total receivables under thirty days, total for thirty to sixty days, and so on. It's usually worth checking out that analysis as well as your overall DSO number to get the full picture of your receivables. The importance of an aging analysis to HR is that it gives you a window into customer behavior; it's one data point in your understanding of how the outside world looks at and responds to your company. The more you understand about the outside world's view, the better job you'll do.

# Creating a Financially Intelligent HR Department (and Organization)

# Financial Literacy, Transparency, and Corporate Performance

**W**e have written this book primarily to help you increase your financial intelligence and become a better manager. We firmly believe that understanding the financial statements, the ratios, and everything else we have included in the book will make you more effective in your job as an HR leader and will better your career prospects. Frankly, we also think that understanding the financial side of the business will make your work life more meaningful. You would never play baseball or backgammon without first learning how the game is played; why should business be any different? Knowing the rules—how profits are figured, why return on assets matters to shareholders, and all the rest—lets you see your work in the big-picture context of business enterprise, which is simply people working together to achieve certain objectives. You'll see more clearly how the company that you're a part of operates. You'll want to contribute to it, and you'll know how to do so. You'll also be able to assess your performance better than you could before because you can see which way the key numbers are moving and understand why they're moving in one direction or the other.

Then, of course, there's the fun of it. As we've shown, the financial report cards of business are partly reflections of reality. But they're also—sometimes very much so—reflections of estimates, assumptions, educated guesswork, and all the resulting biases. (Occasionally, they reflect outright manipulation as well.) The folks in your company's finance organization know all this, but they haven't done a good job of sharing their knowledge with the rest of us. Now you get to ask them the tough questions. How do they recognize a particular category of revenue? Why did they choose a particular time frame for depreciation? Why is DII on the upswing? Of course, once they get past the shock of hearing HR colleagues speak their language, they'll almost certainly be willing to discuss the bases for their assumptions and estimates and to modify them when appropriate. Who knows? The financial folks may even start asking for your advice.

## BETTER COMPANIES

But we have another objective for this book as well, and we believe HR has a critical role to play in it. We believe that businesses perform better when the financial intelligence quotient is higher. A healthy business, after all, is a good thing. It offers valuable goods and services to its customers. It provides its employees with stable jobs, pay raises, and opportunities for advancement. It pays a return to its shareholders. Overall, a healthy business helps our economy grow, keeps our communities strong, and improves our standard of living. It also makes HR work more rewarding: you can focus on growth and skill development rather than on turnover and layoffs.

Financially intelligent managers, in HR and other departments, contribute to a business's health because they can make better decisions. They can use their knowledge to help the company succeed. They manage resources more wisely, use financial information more astutely, and thereby increase their company's profitability and cash flow. They also understand more about why things happen and can lend their shoulder to the wheel instead of just carping about how misguided the senior leadership is. We remember, for example, teaching a class of sales executives, using their company's actual financials. When we got to the cash flow statement—and showed them how the company's cash coffers had been drained to pursue growth by acquisition—one of the sales executives smiled. We asked him why he was smiling, and he laughed. "I've been fighting with the vice president of sales in my division for the better part of a year," he said. "The reason is, they changed our commission plan. We used to be paid on sales, and now we're paid when the sales are collected. Finally, I understand the reason for the change." He went on to explain that he agreed with the strategy of growth by acquisition, and he really didn't mind that the comp plan had been changed to support the strategy—he had just never understood why.

Financial intelligence makes for healthier business in another sense, too. A lot of companies today are governed by politics and power. They reward people who curry favor with their superiors and who build behind-the-scenes alliances. Gossip and mistrust are rife; common objectives get lost as individuals scurry to ensure their own advancement. At its worst, this kind of environment becomes truly toxic. At one company we worked with, employees thought that profit sharing was distributed only in years when employees complained loudly enough that they were unhappy. The purpose of profit sharing, they figured, was to keep them quiet. In reality, the company had a fairly straightforward plan that linked employees' efforts to their quarterly profit-sharing checks. But the politics were such that employees never believed the plan was real.

There's a simple antidote to politics: sunlight, transparency, and open communication. When people understand a company's objectives and work to attain them, it's easier to create an organization built on a sense of trust and a feeling of community. *In the long run, that kind of organization will always be more successful than its less open counterparts.* Sure, an Enron or a WorldCom or a Sunbeam can prosper for a while under secretive, self-serving leadership. But an organization that is successful over the long haul will almost invariably be built on trust, communication, and a shared sense of purpose. Financial training—an increase in financial intelligence—can make a big difference. At the company where employees thought that the purpose of profit sharing was to keep them quiet, those who underwent training learned how the plan really worked. Soon they were focusing their efforts on the numbers they affected—and soon they were getting a profit-sharing check every quarter.

Financially savvy managers can also react more quickly to the unexpected. There's a famous book called *Warfighting*, prepared by staff members of the U.S. Marine Corps, that was first published in 1989 and since then has become a kind of bible for special forces of all kinds. One theme of the book is that marines in combat are always faced with uncertainty and rapidly changing conditions. They can rarely rely on instructions from above; instead, they must make decisions on their own. So it's imperative that commanders spell out their broad objectives and then leave decisions about implementation to junior officers and ordinary marines in the field. That lesson is just as valuable to companies in today's mercurial business climate. Managers have to make a lot of day-to-day decisions without consulting the higher-ups. Many of these key day-to-day issues involve personnel and HR issues. If people in HR understand the financial parameters they're working under, they can make those decisions more quickly and effectively. The company's performance—like the performance of a marine unit on the ground—will be that much stronger.

## TAKING IT TO THE TROOPS

There's a next step here as well. If it makes a difference for managers to understand finance, imagine how much more of a difference it would make if everybody in a department—indeed, everybody in a company—understood it.

The same logic applies: people in offices, in stores and warehouses, on shop floors, and at client sites can make smarter decisions if they know something about how their unit is measured and about the financial implications of what they do every day. Should they rework a damaged part or use a new one? Should they work fast to get as much done as possible or work more deliberately to ensure fewer mistakes? Should they spend their time developing new services or cultivating and serving existing customers? How important is it to have everything a customer might possibly need? Like marines, frontline employees and supervisors should know the broad outlines of what the organization needs so that they can work smarter on the job.

Companies understand this idea, of course, and in recent years have deluged employees and supervisors with performance goals, key performance indicators (KPIs), and other metrics. Maybe you have been the one to inform people of the KPIs they'll be evaluated on; if so, you know that there's typically a good deal of eye rolling and head shaking, particularly if the KPIs this quarter are different from last quarter's. But what if the folks in the field understood the financial logic of the KPIs or the performance goals? What if they understood that they are facing new KPIs this quarter not because some executive randomly decided it but because the company's financial situation had changed? Like the sales executive in the class, most people are willing to adapt to a new situation provided they understand the reason for the change. If they don't understand, they won't be motivated or have the knowledge to do anything about it.

Just as financial intelligence in the managerial ranks can boost a business's performance, so can financial intelligence among the troops. The Center for Effective Organizations, for instance, conducted a study that looked at (among other things) many measures of employee involvement.[1] Two measures in particular were "sharing information about business performance, plans and goals" and training employees in "skills in understanding the business." Both of these were positively related to productivity, customer satisfaction, quality, speed, profitability, competitiveness, and employee satisfaction. The more that organizations trained their people in financial literacy, in other words, the better the organizations did. Other students of management—including Daniel R. Denison, Peter Drucker, and Jeffrey Pfeffer—have studied and supported the idea that the more employees understand the business, the better the business performs. All these findings should come as no surprise. When people understand what's going on, the level of trust in the organization rises. Turnover drops. Motivation and commitment increase. Does anybody doubt that greater trust, motivation, and commitment lead to better performance?

One of us, Joe, has seen all these phenomena firsthand. He and his partners have spent years building a business, Setpoint, from the ground up. Like every start-up, it experienced periodic difficulties and crises, and more than once the company's accountant told Joe that it couldn't survive another period of turbulence. But somehow it always did. Finally, the accountant confessed to Joe, "You know, I think the reason why you get through these difficult times is because you train your employees and share the finances with them. When times are tough, the company rallies together and finds a way to fight through it."

The accountant was right: the employees all do know exactly where the company stands. Sharing financial information and helping subordinates and coworkers understand it is a way of creating a common purpose in a company. It fosters an environment where teamwork can survive and prosper. What's more, it's harder to cook the books when they're open for everybody to see. Enron's employees thought they had a good thing going:

a growing company, rapidly appreciating stock, fat 401(k) plans, plenty of opportunity for advancement. But then, suddenly, the whole thing came tumbling down around their ears and nearly all those employees, HR included, were out on the streets looking for work. A culture of transparency won't always prevent fraud like Enron's, but it might discourage it. Why? Financially savvy employees can serve as one more group of watchdogs. This is not something that is part of people's traditional expectations for HR staff and most other employees in a business. But it is now.

So think what could be gained by a true culture of financial transparency and intelligence—a culture in which people everywhere saw and learned to understand the financial statements as a matter of course. No, we don't expect everyone to become Wall Street analysts or even accountants. We just think that if the financials are out there and the key concepts repeatedly explained, every employee in the place will be more trusting and more loyal, and the company will be stronger for it. To be sure, publicly traded companies can't show consolidated financials to employees except once a quarter, when the information is released to the public. But they can certainly make a point of explaining things when those financials are released. In the meantime, such companies can make sure that employees see operating numbers for the department or facility they work in.

You can see that we believe passionately in the power of knowledge. When it comes to business, we believe most of all in the power of financial knowledge—and the financial intelligence necessary to put it to work. Financial information is the nervous system of any business. It contains the data that shows how the business is faring—where its strengths are, where its weaknesses are, where its opportunities and threats are as well. For too long, a relative handful of people in each company were the only ones who understood what the financial data was telling them. We think more people should understand it—starting with HR and other managers, but ultimately extending out into the entire workforce. People will be better off for gaining that understanding—and so will companies.

If you buy into that vision, you have some exciting work ahead of you.

# Financial Literacy Strategies

If you want to help create a finan-
cially intelligent workplace, your first step is to figure out a strategy for getting there. We don't use the word *strategy* lightly. If you really want to
change the culture, you know that sponsoring a one-time training course
or handing out an instruction book isn't going to do it. You will need a
plan and the time to implement it. You will need resources and support from
others in your department and from higher-ups in the company. We'll outline three approaches—ones that aren't mutually exclusive—that we have
seen work.

## A FINANCIALLY LITERATE HR DEPARTMENT

The following tools and techniques hardly constitute an exhaustive list,
but they are all approaches that you can implement on your own for your
department fairly easily.

### Training (Over and Over)

Training is the first step, just so that everyone speaks the same language,
understands the core concepts of how financial success is measured, and
knows what he or she can do to make an impact.

As training professionals know, people need to be engaged in the learning. For financial training, that means ensuring the learning includes
"doing it" (discussions, exercises, case studies, and so on). It also means

finding (or learning to be) a particular kind of trainer. The trainer must know how to communicate these concepts in a way that doesn't intimidate people. (Remember that many people are afraid of numbers and finance.) The trainer must also be able to show people the WIIFM—what's in it for me. That means showing them how they make a difference, explaining why it is important to understand finance, and making the concepts relevant to them, their jobs, and their company. Good trainers use the spiral method when teaching: they integrate the foundational concepts as they teach the more advanced concepts, repeating and revisiting the basics in different ways each time around.

So start by putting together three short training sessions. We don't mean anything fancy: even a PowerPoint presentation with some handouts works fine (though we would caution you that using PowerPoint for all your class materials doesn't necessarily support lasting learning!). Each session should be between thirty and sixty minutes. Focus on one financial concept per session. Joe, for example, conducts three one-hour courses at Setpoint—on the income statement, on cash flow and project finance, and on the balance sheet. Depending on your situation, you might look at gross margin, selling expenses as a percent of sales, or even inventory turns. Pick the topics and measures that give people an understanding of both their department and the company as a whole. The concepts should be relevant to human resources, and you should show people how they themselves affect the numbers.

Offer these classes regularly, maybe once a month. Let people attend two or three times if they want—it often takes that long for folks to get it. Encourage 100 percent attendance from your direct reports. Create an environment that tells participants that you believe they are an important part of the department's success and that you want their involvement. Eventually, you can ask other people to teach the class—that's a good way for them to learn the material, and their teaching styles might be different enough from yours that they're able to reach people whom you can't.

### Weekly "Numbers" Meetings

What are the two or three numbers that measure the human resource department's performance week after week and month after month? What are the two or three numbers that you yourself watch to know whether you're doing a good job as a manager? Turnover? Productivity? Revenue per employee? Performance to budget? Chances are, the key numbers that you watch relate in some way to your company's financial statements and hence ultimately affect financial performance. So start sharing those numbers with your team in weekly meetings. Explain where the numbers come from, why they're important, and how everybody on the team affects them. Track the trend lines over time.

You know what will happen? Pretty soon people will begin talking about the numbers themselves. They'll start figuring out ways to move the needle in the right direction. Once that begins to occur, try taking it to the next level: forecast where the numbers will be in the coming month or quarter. You'd be amazed how people begin to take ownership of a number once they have staked their credibility on a forecast. (We've even seen companies where employees have set up a betting pool on where a given number will be!)

## Reinforcements: Scoreboards and Other Visual Aids

It's fashionable these days for corporate executives to have a dashboard on their computers, showing where the business's performance indicators stand at any given moment. We always wonder why operating units don't have the same thing out in the open for all employees to see. So we not only recommend discussing the key number or numbers in meetings; we also suggest posting them on a scoreboard and comparing past performance with present performance and future forecasts. When the numbers are out there for everybody to see, it's tough for people to forget or ignore them. Remember, though, that small graphs can be easily ignored—and if they can be, they will be. As with your dashboard, make sure the scoreboard is clear, straightforward, and easy to see.

We also like visual aids that remind people how the company makes money. They provide a context for the day-to-day focus on key numbers. Our own company has developed what we call Money Maps, illustrating topics such as where profits come from. See the sample in figure 30-1: the map traces the entire business process at a fictional company, showing how much of each sales dollar goes to paying the expenses of each department, and then highlighting how much is left over as profit. We customize these maps for our clients, so that everyone can see all the operations in their companies. But you can even draw maps and diagrams yourself, if you know the material well enough. A visual is always a powerful tool for reinforcing learning. When people look at it, it reminds them how they fit into the big picture. It's useful as well. One company we know of put up two copies of the same map. One showed the company's target numbers—what its best branch would do. On the other, managers wrote their own branch's actual numbers. People could see for each critical element how close they were to, or how far away from, the best branch's performance.

In all these approaches, remember that adults learn best if they are doing something themselves. So don't just announce or post the numbers—ask people to do the calculations themselves, to discuss the impact, to explain the meaning. We bet you'll hear some amazing things, like new ideas for how to reduce downtime or improve cash flow. Adults learn especially fast when they see a reason to. If they understand the big picture—and if they understand how what they're learning connects to their job,

FIGURE 30-1

**Money map**

Copyright © Business Literacy Institute. Illustrated by Dave Merrill.

their impact on the company results, and their own financial situation (e.g., job security, the chance for raises)—they'll pay close attention. Just be careful not to make assumptions about what they already know. (Managers often assume their team members know more than they really do.) Instead, teach those basics in a way that ensures no one is embarrassed about what they don't know. Keep the teaching tightly focused, keep it fun, and remember, don't try to make them into accountants!

## AN ORGANIZATION-WIDE INITIATIVE

What you do with the HR department can become a template for a far larger organizational initiative. You'll need a high-level sponsor (such as your CEO or CFO, or an operational VP), and you'll probably need some outside help to develop and deliver the education. One client of ours runs a five-day finance boot camp for its leaders, a two-day course for its managers, and a one-day program for all employees. Everyone speaks the language of finance in that company. Another client includes financial literacy training in its new-employee orientation. Others create videos, use Money Maps, or play games. And still others offer regular classes so that all employees have an opportunity to increase their financial intelligence. Each of these initiatives is focused on ensuring that everyone understands how financial success is measured.

If the culture is right in your company for even more ongoing activities, the opportunity for improvement is huge. At one company we worked with, part of the education process included a change in language (which can be tremendously important in any culture change). It started at one location, where the regional manager began calling employees "business partners." These new business partners took the change seriously, mostly because there were other things going on that told them management truly saw them as partners, and began calling each other business partners. Before long they had even changed the parking lot signs, so that the word *employee* effectively disappeared from the location. Then other locations began to catch on, and soon the president of this national company was talking about business partners in the internal newsletter. The final piece came when a large customer wrote a thank-you to a vice president, calling the employees of this company business partners. The new language, in turn, was reflected in greater commitment, more involvement, and better results.

The keys to a successful companywide initiative are:

- *Top leadership's commitment.* Executives must believe that everyone wants to make a difference, given the knowledge and opportunity.

- *Education.* It is typical to assume people know more than they do when it comes to finance. We are all good at faking it, and most of us are afraid to raise our hand in a meeting and say we don't understand. Don't make any assumptions about what people know.

- *Communication.* As soon as the education is complete, keep the information flowing. Share results, talk about their meaning, and discuss how people make an impact.

We know that we're suggesting an ambitious agenda. But consider the payoffs.

In the not-so-distant past, human resources had a role that was strictly limited to personnel matters—hiring, compensation, and so on. HR people played a correspondingly subordinate role in the organization. Over the years HR's role expanded, and it now includes the many different functions that are often put under the rubric of human-capital management. HR professionals are expected to be conversant with the latest thinking on training and organizational development, recruitment and retention strategies, performance evaluation, and several other specialized topics. At many companies this larger role has earned HR a seat at the strategic table and a part in strategic decisions. The rewards and influence accorded to HR have grown as a result.

We think it can be much the same with financial knowledge. As HR takes on the job of teaching financial skills and helping disseminate financial information, it can become an even more important partner in the business than it is today. An intelligent, motivated, committed workforce, after all, is one of the few advantages that competitors can't easily copy. Financial intelligence adds a critical dimension to employees' skills. The people who help employees learn and maintain those skills will be essential to the organization.

So we urge you to make this book the beginning of a process rather than the end of one. Learn more. Take what you learn, and help others understand it as well. Build a financially literate department. Explore the possibilities for creating a financially literate, even transparent, company. The rewards—to you and your colleagues, to the people you support, and to the company as a whole—will be considerable.

# Part Eight
## TOOLBOX

### UNDERSTANDING SARBANES-OXLEY

If you are anywhere near your finance department, you have heard of Sarbanes-Oxley, also known as Sarbox or just Sox. Sarbanes-Oxley is a law enacted by the U.S. Congress in July 2002 in response to continuing revelations of financial fraud. It may be the most significant legislation affecting corporate governance, financial disclosure, and public accounting since the original U.S. securities laws were enacted in the 1930s. It is designed to improve the public's confidence in the financial markets by strengthening financial reporting controls and the penalties for noncompliance.

Sarbanes-Oxley's provisions affect nearly everyone involved with finance. It creates the Public Company Accounting Oversight Board. It bans accounting firms from selling both audit and nonaudit services to clients. It requires corporate boards of directors to include at least one director who is a financial expert and requires board audit committees to establish procedures whereby employees can confidentially tip off directors to fraudulent accounting. Under Sarbanes-Oxley, a company cannot fire, demote, or harass employees who attempt to report suspected financial fraud.

CEOs and CFOs are greatly affected by this law. These officers must certify their company's quarterly and annual financial statements, attest that they are responsible for disclosure and control procedures, and affirm that the financial statements don't contain misrepresentations. Intentional misrepresentation of financial results may lead to fines, jail time, or both. Also, the law forbids companies from granting or guaranteeing personal loans to executives and directors. (A study by the nonprofit Corporate Library Research Group found that companies lent executives more than $4.5 billion in 2001, often at no or low interest.) And it requires CEOs and CFOs to give back certain bonuses and stock-option profits if their company is forced to restate financial results because of misconduct.

Sarbanes-Oxley requires companies to strengthen their internal controls. They must include an "internal controls report" in their annual report to shareholders, addressing management's responsibility in maintaining adequate controls over financial reporting and stating a conclusion about the effectiveness of the controls. In addition, management must disclose information on material changes in the financial condition or operations of the company on a rapid and current basis.

Sarbanes-Oxley forces public companies to take more responsibility for their financial statements, and it may lessen the probability of undetected fraud. However, it is very expensive to implement. The average cost for companies is $5 million; for large companies such as General Electric, it may be as much as $30 million.

## HR AND SOX

Does Sox really have anything to do with HR? On the surface, no. It is all about finance. But look a little deeper, and you'll see that HR plays a critical role.

First, someone has to set up and maintain the system of anonymous tips about possible fraudulent activities to the company board. That process may involve HR. Whoever is maintaining that system and handling the tips better have some financial intelligence.

Second, we are seeing more and more clients who require their managers to sign certifications about their own department's financials. Those certifications go directly to a committee that includes the CFO. *Everyone* is being held accountable for the accuracy of the numbers.

HR managers need to understand exactly what is going on in their own numbers because they may be asked to certify that the data is correct. (Do you know for sure that the accruals and the depreciation in your monthly budget results are accurate, or do you assume that accounting is taking care of it?) On top of that, HR supports other managers who also must sign certifications. That means understanding the requirements and help-ing the business unit understand what it needs to do before it can sign the certification. We know of one company where the training department (a part of HR) has responsibility, along with finance, for training everyone about the certifications.

# Sample Financials

The following is a sample set of financials for an imaginary company.

### INCOME STATEMENT *(in millions)*

|                                      | Year ended Dec. 31, 2007 |
| ------------------------------------ | -----------------------: |
| Sales                                |                   $8,689 |
| Cost of goods sold                   |                    6,756 |
| **Gross profit**                     |               **$1,933** |
| Selling, general, and admin. (SG&A)  |                    1,061 |
| Depreciation                         |                      239 |
| Other income                         |                       19 |
| **EBIT**                             |                 **$ 652** |
| Interest expense                     |                      191 |
| Taxes                                |                      213 |
| **Net profit**                       |                 **$ 248** |

## BALANCE SHEET *(in millions)*

| | Dec. 31, 2007 | Dec. 31, 2006 |
|---|---|---|
| **Assets** | | |
| Cash and cash equivalents | $ 83 | $ 72 |
| Accounts receivable | 1,312 | 1,204 |
| Inventory | 1,270 | 1,514 |
| Other current assets and accruals | 85 | 67 |
| Total current assets | 2,750 | 2,857 |
| Property, plant, and equipment | 2,230 | 2,264 |
| Other long-term assets | 213 | 233 |
| **Total assets** | **$5,193** | **$5,354** |
| | | |
| **Liabilities** | | |
| Accounts payable | $1,022 | $1,129 |
| Credit line | 100 | 150 |
| Current portion of long-term debt | 52 | 51 |
| Total current liabilities | 1,174 | 1,330 |
| Long-term debt | 1,037 | 1,158 |
| Other long-term liabilities | 525 | 491 |
| **Total liabilities** | **$2,736** | **$2,979** |
| | | |
| **Shareholders' equity** | | |
| Common stock, $1 par value (100,000,000 authorized, 74,000,000 outstanding in 2007 and 2006) | $ 74 | $ 74 |
| Additional paid-in capital | 1,110 | 1,110 |
| Retained earnings | 1,273 | 1,191 |
| **Total shareholders' equity** | **$2,457** | **$2,375** |
| | | |
| **Total liabilities and shareholders' equity** | **$5,193** | **$5,354** |

*2007 footnotes:*

| | |
|---|---|
| *Depreciation* | *$239* |
| *Number of common shares (mil)* | *74* |
| *Earnings per share* | *$3.35* |
| *Dividend per share* | *$2.24* |

## CASH FLOW STATEMENT *(in millions)*

| | Year ended Dec. 31, 2007 |
|---|---|
| **Cash from operating activities** | |
| Net profit | $248 |
| Depreciation | 239 |
| Accounts receivable | (108) |
| Inventory | 244 |
| Other current assets | (18) |
| Accounts payable | (107) |
| **Cash from operations** | **$498** |
| **Cash from investing activities** | |
| Property, plant, and equipment | ($205) |
| Other long-term assets | 20 |
| **Cash from investing** | **($185)** |
| **Cash from financing activities** | |
| Credit line | ($ 50) |
| Current portion of long-term debt | 1 |
| Long-term debt | (121) |
| Other long-term liabilities | 34 |
| Dividends paid | (166) |
| **Cash from financing** | **($302)** |
| Change in cash | 11 |
| Cash at beginning | 72 |
| **Cash at end** | **$ 83** |

# Exercises to Build Your Financial Intelligence

## Income Statement Exercise

The following exercises will give you the opportunity to practice what you learned about the income statement.

Our goals with this practice are for you to:

- *Get comfortable reading an income statement.* Half the battle is simply learning to find the right data, so we'll ask you to find the numbers that you'll need to do some analysis.

- *Begin to analyze the results.* By looking at the trends and doing a few simple percentage calculations, you'll start to see a layer of meaning behind the numbers.

- *Understand the meaning of the numbers.* You will answer a few questions about the numbers that will help you understand their significance.

### EXERCISE DESCRIPTION

There are two income statements, one for Kimberly-Clark and one for FedEx (see appendix C). You can practice with one or both. We've included these two companies because one is a manufacturer and one is a service company. Of course, there are many other types of organizations (retail, banking, nonprofit, and so on), but two will give you a good start.

A few cautions: because one company is in manufacturing and one is a service business, the income statements contain some different line items. Even common line items may be labeled differently. Remember, too, that these two companies are just samples—other manufacturers' and service companies' statements will have slightly different line items and labels. But once you familiarize yourself with the key lines, you'll be able to work your way through most financial statements.

Follow the instructions here, and you'll be building your financial intelligence.

## INSTRUCTIONS

1. Choose which company's financial information you want to work with, and then find the correct table to fill in. The tables are different because the two companies' income statements have different line items. Use the tables to enter your numbers or as a guide to write your answers on a separate piece of paper.

2. Try your hand at the calculations and questions. You'll see the calculation to do (either a "percent of" or a "percent change" calculation), a column for the data, and a column for the results. Pay close attention to the year you are working on, and be sure your data and results match the correct year. That will help you later when you are looking at trends. The tables and questions are labeled for Kimberly-Clark and for FedEx. Doing the calculations and answering the questions will give you an opportunity to think about what the numbers you just wrote down mean.

3. Step back and be proud of your work!

4. Take a look at the answers and see how you did. (Yes, the answers are right here. We don't want you to have to flip back and forth, and it is OK if you peek. The whole point is to learn. This is not a test!)

## CALCULATIONS

Really do try these—you'll be surprised at how easy they are and how much more information you'll have about the company once you do them.

### Kimberly-Clark Corporation
**Percent of:**

|  | 2006 Data | 2006 Result | 2005 Data | 2005 Result | 2004 Data | 2004 Result |
|---|---|---|---|---|---|---|
| Gross profit as a percent of net sales |  |  |  |  |  |  |
| Marketing, research, and general expenses as a percent of net sales |  |  |  |  |  |  |
| Operating profit as a percent of net sales |  |  |  |  |  |  |

**Percent Change:**

|  | 2005 to 2006 Data | 2005 to 2006 Result | 2004 to 2005 Data | 2004 to 2005 Result |
|---|---|---|---|---|
| Percent change in net sales |  |  |  |  |
| Percent change in operating profit |  |  |  |  |

## FedEx Corporation

### Percent of:

|  | 2006 Data | 2006 Result | 2005 Data | 2005 Result | 2004 Data | 2004 Result |
|---|---|---|---|---|---|---|
| Salaries and employee benefits as a percent of revenues |  |  |  |  |  |  |
| Operating income as a percent of revenues |  |  |  |  |  |  |

### Percent Change:

|  | 2005 to 2006 Data | 2005 to 2006 Result | 2004 to 2005 Data | 2004 to 2005 Result |
|---|---|---|---|---|
| Percent change in revenues |  |  |  |  |
| Percent change in operating income |  |  |  |  |

## QUESTIONS

Now let's try answering a few questions. You can answer them for one or both companies:

1. What trends do you see by looking at the income statement itself, the raw numbers? What are they telling you?

   *Kimberly-Clark:*

   _____

   _____

   _____

*FedEx:*

_____

_____

_____

2. Look at your percent of and percent change results. What are they telling you?

     *Kimberly-Clark:*

_____

_____

_____

     *FedEx:*

_____

_____

_____

## CALCULATION RESULTS

## Kimberly-Clark Corporation

### Percent of:

|  | 2006 Data | 2006 Result | 2005 Data | 2005 Result | 2004 Data | 2004 Result |
|---|---|---|---|---|---|---|
| Gross profit as a percent of net sales | 5,082.1 / 16,746.9 | 30.3% | 5,075.2 / 15,902.6 | 31.9% | 5,068.5 / 15,083.2 | 33.6% |
| Marketing, research, and general expenses as a percent of net sales | 2,948.3 / 16,746.9 | 17.6% | 2,737.4 / 15,902.6 | 17.2% | 2,510.9 / 15,083.2 | 16.6% |
| Operating profit as a percent of net sales | 2,101.5 / 16,746.9 | 12.5% | 2,310.6 / 15,902.6 | 14.5% | 2,506.4 / 15,083.2 | 16.6% |

## Percent Change:

| | 2005 to 2006 Data | 2005 to 2006 Result | 2004 to 2005 Data | 2004 to 2005 Result |
|---|---|---|---|---|
| Percent change in net sales | $\dfrac{16,746.9 - 15,902.6}{15,902.6}$ | 5.3% | $\dfrac{15,902.6 - 15,083.2}{15,083.2}$ | 5.4% |
| Percent change in operating profit | $\dfrac{2,101.5 - 2,310.6}{2,310.6}$ | (9.0%) | $\dfrac{2,310.6 - 2,506.4}{2,506.4}$ | (7.8%) |

## FedEx Corporation

### Percent of:

| | 2006 Data | 2006 Result | 2005 Data | 2005 Result | 2004 Data | 2004 Result |
|---|---|---|---|---|---|---|
| Salaries and employee benefits as a percent of revenues | $\dfrac{12,571}{32,294}$ | 38.9% | $\dfrac{11,963}{29,363}$ | 40.7% | $\dfrac{10,728}{24,710}$ | 43.4% |
| Operating income as a percent of revenues | $\dfrac{3,014}{32,294}$ | 9.3% | $\dfrac{2,471}{29,363}$ | 8.4% | $\dfrac{1,440}{24,710}$ | 5.8% |

### Percent Change:

| | 2005 to 2006 Data | 2005 to 2006 Result | 2004 to 2005 Data | 2004 to 2005 Result |
|---|---|---|---|---|
| Percent change in revenues | $\dfrac{32,294 - 29,363}{29,363}$ | 10.0% | $\dfrac{29,363 - 24,710}{24,710}$ | 18.8% |
| Percent change in operating income | $\dfrac{3,014 - 2,471}{2,471}$ | 22.0% | $\dfrac{2,471 - 1,440}{1,440}$ | 71.6% |

## ANSWERS TO THE QUESTIONS

Here are just a few thoughts in response to each of the questions we asked you to consider. There is certainly lots of data to look at, with various conclusions, so there is no one right answer. These answers are just to give you a flavor of what you might look at as you study the results.

1.  What trends do you see in the raw numbers? What are they telling you?

    *Kimberly-Clark:* Kimberly-Clark is experiencing slow top-line growth—probably a bit too low for a manufacturing company of this sort. It appears that profitability is not tracking at the same rate in these years.

    *FedEx:* FedEx looks very strong by the raw numbers. Top-line growth is strong, and the margins seem to be healthy. There appears to be a significant increase in fuel costs relative to net income. All other expenses appear to be in line.

2.  Look at your percent of and percent change results. What are they telling you?

    *Kimberly-Clark:* Kimberly-Clark is growing revenue at 5 percent. Since it is a public company, its executives should probably target growing revenue at 8 percent to 12 percent. Its margins decreased significantly during this period. A concern here is that Kimberly-Clark's product offerings are facing competition, thus driving margins down. Investors might like to see more investment in R&D.

    *FedEx:* FedEx is growing well. Anything over 10 percent is a great growth rate for revenue, and margin improvement is even stronger. FedEx is able to grow and improve efficiency at the same time: it has improved its operating margins even while growing the top line.

## INTERESTING THINGS TO NOTE

- The two companies' year-ends are different. Remember that a company can use any year-end it wants, although it must be consistent and it must disclose any change in year-end.

- The same line items are called different things, both from company to company and within one company. Kimberly-Clark calls sales "net sales" and FedEx calls it "revenues." Kimberly-Clark has "operating profit" as one profit number, but then the bottom line is called "net income."

- Kimberly-Clark shows results from continuing operations and discontinued operations. It does this so that investors and others can see the results from the operations that are going forward versus the operations the company decided to get rid of. There is a benefit to the investor (who can consider more data) and a benefit to the company (whose results look better when it excludes discontinued operations).

- FedEx's statement seems to be a bit clearer, with straightforward line item names. Kimberly-Clark, by contrast, has line items that tend to throw people off, with terms such as "minority owners' share of subsidiaries' net income" and "cumulative effect of accounting change, net of income taxes." These detailed lines are not large items relative to sales and therefore are not material to results.

- Both statements are in millions of dollars except for the bottom section in each. Those bottom sections are "per share"—that is, data based on the number of common shares outstanding. So, for example, the very last line on both statements says "net income," which we have said is the bottom line of a company. However, these are per-share numbers, not the company's net income or net earnings as a whole.

# Balance Sheet Exercise

The balance sheet is a little tougher than the income statement exercise, but remember that this is the statement that outsiders look at first. If you really understand it, you might start doing that, too.

Once again, our goals for you are:

- *To get comfortable reading the balance sheet.* You'll get more practice finding certain numbers.

- *To begin to analyze the results.* You'll do just a little analysis here. There will be more later, in the ratios exercise.

- *To understand the numbers you are finding.* The questions will help you do just that.

## EXERCISE DESCRIPTION

The balance sheets for Kimberly-Clark and FedEx are found in appendix C. Do one or both. The general exercise is the same as in the income statement exercise: use the appropriate table and then analyze the results.

## INSTRUCTIONS

1. Based on the financial statement of your choice, find the appropriate table.

2. Try your hand at the calculations and questions. You'll see the formula, a column for the data, and a column for the result, just as with the income statement calculations. There are only a few calculations to do with the balance sheet for now. You'll do more when we get to ratios. Doing the calculations and answering the questions will give you an opportunity to think about what the numbers mean.

3. Step back and be proud of your work!

4. Take a look at the answers and see how you did.

## CALCULATIONS

Let's do the calculations. For the balance sheet calculations, the names of the categories are the same, so do these calculations for both companies (of course, only if you want to practice).

### Kimberly-Clark Corporation

|  | 2005 to 2006 Data | 2005 to 2006 Result |
|---|---|---|
| Percent change in total assets (total assets are shown but not labeled) |  |  |
| Percent change in total liabilities (you'll need to calculate total liabilities) |  |  |

### FedEx Corporation

|  | 2005 to 2006 Data | 2005 to 2006 Result |
|---|---|---|
| Percent change in total assets (total assets are shown but not labeled) |  |  |
| Percent change in total liabilities (you'll need to calculate total liabilities) |  |  |

## QUESTIONS

Now let's try answering a few questions:

1. What trends do you see in the raw numbers? What are they telling you?

   *Kimberly-Clark:*

   _____

   _____

   _____

   *FedEx:*

   _____

   _____

   _____

2. Look at your percent change results. What are they telling you?

   *Kimberly-Clark:*

   _____

   _____

   _____

   *FedEx:*

   _____

   _____

   _____

## CALCULATION RESULTS

### Kimberly-Clark Corporation

|  | 2005 to 2006 Data | 2005 to 2006 Result |
|---|---|---|
| Percent change in total assets | $\frac{17{,}067.0 - 16{,}303.2}{16{,}303.2}$ | 4.7% |
| Percent change in total liabilities | $\frac{10{,}969.6 - 10{,}745.0}{10{,}745.0}$ | 2.1% |

## FedEx Corporation

|  | 2005 to 2006 Data | 2005 to 2006 Result |
|---|---|---|
| Percent change in total assets | $\dfrac{22{,}690 - 20{,}404}{20{,}404}$ | 11.2% |
| Percent change in total liabilities | $\dfrac{11{,}179 - 10{,}816}{10{,}816}$ | 3.4% |

## ANSWERS TO THE QUESTIONS

As in the income statement exercise, here are just a few thoughts in response to each of the questions we asked you to consider.

1. What trends do you see in the raw numbers? What are they telling you?

    *Kimberly-Clark:* Kimberly Clark is a stable company and is not changing its capital structure. Over these two years, this company appears to be keeping things fairly constant.

    *FedEx:* FedEx is growing its assets. It appears that this is to support its revenue growth. FedEx is also building up cash on its balance sheet.

2. Look at your percent change results. What are they telling you?

    *Kimberly-Clark:* Assets are growing faster than liabilities for Kimberly-Clark. This is a good sign. The growth in both areas is fairly low, implying a stable, slow-growth financial situation.

    *FedEx:* Assets are growing faster than liabilities for FedEx. There is a significant percentage growth in assets year-over-year. Assets grew at three times the level of liabilities. FedEx is lowering its leverage through this trend.

## INTERESTING THINGS TO NOTE

- FedEx shows the details of its property and equipment, but Kimberly-Clark has just one line item. As we've discussed, companies have latitude in how they present their numbers, as long as they are consistent and disclose any changes. But think why FedEx might want to show investors the details of its equipment—the effective delivery of the company's service depends on the equipment it has.

- Neither company provides all the totals that would be helpful in reading the statements. For example, both include but don't label total assets. And neither includes a total liabilities number. Kimberly-Clark's total liabilities number is especially difficult to determine because the liabilities run right into the shareholders' equity. Other companies do provide those totals. One trick to ensuring you have all your numbers correct: add up what you think are all the liabilities, and then add that to the stockholders' equity. If that total is the same as total assets, you have the answer.

- Although some line items are the same, the wording is slightly different. For example, Kimberly-Clark shows accounts receivable as "accounts receivable, net" and FedEx lists it as "receivables, less allowances of $144 and $125." Kimberly-Clark isn't showing the allowances for doubtful accounts here in the statement (although it is probably in the notes), but FedEx did include the amounts. And some line items are completely different. For example, FedEx has a line item called "deferred lease obligation," and Kimberly-Clark doesn't.

- FedEx calls its stockholders' equity section "commitments and contingencies," and Kimberly-Clark does not. Again, you just need to take these documents slowly and figure out what everything means.

# Cash Flow Statement Exercise

OK, let's practice the cash flow statement. Here we'll just look at the numbers and trends but not do any calculations (whew—enough already with the calculator!).

To review, our goals for you are:

• *To get comfortable reading the cash flow statement*

• *To understand the numbers you find*

• *To be able to identify where the cash is coming from and where it is going*

## EXERCISE DESCRIPTION

Once again, pick either Kimberly-Clark, FedEx, or both (see appendix C), and use the tables. Then answer the questions that follow.

## INSTRUCTIONS

1. Using the financial statement of your choice, find each line item listed in the table in the appropriate cash flow statement, for 2006, 2005, and 2004.

2. After you've finished, answer the questions. They will help you think about the numbers you just found.

3. Step back and be proud of your work!

4. Take a look at the answers and see how you did.

## Kimberly-Clark Corporation: Consolidated Cash Flow Statement, in millions

Year ended December 31

|  | 2006 | 2005 | 2004 |
|---|---|---|---|
| Cash provided by operations |  |  |  |
| Cash used for investing |  |  |  |
| Cash used for financing |  |  |  |
| (Decrease) increase in cash and cash equivalents |  |  |  |
| Cash and cash equivalents, beginning of year |  |  |  |
| Cash and cash equivalents, end of year |  |  |  |

## FedEx Corporation: Consolidated Statements of Cash Flows, in millions

Years ended May 31

|  | 2006 | 2005 | 2004 |
|---|---|---|---|
| Cash provided by operating activities |  |  |  |
| Cash used in investing activities |  |  |  |
| Cash (used in) provided by financing activities |  |  |  |
| Net increase (decrease) in cash and cash equivalents |  |  |  |
| Cash and cash equivalents at beginning of period |  |  |  |
| Cash and cash equivalents at end of period |  |  |  |

## QUESTIONS

Now for a few thought-provoking questions:

1.  Where is the cash coming from? Is it from operations (the business of the company), from investing, or from financing? What might that mean?

    *Kimberly-Clark:*

    _____

    _____

    _____

    *FedEx:*

    _____

    _____

    _____

2.  What are the trends in the three categories of cash?

    *Kimberly-Clark:*

    _____

    _____

    _____

    *FedEx:*

    _____

    _____

    _____

## CALCULATION RESULTS

### Kimberly-Clark Corporation: Consolidated Cash Flow Statement, in millions

Year ended December 31

|  | 2006 | 2005 | 2004 |
|---|---|---|---|
| Cash provided by operations | 2,579.5 | 2,311.8 | 2,726.2 |
| Cash used for investing | (1,035.9) | (596.2) | (495.4) |
| Cash used for financing | (1,551.3) | (1,929.7) | (2,174.9) |
| (Decrease) increase in cash and cash equivalents | (3.2) | (230.0) | 303.4 |
| Cash and cash equivalents, beginning of year | 364.0 | 594.0 | 290.6 |
| Cash and cash equivalents, end of year | 360.8 | 364.0 | 594.0 |

### FedEx Corporation: Consolidated Statements of Cash Flows, in millions

Years ended May 31

|  | 2006 | 2005 | 2004 |
|---|---|---|---|
| Cash provided by operating activities | 3,676 | 3,117 | 3,020 |
| Cash used in investing activities | (2,454) | (2,348) | (3,662) |
| Cash (used in) provided by financing activities | (324) | (776) | 1,150 |
| Net increase (decrease) in cash and cash equivalents | 898 | (7) | 508 |
| Cash and cash equivalents at beginning of period | 1,039 | 1,046 | 538 |
| Cash and cash equivalents at end of period | 1,937 | 1,039 | 1,046 |

## ANSWERS TO THE QUESTIONS

Here are our thoughts in response to each of the questions we asked you to consider.

1. Where is the cash coming from? Is it from operations (the business of the company), from investing, or from financing? What might that mean?

   *Kimberly-Clark:* Kimberly-Clark's cash is coming from operations. This is what one would expect from a mature company like this one.

   *FedEx:* FedEx's cash is also coming from operations. These numbers are fairly strong relative to net income. FedEx is in cash-generation mode.

2. What are the trends in the three categories of cash?

   *Kimberly-Clark:* Kimberly-Clark is generating cash and reinvesting some. It is also spending cash on financing. It is paying a large dividend and buying back stock on the financing side.

   *FedEx:* FedEx is using its strong operating cash flow to invest in equipment. It also made an acquisition in 2004. On the financing side, FedEx is paying a modest dividend and keeping things fairly stable.

## INTERESTING THINGS TO NOTE

- Remember that every company uses its own terminology. You can see the minor differences ("cash provided by operations" vs. "cash provided by operating activities"). Don't let that throw you off.

- These statements are well organized. Both statements have a header that organizes the statement by the three types of cash, provides the details, and then gives the total.

- The increases or decreases in assets and liabilities that impact cash are shown very differently on the two statements. Kimberly-Clark lumps them into one category called "decrease (increase) in operating working capital," and FedEx details it all out, with individual line items for receivables, payables, and so on.

- Remember that the cash flow statement is the most difficult to read. But now that we have real numbers, you can see how it works in action. Look at receivables for FedEx. If you look at the balance sheet, accounts receivable went up from 2005 to 2006, so cash went down. And you'll note that the number on the cash flow statement for receivables is in parentheses, which means it is subtracted from cash.

# Ratios Exercise

Now we get to put it all together and calculate some ratios for our two sample companies, Kimberly-Clark and FedEx. Remember what we said when we introduced ratios: that ratios give us more information than the raw numbers alone. So let's see what our ratios can tell us.

Once again, our goals for you are as follows:

- *To find the numbers required to calculate the ratios*

- *To get comfortable using the ratio formulas*

- *To get you thinking about what the ratios mean*

## EXERCISE DESCRIPTION

Depending on which ratio you'll be calculating, you'll be using one or more of Kimberly-Clark's or FedEx's financial statements. Again, you can calculate the ratios for one or both companies. Here it might be really interesting to do both. Some of the differences between a manufacturing company and a service company will reveal themselves in ratio results.

You won't be calculating all the ratios you learned in part 5, just enough to get a good feel for how ratios work and what they might tell you. Also, you won't calculate exactly the same ratios for Kimberly-Clark as you will for FedEx. For example, FedEx doesn't have inventory, so you can't calculate days in inventory or inventory turnover.

You may have noticed in the previous practices that the language in the tables matched the financial statements exactly. That was to minimize confusion. In real life, however, everyone will be using different terminology. So this time our formulas are generic: we use just one word for profit, sales, and so on, and you will need to find the appropriate line item, even if it doesn't match exactly. With as much reading as you've been doing, we are confident you'll master this challenge.

Your next step, after you finish this book, is to get the financials for the company you work for and calculate all the ratios that make sense for your type of organization. That should tell you a lot about your company—information you'll be able to use to improve your work.

## INSTRUCTIONS

1. Calculate the ratios indicated. We've listed the name of the ratio and the formula to use. Then there are columns for the longhand calculation and a column for the result. Use these tables or a separate piece of paper.

2. After you've finished, answer the questions that follow the table. They will help you look at your results with a critical eye.

3. Step back and be proud of your work!

4. Take a look at the answers in the next set of tables and see how you did.

### Kimberly-Clark Corporation: Ratio Table

| | Formula | 2006 Data | 2006 Result | 2005 Data | 2005 Result |
|---|---|---|---|---|---|
| **Profitability ratios** | | | | | |
| Gross profit margin percentage | $\dfrac{\text{Gross profit}}{\text{Revenue}}$ | | | | |
| Operating profit margin percentage | $\dfrac{\text{Operating profit}}{\text{Revenue}}$ | | | | |
| Return on assets | $\dfrac{\text{Net profit}}{\text{Total assets}}$ | | | | |
| Return on equity | $\dfrac{\text{Net profit}}{\text{Shareholders' equity}}$ | | | | |
| **Leverage ratio** | | | | | |
| Debt-to-equity | $\dfrac{\text{Total liabilities}}{\text{Shareholders' equity}}$ | | | | |
| **Liquidity ratio** | | | | | |
| Current ratio | $\dfrac{\text{Current assets}}{\text{Current liabilities}}$ | | | | |

*(continued)*

|  | Formula | 2006 Data | 2006 Result | 2005 Data | 2005 Result |
|---|---|---|---|---|---|
| **Efficiency ratios** | | | | | |
| Inventory days (DII) | $\dfrac{\text{Average inventory}}{\text{COGS/day}}$ | | | | Don't have 2004 data, so can't calculate. |
| Inventory turns | $\dfrac{360}{\text{DII}}$ | | | | Don't have DII, so can't calculate. |
| Days sales outstanding | $\dfrac{\text{Ending A/R}}{\text{Revenue/day}}$ | | | | |
| PPE turnover | $\dfrac{\text{Revenue}}{\text{PPE}}$ | | | | |
| Total asset turnover | $\dfrac{\text{Revenue}}{\text{Total assets}}$ | | | | |

# FedEx Corporation: Ratio Table

|  | Formula | 2006 Data | 2006 Result | 2005 Data | 2005 Result |
|---|---|---|---|---|---|
| **Profitability ratios** | | | | | |
| Operating profit margin percentage | $\dfrac{\text{Operating profit}}{\text{Revenue}}$ | | | | |
| Net profit margin percentage | $\dfrac{\text{Net profit}}{\text{Revenue}}$ | | | | |
| Return on assets | $\dfrac{\text{Net profit}}{\text{Total assets}}$ | | | | |
| Return on equity | $\dfrac{\text{Net profit}}{\text{Shareholders' equity}}$ | | | | |

| | Formula | 2006 Data | 2006 Result | 2005 Data | 2005 Result |
|---|---|---|---|---|---|
| **Leverage ratio** | | | | | |
| Debt-to-equity | Total liabilities / Shareholders' equity | | | | |
| **Liquidity ratio** | | | | | |
| Current ratio | Current assets / Current liabilities | | | | |
| **Efficiency ratios** | | | | | |
| Days sales outstanding | Ending A/R / Revenue/day | | | | |
| PPE turnover | Revenue / PPE | | | | |
| Total asset turnover | Revenue / Total assets | | | | |

## QUESTIONS

Now let's consider the results.

1. What do the ratio results tell you that the raw numbers didn't? For example, what do the profitability ratios tell you that the raw numbers didn't?

   *Kimberly-Clark:*

   _____

   _____

   _____

*FedEx:*

_____

_____

_____

2.  What do you see in the leverage and liquidity ratio results?

   *Kimberly-Clark:*

   _____

   _____

   _____

   *FedEx:*

   _____

   _____

   _____

3.  What are the trends in the efficiency ratios?

   *Kimberly-Clark:*

   _____

   _____

   _____

   *FedEx:*

   _____

   _____

   _____

## ANSWERS

Now let's see how you did.

### Kimberly-Clark Corporation: Ratio Results

| | Formula | 2006 Data | 2006 Result | 2005 Data | 2005 Result |
|---|---|---|---|---|---|
| **Profitability ratios** | | | | | |
| Gross profit margin percentage | Gross profit / Revenue | 5082.1 / 16,746.9 | 30.3% | 5075.2 / 15,902.6 | 31.9% |
| Operating profit margin percentage | Operating profit / Revenue | 2,101.5 / 16,746.9 | 12.5% | 2,310.6 / 15,902.6 | 14.5% |
| Return on assets | Net profit / Total assets | 1,499.5 / 17,067.0 | 8.8% | 1,568.3 / 16,303.2 | 9.6% |
| Return on equity | Net profit / Shareholders' equity | 1,499.5 / 6,097.4 | 24.6% | 1,568.3 / 5,558.2 | 28.2% |
| **Leverage ratio** | | | | | |
| Debt-to-equity | Total liabilities / Shareholders' equity | 10,969.6 / 6,097.4 | 1.80 | 10,745.0 / 5,558.2 | 1.93 |
| **Liquidity ratio** | | | | | |
| Current ratio | Current assets / Current liabilities | 5,269.7 / 5,015.8 | 1.05 | 4,783.1 / 4,642.9 | 1.03 |
| **Efficiency ratios** | | | | | |
| Inventory days (DII) | Average inventory / COGS/day | (2004.5+ 1752.1)/2 11,644.8/ 360 | 58.1 days | Don't have 2004 data, so can't calculate. | |
| Inventory turns | 360 / DII | 360 / 58.1 | 6.2 | Don't have DII, so can't calculate. | |

*(continued)*

|  | Formula | 2006 Data | 2006 Result | 2005 Data | 2005 Result |
|---|---|---|---|---|---|
| **Efficiency ratios** *continued* | | | | | |
| Days sales outstanding | Ending A/R Revenue/day | 2,336.7 16,746.9/ 360 | 50.2 days | 2,101.9 15,902.6/ 360 | 47.6 days |
| PPE turnover | Revenue PPE | 16,746.9 7,684.8 | 2.2 | 15,902.6 7,494.7 | 2.1 |
| Total asset turnover | Revenue Total assets | 16,746.9 17,067.0 | .981 | 15,902.6 16,303.2 | .975 |

## FedEx Corporation: Ratio Results

|  | Formula | 2006 Data | 2006 Result | 2005 Data | 2005 Result |
|---|---|---|---|---|---|
| **Profitability ratios** | | | | | |
| Operating profit margin percentage | Operating profit Revenue | 3,014 32,294 | 9.3% | 2,471 29,363 | 8.4% |
| Net profit margin percentage | Net profit Revenue | 1,806 32,294 | 5.6% | 1,449 29,363 | 4.9% |
| Return on assets | Net profit Total assets | 1,806 22,690 | 8.0% | 1,449 20,404 | 7.1% |
| Return on equity | Net profit Shareholders' equity | 1,806 11,511 | 15.7% | 1,449 9,588 | 15.1% |
| **Leverage ratio** | | | | | |
| Debt-to-equity | Total liabilities Shareholders' equity | 11,179 11,511 | .97 | 10,816 9,588 | 1.13 |

| | Formula | 2006 Data | 2006 Result | 2005 Data | 2005 Result |
|---|---|---|---|---|---|
| **Liquidity ratio** | | | | | |
| Current ratio | Current assets / Current liabilities | 6,464 / 5,473 | 1.18 | 5,269 / 4,734 | 1.11 |
| **Efficiency ratios** | | | | | |
| Days sales outstanding | Ending A/R / Revenue/day | 3,516 / 32,294/ 360 | 39.2 days | 3,297 / 29,363/ 360 | 40.4 days |
| PPE turnover | Revenue / PPE | 32,294 / 10,770 | 3.00 | 29,363 / 9,643 | 3.05 |
| Total asset turnover | Revenue / Total assets | 32,294 / 22,690 | 1.42 | 29,363 / 20,404 | 1.44 |

## ANSWERS TO THE QUESTIONS

To interpret ratios accurately would require that we know a lot about the company in question. We don't work for Kimberly-Clark or FedEx, and we aren't analysts studying the companies over time. The following responses, therefore, are just a few thoughts on the little information that we do have.

1. What do the ratio results tell you that the raw numbers didn't? For example, what do the profitability ratios tell you that the raw numbers didn't?

   *Kimberly-Clark:* Kimberly-Clark has declining profit margins over the period we reviewed. Its leverage is decreasing. Asset management appears to be stable.

   *FedEx:* FedEx is growing its revenue and its margins. While this growth is not significant, it is a very good trend for a mature company like FedEx. The company is lowering leverage as debt is paid off. Its asset management is very strong.

2. What do you see in the leverage and liquidity ratio results?

   *Kimberly-Clark:* K-C seems to be just keeping things constant. Leverage is decreasing slightly, with its debt to equity ratio going down slightly and the current ratio increasing slightly.

   *FedEx:* FedEx is lowering leverage and improving its financial strength. Its long-term debt from 2004 is being paid down significantly.

3. What are the trends in the efficiency ratios?

   *Kimberly-Clark:* Kimberly Clark is keeping things fairly conservative. It has seen its DSO increase by a few days. On the other hand, its total asset turnover improved slightly.

   *FedEx:* FedEx is not changing much. Its DSO went down by a day, but its PPE turnover increased, as did its total asset turnover. The numbers are fairly stable.

# APPENDIX C

# Kimberly-Clark and FedEx Financial Statements

**KIMBERLY-CLARK CORPORATION AND SUBSIDIARIES
CONSOLIDATED INCOME STATEMENT**

| | Year Ended December 31, | | |
| --- | --- | --- | --- |
| | 2006 | 2005 | 2004 |
| | (Millions of dollars, except per share amounts) | | |
| Net Sales | $ 16,746.9 | $15,902.6 | $15,083.2 |
| Cost of products sold | 11,664.8 | 10,827.4 | 10,014.7 |
| Gross Profit | 5,082.1 | 5,075.2 | 5,068.5 |
| Marketing, research and general expenses | 2,948.3 | 2,737.4 | 2,510.9 |
| Other (income) and expense, net | 32.3 | 27.2 | 51.2 |
| Operating Profit | 2,101.5 | 2,310.6 | 2,506.4 |
| Nonoperating expense | (65.5) | (179.0) | (158.4) |
| Interest income | 29.2 | 27.5 | 17.9 |
| Interest expense | (220.3) | (190.2) | (162.5) |
| Income Before Income Taxes, Equity Interests, Discontinued Operations and Cumulative Effect of Accounting Change | 1,844.9 | 1,968.9 | 2,203.4 |
| Provision for income taxes | (469.2) | (438.4) | (483.9) |
| Share of net income of equity companies | 218.6 | 136.6 | 124.8 |
| Minority owners' share of subsidiaries' net income | (94.8) | (86.5) | (73.9) |
| Income From Continuing Operations | 1,499.5 | 1,580.6 | 1,770.4 |
| Income from discontinued operations, net of income taxes | — | — | 29.8 |
| Income Before Cumulative Effect of Accounting Change | 1,499.5 | 1,580.6 | 1,800.2 |
| Cumulative effect of accounting change, net of income taxes | — | (12.3) | — |
| Net Income | $1,499.5 | $1,568.3 | $1,800.2 |
| Per Share Basis | | | |
| Basic | | | |
| Continuing operations | $ 3.27 | $ 3.33 | $ 3.58 |
| Discontinued operations | — | — | .06 |
| Cumulative effect of accounting change | — | (.03) | — |
| Net income | $ 3.27 | $ 3.30 | $ 3.64 |
| Diluted | | | |
| Continuing operations | $ 3.25 | $ 3.31 | $ 3.55 |
| Discontinued operations | — | — | .06 |
| Cumulative effect of accounting change | — | (.03) | — |
| Net income | $ 3.25 | $ 3.28 | $ 3.61 |

See Notes to Consolidated Financial Statements.

# KIMBERLY-CLARK CORPORATION AND SUBSIDIARIES
## CONSOLIDATED BALANCE STATEMENT

|  | December 31, | |
|---|---|---|
|  | **2006** | **2005** |
|  | (Millions of dollars) | |
| **ASSETS** | | |
| **Current Assets** | | |
| Cash and cash equivalents | $ 360.8 | $364.0 |
| Accounts receivable, net | 2,336.7 | 2,101.9 |
| Inventories | 2,004.5 | 1,752.1 |
| Deferred income taxes | 219.2 | 223.4 |
| Time deposits | 264.5 | 212.3 |
| Other current assets | 84.0 | 129.4 |
| **Total Current Assets** | 5,269.7 | 4,783.1 |
| **Property, Plant and Equipment, net** | 7,684.8 | 7,494.7 |
| **Investments in Equity Companies** | 392.9 | 457.8 |
| **Goodwill** | 2,860.5 | 2,685.6 |
| **Other Assets** | 859.1 | 882.0 |
|  | $17,067.0 | $16,303.2 |
| **LIABILITIES AND STOCKHOLDERS' EQUITY** | | |
| **Current Liabilities** | | |
| Debt payable within one year | $ 1,326.4 | $1,222.5 |
| Trade accounts payable | 1,205.6 | 1,055.5 |
| Other payables | 325.2 | 298.8 |
| Accrued expenses | 1,603.8 | 1,399.6 |
| Accrued income taxes | 330.8 | 457.9 |
| Dividends payable | 224.0 | 208.6 |
| **Total Current Liabilities** | 5,015.8 | 4,642.9 |
| **Long-Term Debt** | 2,276.0 | 2,594.7 |
| **Noncurrent Employee Benefit and Other Obligations** | 2,070.7 | 1,782.6 |
| **Deferred Income Taxes** | 391.1 | 572.9 |
| **Minority Owners' Interests in Subsidiaries** | 422.6 | 394.5 |
| **Preferred Securities of Subsidiary** | 793.4 | 757.4 |
| **Stockholders' Equity** | | |
| Preferred stock—no par value—authorized 20.0 million shares, none issued | — | — |
| Common stock—$1.25 par value—authorized 1.2 billion shares; issued 478.6 million and 568.6 million shares at December 31, 2006 and 2005 | 598.3 | 710.8 |
| Additional paid-in capital | 427.6 | 324.6 |
| Common stock held in treasury, at cost—23.0 million and 107.1 million shares at December 31, 2006 and 2005 | (1,391.9) | (6,376.1) |
| Accumulated other comprehensive income (loss) | (1,432.2) | (1,669.4) |
| Retained earnings | 7,895.6 | 12,581.4 |
| Unearned compensation on restricted stock | — | (13.1) |
| **Total Stockholders' Equity** | 6,097.4 | 5,558.2 |
|  | $17,067.0 | $16,303.2 |

See Notes to Consolidated Financial Statements.

# KIMBERLY-CLARK CORPORATION AND SUBSIDIARIES
## CONSOLIDATED CASH FLOW STATEMENT

| | Year Ended December 31, | | |
| --- | --- | --- | --- |
| | 2006 | 2005 | 2004 |
| | (Millions of dollars) | | |
| **Continuing Operations:** | | | |
| **Operating Activities** | | | |
| Income from continuing operations | $1,499.5 | $1,580.6 | $1,770.4 |
| Depreciation and amortization | 932.8 | 844.5 | 800.3 |
| Asset impairments | 6.2 | 80.1 | — |
| Stock-based compensation | 67.4 | 32.4 | 19.4 |
| Deferred income taxes | (208.0) | (142.7) | (19.4) |
| Net losses on asset dispositions | 116.1 | 45.8 | 45.5 |
| Equity companies' earnings less than (in excess of) dividends paid | 26.6 | (23.8) | (30.1) |
| Minority owners' share of subsidiaries' net income | 94.8 | 86.5 | 73.9 |
| Decrease (increase) in operating working capital | 5.1 | (180.1) | 94.8 |
| Postretirement benefits | 33.8 | 40.9 | (54.4) |
| Other | 5.2 | (52.4) | 25.8 |
| **Cash Provided by Operations** | 2,579.5 | 2,311.8 | 2,726.2 |
| **Investing Activities** | | | |
| Capital spending | (972.1) | (709.6) | (535.0) |
| Acquisitions of businesses, net of cash acquired | (99.6) | (17.4) | — |
| Investments in marketable securities | (20.5) | (2.0) | (11.5) |
| Proceeds from sales of investments | 46.2 | 27.3 | 38.0 |
| Net (increase) decrease in time deposits | (35.1) | 75.5 | (22.9) |
| Proceeds from dispositions of property | 44.1 | 46.8 | 30.7 |
| Other | 1.1 | (16.8) | 5.3 |
| **Cash Used for Investing** | (1,035.9) | (596.2) | (495.4) |
| **Financing Activities** | | | |
| Cash dividends paid | (884.0) | (838.4) | (767.9) |
| Net (decrease) increase in short-term debt | (390.5) | 524.3 | (54.7) |
| Proceeds from issuance of long-term debt | 261.5 | 397.7 | 38.7 |
| Repayments of long-term debt | (104.2) | (599.7) | (199.0) |
| Proceeds from preferred securities of subsidiary | — | — | 125.0 |
| Proceeds from exercise of stock options | 331.1 | 142.7 | 290.0 |
| Acquisitions of common stock for the treasury | (761.5) | (1,519.5) | (1,598.0) |
| Other | (3.7) | (36.8) | (9.0) |
| **Cash Used for Financing** | (1,551.3) | (1,929.7) | (2,174.9) |
| **Effect of Exchange Rate Changes on Cash and Cash Equivalents** | 4.5 | (15.9) | 4.1 |
| **Cash (Used for) Provided by Continuing Operations** | (3.2) | (230.0) | 60.0 |
| **Discontinued Operations:** | | | |
| Cash provided by discontinued operations | — | — | 30.0 |
| Cash payment from Neenah Paper, Inc. | — | — | 213.4 |
| **Cash Provided by Discontinued Operations** | — | — | 243.4 |
| **(Decrease) Increase in Cash and Cash Equivalents** | (3.2) | (230.0) | 303.4 |
| **Cash and Cash Equivalents, beginning of year** | 364.0 | 594.0 | 290.6 |
| **Cash and Cash Equivalents, end of year** | $ 360.8 | $ 364.0 | $ 594.0 |

See Notes to Consolidated Financial Statements.

**FEDEX CORPORATION**
**CONSOLIDATED STATEMENTS OF INCOME**
**(IN MILLIONS, EXCEPT PER SHARE AMOUNTS)**

| | Years ended May 31, | | |
| --- | --- | --- | --- |
| | **2006** | **2005** | **2004** |
| REVENUES | $ 32,294 | $ 29,363 | $ 24,710 |
| OPERATING EXPENSES: | | | |
| Salaries and employee benefits | 12,571 | 11,963 | 10,728 |
| Purchased transportation | 3,251 | 2,935 | 2,407 |
| Rentals and landing fees | 2,390 | 2,299 | 1,918 |
| Depreciation and amortization | 1,550 | 1,462 | 1,375 |
| Fuel | 3,256 | 2,317 | 1,531 |
| Maintenance and repairs | 1,777 | 1,695 | 1,523 |
| Business realignment costs | — | — | 435 |
| Other | 4,485 | 4,221 | 3,353 |
| | 29,280 | 26,892 | 23,270 |
| OPERATING INCOME | 3,014 | 2,471 | 1,440 |
| OTHER INCOME (EXPENSE): | | | |
| Interest expense | (142) | (160) | (136) |
| Interest income | 38 | 21 | 20 |
| Other, net | (11) | (19) | (5) |
| | (115) | (158) | (121) |
| INCOME BEFORE INCOME TAXES | 2,899 | 2,313 | 1,319 |
| PROVISION FOR INCOME TAXES | 1,093 | 864 | 481 |
| NET INCOME | $ 1,806 | $ 1,449 | $ 838 |
| BASIC EARNINGS PER COMMON SHARE | $ 5.94 | $ 4.81 | $ 2.80 |
| DILUTED EARNINGS PER COMMON SHARE | $ 5.83 | $ 4.72 | $ 2.76 |

The accompanying notes are an integral part of these consolidated financial statements.

**FEDEX CORPORATION**
**CONSOLIDATED BALANCE SHEETS**
**(IN MILLIONS)**

| | May 31, | |
|---|---|---|
| | **2006** | **2005** |
| **ASSETS** | | |
| CURRENT ASSETS | | |
| Cash and cash equivalents | $ 1,937 | $ 1,039 |
| Receivables, less allowances of $144 and $125 | 3,516 | 3,297 |
| Spare parts, supplies and fuel, less allowances of $150 and $142 | 308 | 250 |
| Deferred income taxes | 539 | 510 |
| Prepaid expenses and other | 164 | 173 |
| Total current assets | 6,464 | 5,269 |
| PROPERTY AND EQUIPMENT, AT COST | | |
| Aircraft and related equipment | 8,611 | 7,610 |
| Package handling and ground support equipment | 3,558 | 3,366 |
| Computer and electronic equipment | 4,331 | 3,893 |
| Vehicles | 2,203 | 1,994 |
| Facilities and other | 5,371 | 5,154 |
| | 24,074 | 22,017 |
| Less accumulated depreciation and amortization | 13,304 | 12,374 |
| Net property and equipment | 10,770 | 9,643 |
| OTHER LONG-TERM ASSETS | | |
| Goodwill | 2,825 | 2,835 |
| Prepaid pension cost | 1,349 | 1,272 |
| Intangible and other assets | 1,282 | 1,385 |
| Total other long-term assets | 5,456 | 5,492 |
| | $ 22,690 | $ 20,404 |

The accompanying notes are an integral part of these consolidated financial statements.

**FEDEX CORPORATION**
**CONSOLIDATED BALANCE SHEETS**
**(IN MILLIONS, EXCEPT SHARE DATA)**

|  | May 31, | |
| --- | --- | --- |
|  | **2006** | **2005** |
| **LIABILITIES AND STOCKHOLDERS' INVESTMENT** | | |
| CURRENT LIABILITIES | | |
| Current portion of long-term debt | $ 850 | $ 369 |
| Accrued salaries and employee benefits | 1,325 | 1,275 |
| Accounts payable | 1,908 | 1,739 |
| Accrued expenses | 1,390 | 1,351 |
| Total current liabilities | 5,473 | 4,734 |
| LONG-TERM DEBT, LESS CURRENT PORTION | 1,592 | 2,427 |
| OTHER LONG-TERM LIABILITIES | | |
| Deferred income taxes | 1,367 | 1,206 |
| Pension, postretirement healthcare and other benefit obligations | 944 | 828 |
| Self-insurance accruals | 692 | 621 |
| Deferred lease obligations | 658 | 532 |
| Deferred gains, principally related to aircraft transactions | 373 | 400 |
| Other liabilities | 80 | 68 |
| Total other long-term liabilities | 4,114 | 3,655 |
| COMMITMENTS AND CONTINGENCIES | | |
| COMMON STOCKHOLDERS' INVESTMENT | | |
| Common stock, $0.10 par value; 800 million shares authorized; 306 million shares issued for 2006 and 302 million shares issued for 2005 | 31 | 30 |
| Additional paid-in capital | 1,468 | 1,241 |
| Retained earnings | 10,068 | 8,363 |
| Accumulated other comprehensive loss | (24) | (17) |
|  | 11,543 | 9,617 |
| Less deferred compensation and treasury stock, at cost | 32 | 29 |
| Total common stockholders' investment | 11,511 | 9,588 |
|  | $ 22,690 | $ 20,404 |

The accompanying notes are an integral part of these consolidated financial statements.

**FEDEX CORPORATION**
**CONSOLIDATED STATEMENTS OF CASH FLOWS**
**(IN MILLIONS)**

| | Years ended May 31, | | |
| --- | --- | --- | --- |
| | 2006 | 2005 | 2004 |
| OPERATING ACTIVITIES | | | |
| Net income | $ 1,806 | $ 1,449 | $ 838 |
| Adjustments to reconcile net income to cash provided by operating activities: | | | |
| Lease accounting charge | 79 | — | — |
| Depreciation and amortization | 1,548 | 1,462 | 1,375 |
| Provision for uncollectible accounts | 121 | 101 | 106 |
| Deferred income taxes and other noncash items | 187 | 63 | (8) |
| Tax benefit on the exercise of stock options | 62 | 36 | 43 |
| Changes in operating assets and liabilities, net of the effects of businesses acquired: | | | |
| Receivables | (319) | (235) | (307) |
| Other current assets | (38) | (26) | 10 |
| Pension assets and liabilities, net | (71) | (118) | 155 |
| Accounts payable and other operating liabilities | 346 | 365 | 841 |
| Other, net | (45) | 20 | (33) |
| Cash provided by operating activities | 3,676 | 3,117 | 3,020 |
| INVESTING ACTIVITIES | | | |
| Capital expenditures | (2,518) | (2,236) | (1,271) |
| Business acquisitions, net of cash acquired | — | (122) | (2,410) |
| Proceeds from asset dispositions | 64 | 12 | 18 |
| Other, net | — | (2) | 1 |
| Cash used in investing activities | (2,454) | (2,348) | (3,662) |
| FINANCING ACTIVITIES | | | |
| Principal payments on debt | (369) | (791) | (319) |
| Proceeds from debt issuances | — | — | 1,599 |
| Proceeds from stock issuances | 144 | 99 | 115 |
| Dividends paid | (97) | (84) | (66) |
| Purchase of treasury stock | — | — | (179) |
| Other, net | (2) | — | — |
| Cash (used in) provided by financing activities | (324) | (776) | 1,150 |
| CASH AND CASH EQUIVALENTS | | | |
| Net increase (decrease) in cash and cash equivalents | 898 | (7) | 508 |
| Cash and cash equivalents at beginning of period | 1,039 | 1,046 | 538 |
| Cash and cash equivalents at end of period | $ 1,937 | $ 1,039 | $ 1,046 |

The accompanying notes are an integral part of these consolidated financial statements.

# NOTES

## Chapter 3

1. Andrew Ross Sorkin, "Back to School, But This One Is for Corporate Officials," *New York Times*, September 3, 2002.

2. Mike France, "Why Bernie Before Kenny-Boy?" *BusinessWeek*, March 15, 2004, 37.

## Part One Toolbox

1. David Harding and Ted Rouse, "Human Due Diligence," *Harvard Business Review*, April 2007, 124–131.

## Chapter 5

1. H. Thomas Johnson and Robert S. Kaplan, *Relevance Lost: The Rise and Fall of Management Accounting* (Boston: Harvard Business School Press, 1991).

2. Dell Inc., Form 10-K, 2006. See "Note 1—Description of Business and Summary of Significant Accounting Policies," 41 and 43.

3. Tyco International, Form 10-K, 2006. See "Note 1, Basis of Presentation, Restatement, and Summary of Significant Accounting Policies," 100.

## Chapter 6

1. Wal-Mart, Annual Report, 2007. See "Management's Discussion and Analysis of Financial Condition and Results of Operations, Overview," 28.

## Chapter 9

1. Ford Motor Company, Annual Report, 2006. See "Notes to the Financial Statements, Note 2, Summary of Accounting Policies," 59.

*Chapter 10*

1. Barnes & Noble Booksellers, Annual Report, 2006. See "Management's Discussion and Analysis of Financial Condition and Results of Operations, Merchandise Inventories," 18.

*Chapter 14*

1. Ram Charan and Jerry Useem, "Why Companies Fail," *Fortune*, May 27, 2002, 50–62.

*Chapter 25*

1. Jack J. Phillips, *Accountability in Human Resource Management* (Houston, TX: Gulf Publishing Company, 1996), 57.
2. Ibid., 300.
3. Marcia Conner, "How do I measure return on investment (ROI) for my learning program?" *Training & Learning FAQs*, Learnativity.com, April 5, 2002.

*Chapter 29*

1. Edward E. Lawler, Susan A. Mohrman, and Gerald E. Ledford, *Creating High Performance Organizations* (Los Angeles: Center for Effective Organizations, Marshall School of Business, University of Southern California, 1995).

# ACKNOWLEDGMENTS

We—Karen and Joe—have been working together for more than ten years. Our partnership began with a chance meeting at a conference and evolved over time into co-ownership of our company, the Business Literacy Institute, and now into coauthorship of the Financial Intelligence books. Over the years, we have met, worked with, and shared experiences with many people who have had an impact on our thinking and our work. This book is a culmination of our education, of our management experiences, of our research, of our partnership, and of all we have learned from our work with thousands of employees, managers, and leaders.

Karen first met John while conducting research for her dissertation. He was, and still is, one of the preeminent experts on open-book management. We kept track of each other through the years and were always interested in each other's work. Karen was delighted when John wanted to be a part of this project. He has been an indispensable part of the team.

Many other people have helped make this book a reality. Among them:

- Bo Burlingham, an editor-at-large at *Inc.* magazine, coauthor (with Jack Stack) of the wonderful books *The Great Game of Business* and *A Stake in the Outcome*, and author of *Small Giants*. Bo graciously shared with us the research and writing on financial fraud that he and Joe had gathered for another project.

- Joe Cornwell and Joe VanDenberg, co-owners of Setpoint along with Joe Knight. (At Setpoint they are referred to simply as "the Joes.") We're grateful for their belief in teaching everyone the financials and for their tireless efforts in encouraging everyone at Setpoint to participate actively in the success of the company. We're glad they let us tell some Setpoint stories. We also want to acknowledge Brad Angus (CEO of Setpoint), Clark Carlile, Machel Jackson, Reid Leland, Steve Nuetzman, Roger Thomas, and all the Setpoint employees.

If you are ever in Utah, you should visit Setpoint; the company's system works, and you'll see both financial intelligence and psychic ownership in action. We suspect you'll be surprised at the employees' depth of understanding of the business and their commitment to its success.

- Our clients at the Business Literacy Institute. Thanks to their commitment to business literacy, we have been able to help spread financial intelligence throughout many organizations. It's impossible to thank them all, but a few who helped us and cheered us on are Dan Leever, Michael Siegmund, Greg Bolingbroke, and Gary St. Pierre of MacDermid Inc.; Shellie Crandall of Brinks Inc.; Mark Boitano, Seema Khan, and Julie Holmes of Granite Construction; Richard O'Donnell of GE, Ron Wangerin, and Melinda Del Toro of ViaSat; Heather Ludwig and Beth Dawson of GMAC ResCap; and Winny Ho of The Enterprise University.

- Our colleagues at the Business Literacy Institute. Rochelle Martel is one of those unique financial professionals who is also a fantastic teacher. Cathy Ivancic and Jim Bado are also both experts in the field of financial education, with the added knowledge of employee stock ownership plan organizations. Scott Blackham and Brad Orton round out our facilitator team with their financial expertise. Sharon Maas's contribution to BLI includes customized content development, training program facilitation, and communication work; her extensive knowledge and experience along with her energetic and positive attitude are inspiring. Stephanie Wexler is manager of client services; her thoroughness and professionalism keep everything running smoothly. Judy Golove, manager of training development, ensures that all our training programs are of the highest quality. Sam Case conducted the interviews for this book, providing us with key data to share with you.

- The HR folks who agreed to be interviewed for this book: Michael Crist, director of human resources at Colorado Energy Management; Larry Godfrey, assistant dean of the College of Human Resources and Labor Relations at General Motors; Connie Haney, vice president of compensation and benefits at Mentor Graphics Corporation; and John Hofmeister, president of Shell Oil Company. Their insights were invaluable.

- Dave Merrill, the creative artist who illustrates our Money Maps. His ability to take our initial rough ideas and bring them to life is a true talent.

- Jacqueline Murphy and Brian Surette, our editor and assistant editor, and the rest of the team at Harvard Business Press. Thank you.

- Roberta Wolff, who generously gave us her time and energy with an outcome that delighted us all.

- And all the others who have helped us along the way, including Deborah Annes, Bonnie Andrus, Helen and Gene Berman, Kelin Gersick, Larry and Jewel Knight, Daniel Kutt, Marty Lasker, Michael Lee, and the Main Graphics team, Don Mankin, Kimcee McAnally, Alan Miller, Annie Petros, Loren Roberts, Marlin Shelley, Brian Shore, and Mike Thompson. Our heartfelt thanks to all.

# INDEX

# ABOUT THE AUTHORS

**Karen Berman, PhD,** is founder, president, and co-owner of the Business Literacy Institute, a consulting firm offering customized training programs, Money Maps, keynotes, and other products and services designed to ensure that people in organizations understand how financial success is measured and how they make an impact. Karen has worked with dozens of companies, helping them create financial literacy programs that transform employees, managers, and leaders into business partners.

**Joe Knight** is co-owner of the Business Literacy Institute and co-owner of Setpoint Systems. He works as chief financial officer of Setpoint and as a facilitator and keynote speaker for the Business Literacy Institute, traveling to clients all over the world to teach them about finance. Joe, who holds a master's of business administration from the University of California at Berkeley, is a true believer in financial transparency and lives it every day at Setpoint.